OVERCOME

OVERCOME

My Life in Pursuit of A Dream

Ellamae Simmons, M.D.
with Rosemarie Robotham

Mill City Press · *Minneapolis*

Mill City Press, Inc.
322 First Avenue N, 5th floor
Minneapolis, MN 55401
612.455.2293
www.millcitypublishing.com

Unless otherwise sourced in the Endnotes, the material
contained in this book is based on the recollections of
Ellamae Simmons, M.D., as recorded in her correspondence,
notebooks and journals, written speeches and personally
archived documents. Additional material was gathered through
extensive interviews with Dr. Simmons, her family members,
friends, colleagues and other witnesses to her life and times.

ISBN-13: 978-1-63413-988-5
LCCN: 2016902776

Cover image: Ellamae Simmons, age 9
All photographs courtesy of Ellamae Simmons, M.D.
Typeset by M.K. Ross

Printed in the United States of America

DEDICATION

To Gus and Ella, my first and greatest inspirations,
and to Varian, Shawna and all those who helped me bring
this long-dreamed book into being.

Oh, deep in my heart I do believe
We shall overcome someday.

Negro Spiritual

Contents

Ellamae Simmons, M.D., Oakland, California, February 2015.

PREFACE

The Girl in the Painting

By Rosemarie Robotham

In the summer of 1964, Dr. Ellamae Simmons got behind the wheel of her white Porsche 356C in Denver and headed across the country to California. For the trip west, she had chosen to wear a lemon-yellow sundress and white-framed sunglasses, a silvery blue scarf around her neck. She was headed to San Francisco, after all, and that inspired a certain jauntiness. Slender in frame, with skin the rich polished brown of roasted pecans, she looked at least a decade younger than her 46 years, as much the effect of good genes as the resolute air of adventure she exuded.

She was driving to the Bay Area to interview for a position as a physician specializing in asthma, allergy and immunology with the giant of pre-paid healthcare, Kaiser Permanente. She knew Kaiser had never hired a black female doctor, but why shouldn't she be the first? She drove for two days, hardly stopping to rest. It had been a violent year on the civil rights battlefront, and she saw no reason to chance the reception a Negro woman alone might receive in the vast lonely swaths of the American heartland.

Down South, Freedom Summer was in full swing, with hundreds of volunteers arriving in Mississippi by the busload to register blacks and poor whites for the vote. The backlash from white Southerners during the ten-week project had been sustained and brutal—thousands arrested, hundreds beaten, and homes, churches and businesses burned to the ground. Also during that blood-soaked summer, three young men—James Chaney, Andrew Goodman and Michael Schwerner, a black Mississippian and two Jewish volunteers from New York—were abducted and shot by the Ku Klux Klan, their bodies discarded in an earthen dam.[1]

Ellamae was no stranger to the cruel realities of race in
America. As one of a handful of black medical professionals who
had served during World War II, she'd encountered her share of
racial violence, and she had learned to give trouble a wide berth
when engagement wasn't absolutely necessary. As it was, too
often in Ellamae's life, engagement had been not only necessary
but also critical. At those times, she did not hesitate to square her
shoulders and meet the challenge.

She had been one of eight Negro nurses chosen to integrate
the Army Nurse Corps during the war, and now she was near to
completing a subspecialty in asthma-allergy at the world-famous
National Jewish Hospital at Denver. Married only two years
prior to former Tuskegee Airman Col. Price D. Rice, Ellamae was
ready to reinvent herself in the Bay Area, which happened to be
as far away from her home state of Ohio as it was possible to get
without moving overseas. The position at Kaiser was her dream
job, one she had coveted ever since learning as a graduate student
in social work about Kaiser's bold experiment in pre-paid healthcare plans. In the 1960s, Kaiser was not just the largest hospital
system in the state of California; the Kaiser Foundation was also
in the midst of expanding its pre-paid concept to the rest of the
country, with a goal of making first-rate medical care available to
a truly diverse population rather than just a privileged few who
could afford it.[2]

Ellamae's goal to become the first African American woman
on staff in any of Kaiser's clinics was not so farfetched. She was
already the first and only black woman allergist in the country,
studying under the eminent immunologist Dr. Irving Itkin. Today,
the field of asthma, allergy and immunology is a major medical
specialty, with physicians diagnosing and treating some 50
million affected Americans.[3] But in the late 1950s, when Ellamae
graduated from Howard University medical school, the field was
still in its infancy, controlled by a handful of white male physicians. Dr. Itkin was among the most respected of this group, and
after working with Ellamae during her chest medicine residency

in Denver, he had invited her to train with him. He considered her one of the most gifted physicians he had ever encountered, and in the early 1960s, with racial and gender barriers in medicine beginning to crumble, he was fully on board with the idea of Ellamae Simmons, M.D., as the foremost black female allergist in the nation. His recommendation of her had been unreserved. Ellamae suspected it was the whole reason that his famous colleague Dr. Benjamin Feingold, the founder and chief of allergy medicine at Kaiser, had agreed to meet with her.

As Ellamae recalls it, after their first meeting Dr. Feingold evaluated her candidacy for four straight days while she waited at an airport motel to be called for a follow-up interview. On the fifth day, he brought her into his office and peered at her from across his enormous desk. With a swept-back mane of silver hair and aquiline features, he was as distinguished looking in his way as the composed physician in the crisp blue suit seated opposite him. Holding Ellamae's application papers in his hands, he regarded the woman in front of him for several moments before speaking. Finally he cleared his throat and told Ellamae that while he could not take issue with her knowledge, training and character, he had determined that he could not hire her for a position with Kaiser because she was not sufficiently experienced.

Ellamae listened, her gaze level, her posture deceptively relaxed. She responded calmly: "You know, Dr. Feingold, I am not in the habit of applying for positions for which I am not qualified. So what is the truth? Have you decided not to hire me because I am black?"

Feingold, who would go on to publish groundbreaking research on the link between diet and hyperactivity in children,[4] later confessed he'd been startled by Ellamae's forthrightness, but he had admired it, too. Being Jewish, perhaps he understood something of how it felt to be discriminated against. In the moment after Ellamae challenged him, he reasoned that just because he had never hired a black physician at Kaiser did not mean he should not do so now. In the brown-skinned allergist, with her upright bearing and steady eyes, he saw an opportunity to make history.

For her part, Ellamae Simmons did what she had always done: She shouldered open the door that had previously been closed to her and strode on through.

This is just a bare bones account of the historic meeting between Drs. Simmons and Feingold, which, as this book will show, was a far more layered encounter. But this account explains how Ellamae came to be walking in downtown San Francisco on a Sunday afternoon in the summer of 1965. She had moved to the Bay Area just weeks before to take up the job at Kaiser. She was alone in the city, as her husband Price, the Tuskegee Airman, had remained in Denver to finish up a tour of duty at the military base there, and to oversee moving their furniture. Even though stores were closed on Sunday afternoons, Ellamae thought she would wander and window-shop as a way to become more familiar with her new town. She remembers turning a corner and finding in the window of an art gallery a framed lithograph that stopped her cold. Her heartbeat quickening, Ellamae stared at the picture, a full-sized reproduction of a painting by the artist Norman Rockwell. She actually felt little pinpricks of recognition along her neck and arms, and she shivered slightly in the balmy July afternoon. She stood for a long time looking into the store window at the lithograph, a limited edition print that had been signed by the artist himself.

Rockwell had titled the painting *The Problem We All Live With*. In it, he had depicted a little black girl of about six years old, wearing a starched white dress and white ribbons in her hair, carrying school composition books and a ruler in one hand. U.S. Marshals in business suits escort the child, two in front and two behind her. On their arms are yellow armbands announcing their official mission, but their faces are cropped out of the frame, rendering them as anonymous symbols of law enforcement. The effect is that the viewer's focus remains squarely on the child, her posture strong and purposeful. The child walks in profile, eyes determinedly forward, her courage visible in her sure stride—and implied by the word "Nigger" and the acronym "KKK" scrawled in graffiti above her head, and the tomatoes spattered on the wall behind her.

Ellamae noticed how the red spatter fanned out to resemble both a trail of blood and an angel's wing. What Ellamae didn't know as she gazed at the painting was that it had been a radical departure for the artist, who had made his reputation painting small-town American scenes populated almost exclusively by whites, with blacks appearing only in positions of servitude. Some art historians say this was a mandate given to Rockwell by his editors at the *Saturday Evening Post*, which had engaged him to do cover illustrations for more than a decade. But the artist had recently ended his association with the *Post* and had joined the *Look* magazine roster. He'd been deeply moved by photographs and accounts of a black child named Ruby Bridges, who despite the jeers and threats of angry white mobs had integrated William Frantz Elementary School in New Orleans, Louisiana, in 1960. The artist expressed to his editor at *Look* a desire to commemorate the child's bravery.[5] The result was this painting that rooted Ellamae to the spot on which she stood.

Ellamae decided right then she had to have the Rockwell print. It was way more than she could afford on her still-meager earnings, but she went back to the shop the next day and made a down payment. She returned every two weeks for three months to make further payments until she had purchased the signed lithograph. She took it home to the apartment she had rented and hung it above her bed. She would place that painting in the same honored position in every house she lived in for the rest of her life.

What was it about this now-famous painting that had so moved Dr. Ellamae Simmons? "I am the little girl in the picture," she explained, one hand spread over her heart. "She talks to me. That painting is the entire story of my life."

With the family dog in Mount Vernon, Ohio, circa 1926.

INTRODUCTION

Life, How Precious

I don't recall exactly when I first started writing this narrative. Perhaps I began when I was 11 years old and about to enter the sixth grade. My classmate Janet Graham came to me on the first day of school and said, "Ellamae, I can't be your friend anymore. My mother says I'm not supposed to play with colored people." The year was 1929, and I was living with my family in Mount Vernon, a small Ohio town that had once been a stop on the Underground Railroad. Not many of the black people fleeing slavery had actually settled there; most found their way farther north, to Cleveland or beyond, to Canada. The year I entered sixth grade, Mount Vernon, located some fifty miles northeast of Columbus, was home to just ten or so black families. We represented less than two percent of the town's ten thousand inhabitants.

Throughout my childhood, there had never been more than two or three black children in my class. Most years, I was the only one. I never paid that any mind, however, because all my classmates had played easily together, and no one was excluded. But now we were on the verge of adolescence, and a girl with whom I'd been close from the time we met in kindergarten was trying to explain that her mother no longer wanted her to have anything to do with me because I was, as we referred to ourselves then, a Negro.

As incredible as it now seems, I had not understood before that moment that my family was any different from the other families in our neighborhood, all but two of them white. But on that day I looked at my friend as if seeing her for the first time. I had always recognized that our complexions were not the same, of course. And certainly I noticed the difference in the texture of our hair, hers straight and straw-colored and in a loose ponytail, mine kinked and fluffy as soft, dark wool, caught in three braids with silk ribbons at the ends. But I hadn't realized that these distinctions were of any consequence whatsoever, not until that morning when I lost my friend.

Confused, I simply said, "Well, Janet, that's all right."

The truth is I didn't really believe what she was telling me, but Janet never again sat with me at recess or walked home with me after school to do homework and jump rope in the yard. We would never again dig our bare toes into the sandpile behind my house, or go for rides in my father's hay wagon, or take mutual pride in our straight-A report cards. Nor would we ever again giggle over shared confidences while perched on low-slung branches of the sugar maple in the park across the street.

In all my decades of life since, I have never forgotten Janet's words to me that morning. This girl, at such a tender age, defined for me the entire racial tenor of the country. Her simple statement marked the watershed between a somewhat charmed and oblivious childhood and the harsh, inevitable realities of being a black person in America. All these years later, Janet's comment still echoes in memory, confirming my belief that racism is taught to children by adults. By themselves, children know no prejudice. Indeed, for the first ten years of my life, I was in and out of white children's homes and they were in and out of mine. We walked to school together, held membership in the same school clubs and played together in neighborhood games. Often, inside our home at 110 East Pleasant Street, my mother would place several white children on the living room floor alongside her own children for afternoon naps.

It was not lost on me that some of my playmates had far more privileges, more toys, more wealth and more liberty to roam than my siblings and I did. My white friends often went to the cinema together; they were allowed to hang around snack shops and restaurants that my parents thought questionable; and they often spent afternoons at the town pool and stayed in the park until well after dark. When my siblings and I complained to our parents, my mother would say, "We expect more of you. Those children are not your example. Set your own course." Our parents never bothered to remind us that most of the places we hankered to be let into were segregated. We would not have been allowed in anyway.

And yet my childhood was not unhappy. My parents very deliberately set the tone. Far from expressing bitterness about the scourge of racism that ran through every seam of American life, my parents professed to love their country. Their faith in American democracy, and in what they saw as the inherent virtues of this nation, was unshakable. They believed in the party of Lincoln; my father in particular consistently voted the Republican ticket, citing the fact that Abraham Lincoln's administration had ended slavery on January 1, 1863, a mere fourteen years before he was born.

My mother on the other hand always voted in the interest of religious liberty. Although my parents practiced different faiths— my father was a pillar of the African Methodist Episcopal (AME) church while my mother was a devout Seventh-day Adventist— both gained strength and optimism from the Bible. When it came to confronting the nation's racial prejudices, both Augustus and Ella Simmons held that religious faith, hard work, good citizenship and a college education would triumph over ignorance and bigotry. They believed this in their bones, even though my father was an Ohio farm boy with an eighth-grade education. My mother had gone further: A high school graduate, she had earned a diploma in practical nursing from the Colored High and Training School in her native Baltimore, Maryland.

In encouraging her four children to improve their behavior, Ella often fell back on one of her favorite quotes: "Assume a virtue if you have it not." She was a master at exactly that. She schooled us in the manners of polite society and exposed us to the writings of a wide range of black and white scholars, philosophers and poets, among them Booker T. Washington and W. E. B. Du Bois, Paul Laurence Dunbar, Frederick Douglass, Henry Wadsworth Longfellow, Shakespeare, Milton, Edgar A. Guest, Paul Robeson, Alexandre Dumas, Roland Hayes, Chaucer, Edgar Allan Poe and many others. She sent her children out each day neatly pressed and well read, and she expected us to bring home grades that surpassed those of our classmates.

Certainly my parents did not see other people's bigotry as an excuse not to excel. They expected us to pursue grand ambitions and make good lives for ourselves. Further, they instilled that we must take care never to commit any offense that might reflect unfavorably on black people, and as a representative of any business or profession, we should never behave in a manner that might prevent another motivated member of our tribe from entering that business or profession as well.

It wasn't until I was an adult that I began to understand that my parents' dreams for personal fulfillment could only be satisfied through their children. I can see now that my mother's ambition for me fanned the earliest embers of my own desire to achieve. Her pleasure in me when I brought home my stellar report cards was a powerful affirmation that I was capable of pursuing any career path I might imagine. Not surprisingly, because I hero-worshipped my intellectually brilliant mother, I knew from the time I was very young that I wanted to follow her into the healing arts.

I am sure that my mother was the first person for whom I wanted to write this book, perhaps to set down as a record that her dreams for me and belief in my abilities had been well placed. Later, when I looked back at the unexpected twists and turns my life had taken, the hard passages and the moments of pure grace, I realized that I also wanted to make this record for myself, and for all those who ever had a moment's doubt that their goals could be achieved. Certainly no one expected a little black girl from Mount Vernon, Ohio, to become the first African American female allergist in the country, even if that little girl had been always at the top of her class. Growing up, I had never seen a black physician. I had never met a female physician. I had never even known a black person who had earned a college degree. The field of allergy medicine did not yet exist! And yet I had lofty dreams, and I pursued them with a whole heart because my parents had told me that I could.

When I first began this book, I wrote in fits and starts, in a kind of fever to get the story onto the page. For the most part, I have used the terms *black* and *white* to refer to race, occasionally employing other descriptors that were common to the particular time period about which I was writing—using, for example, *Negro* and *colored* during the early years and switching to the current usage of *black* or *African American* later on. At times, I let the story lie fallow for many years as life and career demands absorbed me. Finally, in the 1990s, shortly after my formal retirement from medicine, I turned back to my narrative. Upon review of what I had so far written, I realized I was angry.

Psychologists will tell you that, frequently, anger and rage are expressions of hurt or sorrow turned inside out, so perhaps I was still smarting from the numerous racial injustices I had encountered along the way, beginning in sixth grade with Janet Graham turning away from me because of the color of my skin.

And so for several years I put the writing aside again, coming back to it only intermittently to record personal travails as a way to make sense of my experiences. I knew I did not want to write my life's story from a place of bitterness, frustration or anger. Even so, I understood that I had to tell the truth, and that it would serve no one for me to sugarcoat it.

I am almost one hundred years old now. With the passage of years I have developed a hard-won peace and a deep sense of gratitude for the great gifts that have been bestowed on me in this life. I now want nothing more than to share the bounty of my experiences as evidence that no matter how bleak the moment we are living through, we can overcome. We *will* overcome. But we may need the help of another person who believes in our vision as strongly as we do. I have come to appreciate that in medicine and in life, our greatest human need is for the hand that reaches out to touch another; the hand that closes around another's and pulls that person forward in a supportive embrace.

I am driven to write my story now, not out of spite but out of forbearance; not out of anger but out of forgiveness; not out of frustration but out of hope; not out of disagreement but out of understanding; and not out of vengeance but out of love. I write now from a place of wonderment at a spiritual and professional journey that has given me perhaps more than one person deserved. Life, how precious, how fragile, yet how enduring!

My father, Augustus Lawrence "Gus" Simmons, circa 1911.

My mother, Ella Sophia Cooper Simmons, circa 1913.

CHAPTER 1

At First Light

In July of 2000, I set out to find the ruined churchyard in Captina where Cousin Vera, our family historian, had told me our ancestors lay buried. I was 82 that year, and had traveled back to my native Ohio to attend the ninetieth Simmons family reunion. Of late, I had felt a strange yearning to stand before the graves of my paternal grandparents and see for myself their names carved into stone. My cousins Jim Payne and Harold Turner, both a good ten years younger than I was, had agreed to accompany me. They were Vera's son and son-in-law, and so they were well acquainted with such excursions.

Our search that warm Midwestern afternoon led us many miles away from the reunion festivities, through a country wilderness of dusty, unmarked roads, into rocky, hilly terrain. At length, we came upon a grassy slope dotted with crumbling headstones, overrun by a thicket of weeds, thorns and wildflowers. As I picked my way among the grave markers, I saw the family names I had heard spoken in my childhood: Myers, Newsome, Turner, Briggs, Hamilton.

And then I spied the prize of my search, the headstones of Abraham Simmons and Amelia May Briggs Simmons, my father's parents. Their names were clearly visible, despite the ravages of weather and years, and the thorny vines colonizing the stone. For a long time, I stood in that hallowed place, gazing at the headstones, remembering the stories, and listening to the whisper of my own mortality.

A little farther up on that shaded, unkempt hill, a few foundation stones were all that were left of the red oak church and school our forebears had built at the northern edge of the Underground Railroad. I wandered away from Harold and Jim, who stayed lower down on the slope, leaning against the car. On a stony outcrop, I sat down on a rock, and from beneath the straw brim of my sunhat, I took in the full sweep of the unforgiving

1

hillside, where the first Simmons to arrive in Ohio had scrabbled together a life for the rest of us. I said a prayer of thanks for their resourcefulness, and I marveled at how far I had traveled to get back to the very beginning.

I am often asked how it was that the Simmons family came to be one of a handful of African American families who settled in Mount Vernon in Knox County, Ohio. It is a question that genealogists within my family have endeavored to answer ever since Abraham and Amelia Simmons' eight children initiated the annual Simmons family reunion in 1909 in Barnesville, Ohio. The event has drawn generations together every year since then, except for one year during World War II when we did not meet because of restrictions imposed by government rationing. Over the years, relatives have combed through state, county and family archives to piece together the Simmons family history. Continually updated versions of that history are recounted at the reunion every year as a way to honor the ancestors and to recognize new births.

From that history, we learned that the Simmonses of Ohio are descended from two African princes, the sons of a royal chieftain from the kingdom of the Gold Coast, now the West African nation of Ghana. The chieftain dealt in gold and ivory, and in the year 1775, he and his family, along with several attendants, went aboard a British cargo vessel intending to trade their wares. Bearing two large wooden chests filled with merchandise, they fully believed they were engaged in a commercial transaction, as indeed they were, although not of the kind they had envisioned. As they stood aboard the ship bartering with its captain, the vessel headed out to sea and was far from shore by the time the chieftain and his family understood they had been taken prisoner. The ship was a slaving vessel, and the royal family and their companions were chained in the cargo hold along with an unknown number of other Africans. The story goes that the chieftain became so distressed upon realizing that slave traders had seized his wife and young sons that he died of a broken heart. It is thought that his wife perished, too, as there is also no record of her surviving the treacherous Atlantic crossing.

The ship carrying the princes eventually landed at a small port city on the coast of North Carolina. The two children, still in possession of the large wooden chests, were sold at auction to Quakers, also known as the Religious Society of Friends. This was fortuitous for my family, because Quakers were deeply opposed to slavery and were at the forefront of the American abolitionist movement, adopting the first formal antislavery resolution as early as 1688 in Germantown, Pennsylvania. The Quakers believed the Inner Light of God resided in all humans, regardless of race or creed, and they had a practice of buying captive Africans from slaving vessels so as to immediately set them free. The Quakers were also well known as conductors on the Underground Railroad, which was not a railway at all but a network of secret routes and safe houses operated by individuals who knew exactly which barns, attics, cellars, corn shacks and churches would provide sanctuary to people of African descent fleeing the slave states of the South.

The two princes remained in the Carolinas until they became young men. Raised by a Quaker family, they were given the names James and York Simmons, and they were schooled in the fundamentals of reading, writing and arithmetic. At around age 13, they went to work doing odd jobs for the Society of Friends. Not only were they paid for this labor, but they were also instructed in the importance of being frugal so that they would one day be able to independently manage their own homes. When they came of age, both brothers wanted to marry, and their benefactors resolved that the time had come to ferry them to free territory farther north. They knew that any child born to a person of African descent in a Southern slave state would be a slave, even if the parents were free. So as soon as the brothers had saved enough money, the Quakers sent them and their wives through on the Underground Railroad to the rich country of the Ohio River Valley to start life anew.

The region was at that time part of the Northwest Territory. It was here in the east central part of what would become the State of Ohio in 1803[6] that the brothers purchased small plots of land on which to support their families. The land was located in modern-day Belmont County. The exact locale was about six miles south of Barnesville, in an area then known as Captina. The ground was hard and inhospitable, with only thin pockets of soil; by no means was it prime real estate, but it was all theirs. York and James Simmons immediately set about clearing and farming their modest acreage. They felled trees, built log cabins, constructed a church and a schoolhouse, and tilled the soil to raise tobacco and corn, and enough fruits and vegetables to feed their growing families.

This was the genesis of the Simmons family in Ohio. The person responsible for reconstructing most of this history was my dear late cousin, Vera Wooten Payne. Cousin Vera was born July 2, 1891, and died a few months short of a century later on October 20, 1990. She was alert and mentally clear until the end, and she never lost her passion for the detective work of Simmons genealogy, tracking down and sharing the details and documents that told our family's story. As a child, she had seen one of the wooden chests that the princes brought with them from Africa. It was filled not with gold and ivory but with the coins and now-rusted tools for which they had traded their treasure.

Cousin Vera always emphasized that although the brothers had arrived in the New World aboard a slaving vessel, they and their descendants had never been slaves. The princes had birthed all their children in non-slave-holding territory before the onset of the Civil War, and subsequent generations had remained in Ohio. It was perhaps the reason that my father, Augustus Lawrence Simmons, revered his home state. He was as proud as his cousin Vera of the fact that in Ohio, his forebears had been self-sufficient farmers who had always lived free. My father, whom everyone called Gus, was only two generations removed from the slave ship that brought the princes to America. How different our story could have been had the brothers not been bought and freed by Quakers!

County records show that Gus' father Abraham was born to York Simmons and his wife Juliann in 1829. Abraham died in 1907. Gus' mother, Amelia Mae née Briggs, was born in 1837 and died in 1929. Gus was one of Abraham and Amelia's eight children born in Captina, which was later incorporated into the town of Barnesville. My father arrived on July 25, 1877, a little more than a decade after President Lincoln signed the Emancipation Proclamation into law. Gus and his siblings were reared on the family farm in Belmont County that Quakers had helped his grandfather York to secure. Gus attended school only through the eighth grade, leaving after that to help out on the farm.

On November 26, 1900, when he was 23 years old, my father married a young woman named Fina Alexander from nearby St. Clairsville, Ohio. The details of their meeting and courtship are lost to history, but their elaborate framed certificate of marriage hung for many years in the library of my home. The newlyweds soon moved to Mount Vernon in Knox County, where Gus found work as a janitor at the state sanatorium. Some of my older relatives remembered Fina well, and everyone spoke very highly of her. But her marriage to Gus lasted just ten years before she died at home of a ruptured appendix. No children were born to their union.

A year later, Gus, a devout follower of the AME church, was introduced to Ella Sophia Cooper at a church gathering in Mount Vernon. My mother was a striking young woman, tall and slim with a refined bearing, always beautifully clothed in the style of the day. Gus was smitten at once with the preacher's daughter from Baltimore. Ella, too, had been married before, to a brick mason named Miles Carr, and she had given birth to their daughter Georgeanna on October 19, 1908. Ella had moved from Maryland to Ohio with Miles, who went to work in Mount Vernon laying bricks for the many cobblestone streets. But Miles had a drinking problem and was something of a ladies man. By the time Georgeanna was two years old, Ella had gathered up the child and left the marriage. When Gus first laid eyes on her at that church outing, she was 22 years old, already divorced, and working as a domestic for a family named Hagan, who ran a local well-drilling business. Her little girl lived in with her on the Hagan estate.

In his unassuming way, Gus cut a dashing figure in his dark three-piece suit, set off by a handsome handlebar mustache and a lean workingman's build. His hands were big and gnarled, but he wore his starched white shirt and black church bowtie comfortably as he tipped his fedora to my mother. Ella would have been impressed by the fact that Gus Simmons was a man shaping his own destiny, an entrepreneur before anyone coined the word. But even more important to Ella was the kindness Gus showed to her little girl, who took an immediate liking to the tall man with the gentle voice.

By the time my parents met, Gus had already decided that he would be his own boss, and he had made good on that promise by investing in a wagon and a horse named Topsy, which he had used to start the Simmons garbage business. Over the next several months, Gus rode Topsy regularly to visit Ella, wooing my mother with promises to take her "out of white folks' kitchens." At the time, in addition to his garbage business, Gus was working as a waiter in town at a restaurant called Roy's, which was owned by a black family. It was at Roy's that Gus met a one-armed lawyer named Charlie Bermont, who was one of the restaurant's regular white customers. Bermont had been impressed by Gus' work ethic and general affability, and the two men became friends. The lawyer later agreed to deed to Gus a plot of land at 110 East Pleasant Street; it was here that Gus would build the two-story, blue-and-white clapboard house in which he would raise his family.

Gus formally proposed to Ella at the end of 1913. They jumped the broom and began life together with Georgeanna on East Pleasant Street the following February. Soon, three more children joined the family—my brother Lawrence, born on December 18, 1914; my sister Rowena, who arrived on November 30, 1916; and me, a complete surprise to my parents, who had decided after Rowena that three children were enough. Eighteen months later on March 26, 1918, I was born anyway.

Everyone in Mount Vernon knew my father as the trash man. As a child, I wondered why did *my* father have to be the one to haul garbage. I was frankly ashamed of his work, especially when I compared it to the labor of my friends' fathers, who went to their jobs in suits and ties while my father wore overalls and plaid flannel shirts and work boots covered in dried manure and mud.

I was totally ignorant of how difficult and even impossible it was for a black man to gain access to the white-collar jobs held by white men in our town. Had I not been so oblivious, I would have recognized that my father was a self-made man in a racial environment that left him no other choice.

From the time he was a boy, Gus learned to make a buck any way he could, and he knew better than to be embarrassed by honest labor. My father was the original recycler, a man far ahead of his time. He salvaged discarded items from his garbage hauls and stored them in the barn and on the side porch until he could find a use for them or offer them for resale. He also bundled and sold old newspapers, magazines, rags and scrap metal. When I asked him why he collected what appeared to me as junk, he would say, "It'll come in handy someday, baby. Someone can use it." And indeed, people looking for some odd item or part needed for a repair knew to seek out my father. They would usually find just what they wanted among his scavenged materials.

Gus Simmons also farmed fruits and vegetables, and he kept horses, chickens and cows. His cows were pastured on rented fields that lay just beyond the edge of the neighborhood. Every day my father would rise before daybreak and trudge to the pasture to milk his three cows. He could be seen setting off each morning at first light, wide-brimmed hat on his head, milk buckets in hand, our family's Doberman-collie mix Jan, and later Trixie, Lassie or Skipper, trotting along beside him. Through snowstorms and torrential rain, frigid winter temperatures and sweltering summer heat, nothing deterred my father. The cows had to be milked daily and that was all there was to it. The milk he collected and the produce from his truck farming business supplied our family's needs year-round. Other families in town also relied on my father's milk, fruits and vegetables, as well as on the canned goods my mother made from the produce he harvested.

Ella Sophia had a large steamer that held thirty-two quart-sized Mason jars for canning. Preservation by freezing was unheard of in those days. During the summer months, Mother would put us children to work preparing the fruit and vegetables for the canning process. Under her no-nonsense supervision, we would cut corn kernels off the cob and fill Mason jars with them; string and break green beans; shell peas and lima beans; peel tomatoes, peaches, pears and quinces; steam cherries; cut rhubarb; and dig up and cut asparagus. My mother would take the fruits of our labor and turn them into an endless supply of canned produce that my father sold off the back of his truck or gave away to the town's poorer residents.

There was also plenty of milk and milk products to go around. My brother, Lawrence, who at age five began helping to milk the cows, remembers that as he and Gus ferried the full buckets home from the pasture each day, neighbors would come out to the street with a pitcher and a few coins to buy fresh milk.

By the time Gus and Lawrence arrived home, my mother would have everything ready to strain and process the remaining milk. She would skim the cream from the milk, and each child would take turns at churning the cream to butter. Mother would wash away the churnings and store the butter in an icebox that stood on our back porch; to ensure the dairy products stayed fresh, an iceman regularly delivered fifty- or one hundred-pound blocks of ice to be placed in the top compartment of our icebox. We also stored glass bottles of buttermilk left over after the cream had been churned; we called it "clabber" and enjoyed it warm and thickly curdled. Mother would regularly process a portion of this thickened, soured milk, draining away the whey and making cottage cheese from the curds. All these products we sold to regular customers.

Because my dad was a farmer and my mother a practical nurse, our family was able to weather the Great Depression of the 1930s relatively well. Many people in our town were not so fortunate. In those years, a small establishment called Doup's Bake Shop stood across the street from our home, and every evening, raggedly dressed children would forage in barrels for day-old bread and other baked goods that had been discarded. My mother watched them from our porch for several days, her lips pursed and brow furrowed, her hands resting in the pockets of her floral kitchen apron. One day, she called out to the children and asked if they would like some milk. After that, several times each week, these children would crowd onto our porch and Ella would send them on their way with bottles of milk and sometimes a jug of clabber or cottage cheese. Many of our white neighbors, too, would bring their empty milk bottles, and if they had fallen on hard times, my parents would fill their containers free of charge and throw in a bag of eggs, lima beans, tomatoes, rhubarb, peas, squash, whatever was on hand from the farm.

But as busy as my father's farming activities kept him and the rest of the family, it always seemed to me that his primary occupation was collecting garbage. I did not wish to be associated with his horse-drawn garbage wagon ambling through the streets of our town. If I saw manure lying in the street, I was sure my father had collected garbage nearby, and that it was his horses that had left that pile of manure.

One day I asked, "Dad, why do you haul garbage?"

I was 11 years old. At the start of that school year my friend Janet had told me her mother had forbidden her to play with "coloreds." My eyes newly opened by this, my first direct encounter with American racism, I had begun to make comparisons between my family and our white neighbors.

"Well, baby," my father responded, "someone has to haul the trash. Everybody has garbage and someone has to haul it away. You can't let it just pile up. Hogs out in the country feed on garbage."

Gus' voice as he explained this to me was kind, even tender. I have no doubt that my wise and gentle father knew I felt demeaned by the work he did, but he did not chastise me. And yet, his words fell on the deaf ears and closed mind of a sullen daughter. I rebelled against the sight of that garbage wagon, and that rebellion clouded my early relationship with my father. Our bond was not to be repaired until many years later, after I moved away from home and was training as a student nurse in college. Only then did I begin to understand the world in which my father and men like him were forced to operate. I realized that I had allowed myself to be blinded by what I saw as my father's humble station in life, and I had failed to recognize his goodness, his resilience, his creativity and his great love for his family that led him to do whatever he could to provide for us. My father was unschooled and unassuming in his demeanor, but I see now that he was of superior entrepreneurial intelligence. I wonder to this day how he knew so much about so many different issues; no doubt he gleaned much from the newspapers and magazines he liked to read while sitting in the front porch swing, but he was also a quiet student of human nature. And he was generous of spirit. I greatly admired his quality of never speaking disparagingly of anyone.

I know now that a big part of the reason I didn't understand how restricted opportunities were for men like my father back when I was coming of age in Mount Vernon was that I saw so few black men. My parents did their utmost to shelter us from the harsher realities of race relations in America, with the result that as a child, I didn't appreciate how very limited educational options were for all black people, nor did I realize the extent to which my father, this very versatile and practical man, had grasped the crumpled card of discrimination dealt to him and, with the most meager of provisions, made a successful life.

I can still see him sitting high up on his hay wagon drawn by his two horses, Dan and Mollie. During the summer haying season, my father would load his wagon with large quantities of freshly mown hay from surrounding pastures, and he would transport it back to our barn. There, with a forklift and pulley, he would hoist the haystacks to the barn loft for winter storage. In the warmer months, my father offered hayrides, layering the haystacks on the bed of the same horse-drawn wagon that was the mainstay of his garbage and salvage business. The hayrides didn't hold the same allure for me as they did for other neighborhood children, who would climb aboard and trundle through the streets of the town in the wagon, attracted by the horses and doubtless also by my father's genial manner. There is a famous newspaper photograph of a young black boy and four white children on a wagon ride with Gus; the picture was taken for the local paper when some townspeople took up a collection to buy my father a new horse after one of his old ones had died. The whole town depended on Gus and his wagon.

My father also maintained a horse-drawn bobsled, which he rented out for rides at birthday parties, church outings and civic events. On clear, cold, moonlit nights, I could always tell when my father was nearing home after a bobsled party, coming down the alley on his sleigh toward the barn. From my bedroom window on the second floor of our house, I could hear the neighing of his horses and see their frosty breath swirling above their heads. I could pick out the distinctive ring of the brass sleigh bells, and count the heavy *clop clop clop* of the horses' hooves upon the snow-covered street. Gus would park the sleigh, unharness the horses and bed them down in the barn for the night. Before closing up, he would extinguish the kerosene lanterns that hung front and back as head- and taillights for his sleigh; I still have two of those lanterns in my home. As soon as he came inside the house, he would head to the basement to add more wood and coal to the furnace. Then he would eat a bite of dinner and relax on the porch swing or settle into his favorite chair to read the evening paper before retiring to bed.

I was always glad to sit with my father after the bobsled parties; he seemed at his happiest then. I usually peppered him with questions: Who was at the party? What games did they play? What kind of food did they have? And what did he do while the party guests were eating? I knew that in Mount Vernon, Negroes could not be served in any white-owned establishment, which meant Gus was usually relegated to his wagon to wait in the cold while dinner was served. This treatment of my father upset me deeply, although I don't think I was fully aware of it back then. But perhaps my father had some idea, because he always deflected that particular question by saying quickly, "Oh, they brought me some food out," or "I wasn't hungry."

Ella Simmons and her four children, Georgeanna,
Lawrence, Rowena and me, in 1925.

CHAPTER 2

East Pleasant Street

I suppose that by most standards, our family was poor. And yet we always lived in a mortgaged house and never in a rented one. My father constantly drilled into his children the gospel of home ownership. "When you rent, you're just buying another man's house for him," he used to say. "Don't buy another man's house. Buy your own."

We were the only black family on our street, and my father was the longest-standing property owner on the block. No doubt this was because our white neighbors could pick up and move houses when they got a notion, while a black man did not have such freedoms. Even so, Gus had set himself up as a homeowner at a time when most black families could not do more than rent. It was just one more example of my father's determination to be—as singer Billie Holiday famously crooned—the God-blessed child "who's got his own."

Our family home at 110 East Pleasant Street was a fairly large three-bedroom, one bathroom, two-story clapboard structure on a spacious lot that accommodated a barn for my father's horses and a yard with carefully tended rose bushes, peonies and a vegetable garden. My parents never occupied the same bedroom. Growing up, I thought this was normal. My father slept year-round on the screened but unheated sleeping porch upstairs, while my mother and my oldest sister Georgeanna slept in the front bedroom, the windows overlooking Doup's Bake Shop across the street and the parkland beyond. Georgeanna and our mother had always been great buddies. As a child, I envied the closeness of their relationship, which had no doubt been cemented in the years when it was just the two of them, before our father and the rest of us entered the picture. The truth was I craved Mother's attention. My brother, four years my senior, seemed to identify most strongly with our father, but as he was the only boy, I secretly suspected both parents favored him. Lawrence was the only member of the family who did not have to share a room. He slept at the back of the house, in a narrow bedroom overlooking the alleyway and Gus' barn.

Then there was Rowena, who was only eighteen months older than me. We could not have been closer as children, although our interests began to diverge as we grew older. Rowena and I shared the side bedroom with its two matching cots and a dresser. If a guest came to visit us, Rowena and I would give up our bedroom and sleep downstairs in the living room or in the sitting room next to the kitchen.

By the time I was six, Georgeanna was 16 and out of the house attending a Seventh-day Adventist junior college in Alabama. In the summers when she came home, she no longer slept with Ella but opted to share the side bedroom with Rowena, leaving me to sleep in the front bedroom with my mother. I felt like the chosen child during those summers when I slept in Ella's room. But I worried about my father being cold out there on the side porch. Nightly in winter months, he would prepare ceramic-clay hot-water bottles and heat soap stones over the fire and place them under the covers to warm his bed before he climbed in. I remember I once asked him why he slept on the cold sleeping porch instead of in the bedroom with Lawrence. My father responded that he liked the bracing night air, and that it was healthier for the lungs to sleep in the cold.

We children were aware of the distant, strained relationship between our parents, but I never fathomed its cause until much later. Gus and Ella existed in a state of civil indifference. Both were devoted to their four children. In their love and care for us, they were completely united. But when it came to religious and civic events, they functioned independently of one another. They never accompanied each other to church or to local gatherings, and I never once saw them share a kiss or an embrace. Even their meals were taken separately. We children ate supper with my mother at around six each evening in the dining room, but my father worked long hours and usually dined alone at the kitchen table when he came home. At times, Mother could become abrasive, scolding and even belittling my father for some petty infraction. Typically, he would acquiesce to whatever her demand or walk away muttering, "Oh, Ella!" He simply refused to respond in anger. The harshest reprimand I ever heard from my father was, "Oh, thunder!" It was the closest he ever came to cursing.

The hard truth is that my mother considered my father and his people to be her social inferiors, because they were largely unschooled and had been dirt farmers, scratching out a living on inhospitable terrain. I wondered sometimes if she blamed Gus for his inability to deliver the social and economic comforts she had wished for herself. She often said she would have left my father were it not for their children. I didn't believe this, however. In response, my father declared that he would never let anybody separate him from his children or from his home. This, I did believe. Gus often said his family was his kingdom.

If her in-laws had been poor country farmers with little in the way of formal schooling, my mother came from people who had been well educated for generations. Her father, the Reverend William A. Cooper, had earned his doctorate in divinity from Temple University and had been an AME minister back East. On his retirement, Grandpa Cooper was given a plaque for his service to the Asbury Park African Methodist Episcopal Church in Baltimore; that plaque hung in my music room for decades. His brother was also a minister, and his sister, an accomplished pianist, taught music. My maternal grandmother, Bessie Christy Cooper, never worked outside the home. Instead, she busied herself with her duties as first lady of the church, planning events for her congregation, holding afternoon teas and bake sale fundraisers, and teaching piano and playing for the choir during service on Sunday mornings. Big-boned and lighter-skinned than her compactly built husband, she was the only daughter born to an Irish mother and a black father in Washington, D.C. As a child, I can remember my grandmother at the keys of our piano for hours when she came to visit, and I recall her exquisite and expensive wardrobe.

My own mother, born February 23, 1889, had been raised as an only child after her younger sister succumbed to scarlet fever when Ella was four. Mother was academically brilliant, especially in math and literature, and in another age, she might have become a doctor. None of her children equaled her intellectually. She maintained a meticulous accounting of the family's limited income, and she tithed every penny she earned. I have a vivid memory of my mother frequently reminding my father that taxes were due. She was a self-taught Bible scholar and regularly demonstrated this acumen in her church.

Although she had never gone to college, white children from the neighborhood came to her for help with college algebra and geometry, and she discussed their literature assignments with them insightfully. Yet there was never any certificate or diploma attesting to the brilliance of Ella Sophia Cooper. All that existed were her junior and senior high school diplomas from the Baltimore public school system. I remember that when I first read my mother's diploma from the Colored High and Training School, I found the wording demeaning. It said my mother had "pursued and satisfactorily completed an Approved Curriculum." There was no hint anywhere of the hospital courses she had taken during and after high school in order to qualify as a practical nurse, no reflection of her true intellectual abilities, and no further course of study she could undertake to develop her vast potential. I almost cried.

In the years when Mother could not find jobs as a practical nurse, she would work in white people's homes as a domestic servant. On weekends, she would do the washing, ironing, cooking and canning for our family, but as we children grew older, these duties fell to us. Even though we were expected to complete our assigned chores and to keep our rooms clean,

Ella was always more concerned with our schoolwork than our housework, which meant our home was often disheveled while we escaped into reading books. More than once I was able to successfully shirk my own household chores by pleading a heavy homework load. Our education was paramount.

Throughout my childhood, both Gus and Ella were sustained by their deeply rooted religious convictions, and they each clung tenaciously to their respective faiths. Ella had joined the Seventh-day Adventist church when I was two years of age, and she took all four of her children to services each Saturday. We were the only black members of the church, which made me silently question my mother's religious choice. I hated going to her church—I never thought of it as anything other than "her" church. I felt different and separate from the other children, which is odd, because other than my siblings, I was the only child of color in many other areas of my life—in my classroom at school, in my neighborhood, among my friends—and I had never felt the sense of being an outsider anywhere as keenly as I did at the Adventist church. Not that there was ever any racial confrontation. As the only blacks in the congregation, we were treated with scrupulous politeness and were welcomed into all facets of church life. I secretly believed that mother appreciated our being the only black family there. Gus never came to Seventh-day Adventist services with the rest of us, and I suspect that satisfied Ella, too.

We would begin observing the Sabbath on Friday night by singing gospel hymns while my mother accompanied us on our Gulbransen baby grand piano. Before this evening worship, we would have prepared enough food to last through the end of the Sabbath at sunset on Saturday evening. We would end our Sabbath observance in the same way we had opened it, by singing hymns and praying around the piano. During these devotions, my father might be out front on the porch swing, reading from his Bible, or out in the barn, tending to his horses. I never ceased from wishing that he would join us, and that we might all worship together, as I had seen other families do.

Many years later, I became privy to some town gossip that my mother had left the AME church because she was jealous of "sensuous" women in the congregation who she felt were overly friendly with her husband. In joining the Adventist church, she had divorced my father in a religious sense, because the Adventists did not recognize marriage to a person who was not a member of the church. Church leaders often quoted 2 Corinthians 6:14, which said, "Be ye not unequally yoked together with unbelievers, for what fellowship hath righteousness with unrighteousness, and what communion hath light with darkness?" I had silently blamed the Adventist church for alienating my father but came to see that it was my mother who had made it explicitly clear that the Adventist church was her sovereign domain.

Mother's entire social life was her church. This had the effect of isolating her from the black community in Mount Vernon, but it was an active choice rather than a passive one. Ella overtly divorced herself from most local black people as she read, studied and lived by the Bible. "Be ye in the world but not of the world and come ye out from among them and be ye separate," was an often-repeated quote of my mother's. While she was never unkind to people outside of her church, Mother did not seem to truly enjoy social discourse unless with Seventh-day Adventists. She shunned the "worldly ways" of those outside of her church and, in accordance with Adventist teaching, wanted her children to do likewise, dressing simply and modestly, avoiding amusements such as theater and dance, and eating no pork or shellfish. Only seafood with "fins and scales" was acceptable. Mother also saved her pennies to send her two oldest, Georgeanna and Lawrence, to the Seventh-day Adventist Academy and had initially intended to enroll Rowena and me at the school as well.

Her experience with Georgeanna changed her mind. My oldest sister had graduated from the Adventist Academy in 1926 and had gone on to attend a prestigious Adventist school, Oakwood

Junior College in Huntsville, Alabama. While there, she met and married a fellow student from Columbus, Ohio, who, like her, had been raised in the Seventh-day Adventist faith. To my mother's dismay, Georgeanna abandoned junior college and moved back to Ohio with her husband immediately after the nuptials, settling in Columbus. But the marriage didn't last; the two divorced a short time later, without having children. By then, Georgeanna had left the Adventist church. To support herself, she fell back on skills she had honed in junior college, becoming a stenographer and clerk-typist for a famous numbers runner in town. After a second failed marriage, to a man named Bill Skinner, whom the family adored, she would eventually wed Braxton Mitchell, the porter for an exclusive men's club in town. For Georgeanna, the third time turned out to be the charm. She and Braxton would move out west to Los Angeles together in 1960, and Georgeanna would study for her real estate license at a school there. Working as a broker, she would preach Gus' gospel of home ownership until retirement, which made our father proud.

But back when Georgeanna had dropped out of Oakwood, our parents were anything but pleased. The rest of us secretly cheered, however, because our sister's decision made our mother vow never to waste another penny on sending her children to Adventist schools. That, and the fact that our family's finances had been increasingly strained by junior college tuition bills, led my mother to summarily pull Lawrence out of the Academy and enroll him in the local public high school. Lawrence had pleaded for this for years; he hated the strict atmosphere of the Adventist school. Rowena and I also attended the public school. From then on, our Sabbath services on Saturdays and our devotions at home would have to suffice as our religious training, along with the annual Seventh-day Adventist summer camp meeting that convened in Mount Vernon.

The summer camp meeting was my favorite activity on the Adventist church calendar. Families came from all over Ohio, among them several Negro families with children near my age.

I looked forward to these meetings every year, because here at last were children with whom I had something in common. Of course, we had to attend the religious sessions, even though I was somewhere on the scale between indifferent and unaccepting when it came to the teachings. I viewed the Seventh-day Adventist religion as presenting more exclusions than inclusions. Still, it was a rare privilege for me to be able to play with even a few other black children my age. It was years before I realized the social dynamics at work here—the isolation I usually felt in the midst of our home congregation, and my hunger for the company of children who looked like me and experienced the world as I did. I was always sorry when the summer camp meetings came to an end.

My father was also deeply devoted to his church. As long as I could remember, he had been a member of the AME church, which was attended by the handful of black families in and around Knox County. Gus practiced his faith in all his daily activities, serving as a church trustee and Sunday school superintendent and singing in the church choir for fifty-five years. Church and family were the bedrocks of his life, his whole reason for getting out of bed each day. Gus took care of his church in the same way that he took care of his home. When a heavy snowfall came, my father would shovel the front path and steps to our house, and then he would head over to the church with my brother, shovel over his shoulder, to clear its steps, too. Gus also served as the vice president of the United Young People's Society, which was an interracial Methodist group in Mount Vernon. Always well respected among whites in the town, my father was a cornerstone of the black church community of Mount Vernon.

To my mind, both my parents were of superior character, goodness and wisdom, but they did not readily express these qualities toward each other. My father was patient and industrious and mechanically inclined, while my mother was highly literate and socially astute; she could very quickly size up a situation. Each seemed to have qualities the other lacked, which should have made them formidable together. But they failed to mesh their talents into a harmonious marital relationship. Mother always seemed to hold my father and his large extended family at arm's length.

I have come to believe that both my parents were silently troubled by the cruel indignities that ensued from the unaddressed racism of their day. In retrospect, it was everywhere, but in my innocence, I did not recognize it until early adolescence. It was then that I began to grasp that a portion of the difficulty in Gus and Ella's marital relationship was most certainly the outgrowth of a closed racist economy and the stresses it imposed upon black families. I can recall, for example, white men of some wealth approaching my father to hire him for hauling jobs or other work. Most of these men liked and respected my father, but they were nevertheless the ones in the position to do the hiring and not the other way around. One such man often frequented our home. He had bulging, watery eyes and a red, mottled face, and a cigarette dangled constantly from his lips. I realize now he was an alcoholic, but at the time, I only noticed that he talked to my father in a manner dripping with contempt. I silently determined that for all his wealth and status, this man was crude.

As I got older, I understood that he considered my father to be his servant and treated him as if he were beneath him. Yet my father maintained a scrupulously courteous demeanor in all interactions with this man. Later, looking back on my parents' relationship from an adult perspective, I was pained to realize that my mother did not fully respect my father. Perhaps she was as embarrassed as I was at the mildness of his response when white men spoke down to him. Perhaps, as I did back then, she saw his civility as weakness rather than what it truly was, a canny instinct for survival born of self-determination and fortitude. Or perhaps the wedge had been driven into the heart of their marriage years before when they had parted faiths, my mother decamping to the Seventh-day Adventist church, my father staying put in the AME church, where he worshipped every Sunday with Lawrence alone at his side. Whatever the reason for Ella's aloofness toward Gus, there was never any doubt in my mind that my father worshipped my mother and would have done anything she asked of him. His lifelong love and admiration for her was not diminished by the fact that Ella seldom returned the favor.

In navigating around the strain of our parents' marriage, we children tended to align ourselves with the parent of the same gender, none of us more so than my brother, Lawrence, who as the only boy in the family became my father's shadow. I confess I was jealous of my brother, who it seemed to me had the freedom to explore his place in the world in a way that we girls couldn't, at least when we were growing up. My dad made Lawrence his side-kick from the time my brother was five or six, pressing him into service to help fire the furnace each Sunday at church. Lawrence would also carry buckets of water to the horses and chickens in winter, and water the animals using the garden hose in summer. On days off from school, he would travel with my father on his wagon during garbage hauls, and he would even accompany him to nighttime bobsled parties.

Lawrence had clearly inherited our father's entrepreneurial spirit. When he was 10 years old, my brother convinced our parents to let him have his own horse and cart, which he quickly put to good use. In an era when few people owned cars, Lawrence would meet the incoming trains and rent out his cart to haul people's trunks to their homes. With that same cart, he started a taxi service while still in his teens, delivering merchandise and appliances for local merchants and ferrying people to appointments in and around town. Guided by Gus, Lawrence purchased his first car when he was 17, doing yard work all summer to afford it. The car was an old Model T junker, but it drove just fine, and in those days you didn't need a license to operate a vehicle. My brother used that car to drive local businessmen to surrounding towns like Columbus or Mansfield to take meetings or catch trains.

By the time he turned 21, he had saved enough to purchase

his first truck. During the day, he hauled townspeople's garbage as Gus had done for years, and after hours he delivered large electrical appliances like beer coolers, refrigerators and washers for local dealers. In 1939, when he proposed to and married Isabelle Crowder, a young woman from the neighboring town of Marion, Ohio, whom he'd met at a dance, Lawrence again followed the gospel preached by our father, building his own house on a lot just down the street from his childhood home. He had asked a white associate to act as his proxy to help him secure bank financing. In this way, Lawrence was able to make a comfortable life for his wife, Isabelle, and their daughter, Varian, who was born in 1941.

As young women, my sisters and I did not have the same opportunities available to us that our brother did. As we came of age, it seemed the only path open to us was to take care of white people's children or their homes, a life sentence that would only be lifted by marriage to an economically successful man. My sister Rowena and I traveled this road for a while, but I knew it was not for me. My mother's thwarted ambitions had provoked in me a desire for a larger intellectual life than seemed possible for a black woman in Mount Vernon. I decided I would be the first in my family to finish college. I wanted to live the life that had been denied my mother. I would become a nurse.

Rowena and me (in plaid dress at age nine) with a friend in front of our family's East Pleasant Street home.

CHAPTER 3

Colored Girl

On the surface, Mount Vernon during the 1920s was a bucolic Middle American town, its streets completely safe for children of all colors to ride bikes and play ball games, with white townspeople coexisting mostly serenely with the two hundred or so black residents. In his *History of Knox County, Ohio 1876-1976,* Frederick N. Lorey notes that, "In some areas the Negro has been accepted as an individual rather than as a member of his race,"[7] meaning it was possible for some whites to appreciate individual black people while maintaining a prejudice against the race as a whole. This was often true in Mount Vernon, where white neighbors greeted my parents warmly, even as the oppressive currents of discrimination played out continuously.

A full awareness of America's pervasive racism was still in my future, however, because Gus and Ella did all they could to ensure that my dreams for my life would remain protected. Even the resurgence of the Ku Klux Klan in Ohio in the 1920s[8] barely pierced the bubble my parents had so carefully constructed around us. But a march of Klansmen through our streets to the local fairground when I was five did leave me wondering what all the costumes were about, and why black people in Mount Vernon weren't allowed to join in. I have a clear image of an orderly line of robed and hooded Klansmen marching through our town. There were maybe a hundred of them, walking in twos. Lawrence insisted later that we didn't actually see them, which means the mental picture I have of the event must have been etched in memory by a photograph that ran in one of my father's newspapers.

On the day itself, Gus and Ella gathered their children around and told us in no uncertain terms to stay indoors. It was a Saturday, and I found it strange that we were missing Sabbath services because of a fairground parade. From the window of my mother's bedroom upstairs, I could hear cheers and songs reverberating through megaphones in the distance, and come evening I saw an orange glow bloom across the darkened sky. I thought it was a bonfire and I couldn't understand why we were forbidden to go, nor could I explain the tense quiet and pinched looks my father and mother wore all evening.

At school that Monday, some of my classmates talked about being with their parents at the fairground. They described how the men in long white robes and peaked hoods had formed a circle in the park as night fell. I know from later readings that they would have made hateful speeches against not just Negroes, but also Jews, Catholics, foreigners, even urban intellectuals who they found guilty of consorting with people other than "pure" rural Aryan whites like themselves. At the center of the field, a large burlap-wrapped, oil-soaked wooden cross would have been staked into the ground.[9] At some point, they set that cross on fire, and then watched and yelled and generally whooped it up as the flames licked the night. When the cross was burned to char and ash on the grassy field, only then did they disband the meeting.

In the decade after I was born, such marches were happening regularly throughout Ohio, which had become a stronghold for the resurgent Ku Klux Klan. Our immediate next-door neighbors, the Garvins, were known to be Klan members, with white-robed men coming and going from their house every weekend. I can recall at least one cross-burning rally in the park across the street from our front yards, the atmosphere not unlike a rowdy, beer-drinking barbecue—except of course for the fiery cross and the ugly jeers. The stench of gasoline used to drench the wood of the cross seemed to settle in every corner of our house. To this day, the smell of gasoline is a visceral reminder of that afternoon. I was only eight years old, but by then I knew enough not to set foot outside. We didn't believe the Garvins would allow their Klan visitors to actually harm us—after all, they brought over empty jugs to be filled with fresh milk just like everyone else in town—but we kept a wary distance anyway.

During those years, the Klan was simply a fact of life in the rural Midwest. The white supremacy group, founded after the Civil War to oppose Southern Reconstruction and its new freedoms for blacks, had all but disappeared by the late 1800s. But with the 1915 release of D.W. Griffith's film *The Birth of a Nation*, formerly titled *The Clansman*, it had come roaring back. And this time, the group had found its way into mainstream American life, pulling sheriffs, doctors, lawyers, businessmen and ministers into its ranks. In Ohio alone, the clandestine group's numbers ballooned to an estimated four hundred thousand, with the Klan infiltrating every level of state and local politics. As author David M. Chalmers wrote in *Hooded Americanism: The History of the Ku Klux Klan,* "... during the 1920s ... it seemed that mask and hood had become the official symbol of the Buckeye State."[10]

I remember when I asked my parents about the cross-burning rally in front of our house, their reactions were determinedly stoic. "Those people are ignorant," Ella said. "Don't pay them any mind." This would always be their first response when prejudice reared its head. Once, when my father was giving a hayride to local children, white and black, he stopped at an ice cream parlor downtown to give his young passengers a treat. The owner refused service to the black children in the group but allowed the white children to have ice cream cones. Confused, I searched my father's face. "That's just the way it is," he told me, his eyes straight ahead, his voice merely matter-of-fact. "But you don't allow yourself to be destroyed by it."

With this coaching from my parents, I gave little thought to my skin color or to the fact that almost all of my childhood friends were white. Since I was always at the top of my class in school, I failed to grasp that there were people who considered me of lesser intelligence and unworthy of the same legal and civil protections as my white peers. I loved school, and knew quite clearly that no one was any "better" than I was. To their credit, my teachers treated me the same as my white classmates. I liked them and believed they liked me. Some of them even hinted that I was one of their favorites, which made sense to me, because I was a hard worker and a generally cheerful and obedient child. I knew that my mother was very smart, and I wanted nothing more than to be like her. It helped that my parents fully supported my teachers in discipline, grading and homework. If any one of the Simmons children was not doing well in school, my mother was the first to know about it.

Back then I had no idea what a second-class citizen was. If people ever discussed the term in my presence, I looked around to see who they might be talking about. Still, as had happened with the Klan rally, there were moments in my childhood that left me squirming, and I knew they had to do with the fact that my skin was of a darker shade than that of my friends. Whenever we sang popular folk songs in school, for example, I became embarrassed and would slink down in my seat, trying not to be noticed. The song lyrics that evoked this reaction included "Old Black Joe" (*Gone are my friends from the cotton fields away*); "Old Folks At Home" (*Oh! darkies how my heart grows weary*); "My Old Kentucky Home" (*'Tis summer, the darkies are gay*); and "Without A Song" (*A darky's born but he's no good no how, without a song*).

But if music class at my local public school was uncomfortable for me, elsewhere in my young life, music was my joy and my refuge. For ten years, from age seven through age seventeen, five days each week, I practiced the piano in the home of my music teacher, Gertrude Jones, who lived one street over. Mrs. Jones and her husband, Dana Jones, were the only other black family in our neighborhood. This dear lady became a second mother to me, and she remained an inspiration, mentor and dear friend until her death in 1965. Mrs. Jones would call me, "My child, my darling child," and she could not have treated me with more love and care if I had indeed been born from her body. She had wanted children but had been unable to conceive, and so I happily filled that yearning place in her life. To instill in me an appreciation of the classics, she took me to the Community Concert series in Mount Vernon to see recitals by people like Madame Schumann-Heink, Jascha Heifetz, Ignacy Jan Paderewski, Roland Hayes, Lotte Lehmann, Marian Anderson and Paul Robeson. At small recitals in her home and sometimes at my high school, I would play Beethoven's "Moonlight Sonata"; "Rustle Of Spring" by Christian Sinding; "Juba: Dance" by R. Nathaniel Dett; Franz Liszt's "Hungarian Dance #5"; "Prelude in C Sharp Minor" by Rachmaninoff; and other pieces. She saw to it that I was the pianist for the girls' glee club at my school, and I often played solos during their concerts. I thought nothing of the daily rigor of my music instruction. I practiced and studied and played recitals and did what was expected of me by my music teacher and also by my parents, especially my mother.

It was Mrs. Jones who introduced me to whatever black culture I was exposed to as a child. She often advised, "Baby, you must go South to find your roots in black culture." And she would add, "Good blacks like me hail from the South." Often, she would arrange for me to play the piano for local black Baptist or AME church programs. She felt that I needed to interact more with the black people in Knox County, and she created opportunities for me to know them, and for them to know me. Somehow, she did this while always deferring to my mother and her teachings for her children.

While I knew Mrs. Jones felt that Mother's talents were needed in the black community, I sensed rather than observed her subtle reproach at the way my mother kept herself apart. Mrs. Jones was founder of the Twentieth Century Club of Mount Vernon, a black women's club seeking civic improvement for our town; the group later became a branch of the National Association of Colored Women's Clubs, Inc. With a slogan of "Lifting As We Climb," the consortium of women's groups proudly claimed "continuous service to humanity since 1896." Mrs. Jones often invited my mother to join the group, but her effort was in vain; Ella wanted nothing to do with civic meetings. Still, Mrs. Jones made a point of vocally admiring my mother's superior intelligence and praising her capabilities and poise.

Mrs. Jones also had great respect for my dad. She spoke very highly of him, as did everyone else in Mount Vernon. She would admit that she wished my father had more help from my mother when it came to his work for the AME church and for Mount Vernon's small black community. But she managed to make this sound wishful rather than like a complaint. That was who Mrs. Jones was; her outlook was relentlessly optimistic. My very fondest childhood memories are of the time I spent in her home. In addition to teaching music at local black churches, Mrs. Jones worked as a caterer for well-to-do Mount Vernon families, preparing her menus at home and conveying her magnificent spread to the host's table. Often, as I practiced my music on the baby grand in her attractively furnished and immaculately maintained living room, mouthwatering aromas would waft from her kitchen and tease me. Sometimes she would let me taste the black beans, the succulent meats, freshly baked bread, her famous fried chicken and beef stew as she prepared her robust feasts.

She never fed me her renowned baked Springfield ham, however, because she knew I attended the Seventh-day Adventist church, which forbade the consumption of pork. Although I often tried to convince her to let me have just a morsel of the delicious-smelling ham, she stood firm, knowing my mother would not approve. She was respectful of my parents' choices, but at the same time, she gave me a place to safely unburden whenever I became angry with Ella or Gus or felt excluded from social activities at school. Mrs. Jones would listen to my woes and offer measured advice that was considerate of all parties involved. She gave me the kind of tender motherly attention that no one else could, including my pragmatic, unsentimental mother.

I assumed her cultural pride and social and artistic refinement had been nurtured in a middle-class upbringing in the heart of the black South. But this was not the case. I later learned she had been born and raised in Yellow Springs, Ohio, in the humblest of circumstances. Her husband Dana was a chauffeur for the Ring-wald family, who owned the local department store. He was not as cultivated as his wife was, and he was somewhat reserved, but it was obvious that they were a team, devoted to each other and working together for the betterment of their community. Unfortunately, Mr. Jones was a chain smoker. Seldom did I see him without a cigarette in the corner of his mouth, and I hated the tobacco odor that clung to him. Mr. Jones eventually died of lung cancer that had metastasized to his liver. This was in the mid-1950s, before the lethal effects of tobacco smoke had been properly publicized.

It was not until I was a resident in chest medicine in 1963 that I learned of the evils of tobacco. The surgeon general at the time, Dr. Luther Terry, had begun warning the nation of the deadly effects of cigarettes in the early 1960s. But the public refused to believe him or to act upon his advice. Even physicians ignored him, many of them continuing to smoke themselves and to tolerate smoking in their patients, instead of taking a firm stand against the use of tobacco. As a resident in asthma-allergy who had seen firsthand the damage wrought by cigarettes, I viewed smoking as suicidal for the smoker and chronic illness-producing for those forced to inhale secondhand fumes. I have been on a perpetual soapbox since the 1960s, berating smoking (but never the smoker). To this day, I forbid anyone to smoke in my presence, and I have had friends accuse me of being fanatical on the subject. If I am, I am sure it has something to do with watching the pain my adored music teacher endured at the loss of her husband to lung cancer.

Mrs. Jones, more than anyone, helped to anchor me as I grew older and the world around me began to feel less welcoming, less safe. No matter what was happening outside of Mrs. Jones' home, I knew I could always go to her living room and find a corner of security, where I could make beautiful music under her tutelage and bask in her love. Mrs. Jones gave me a sheltered place to develop myself creatively and to explore my ambitions. She is the whole reason that playing the piano was and remains to this day one of the most fulfilling activities of my life, an escape from all worldly cares.

Those cares increased for me as I entered puberty. That was around the time when my childhood friends began to pull away. In retrospect, my high school years were a lonely time. My older siblings were off living their own lives—Lawrence was already pursuing his own business ventures; Georgeanna was married and living in Columbus; Rowena was involved with her own friends—and my schoolmates, although pleasant enough in the classroom, no longer included me in any extracurricular plans. Work became my sanctuary. I buried myself in my studies, earning grades at the very top of my class. My report cards from high school show a constellation of As, with the average marks in my exams hovering at 98 percent. I lost myself in dreams of the future, visualizing a life in the medical field in vivid Technicolor. I started doing childcare in my free time as a means of saving money for college, and I was thrilled when our long-time family doctor hired me as the regular babysitter for his younger child, a five-year-old boy.

Every day after school I would walk to the family's home a few neighborhoods away to take care of this little boy. The father was the only doctor for miles around who would see colored patients as part of his practice. I admired him a great deal; perhaps I even idolized him, because he openly applauded my goal of entering the medical field, and he even discussed his cases with me. He told me I was a bright young woman, and that I would make an excellent nurse, and his encouragement meant everything.

Imagine me back then, a lonely teenager with an outsized dream, a colored girl in a small and overwhelmingly white Midwestern town, and you'll begin to understand just how vulnerable for affirmation I was, especially from a man such as he was, a medical doctor and a prominent figure in our town. The fact that I had found someone outside of my parents and Mrs. Jones who not only believed I could achieve my ambition, but who also actively encouraged it, going so far as to solicit my thoughts on his medical cases, well, I would have done almost anything he asked of me to have it continue. As it turned out, the good doctor didn't ask for what he wanted. He simply took it from me.

I had fallen ill with scarlet fever. My mother took me to the doctor's office downtown for treatment. The first time, she stayed in the room with me as he examined my chest with his stethoscope. But a few weeks later, when I had recovered and went back to see the doctor for a follow-up visit, my mother was working, and so she sent me there on my own. She trusted this man, and so did I. After all, he knew the family; I babysat for his son. It is true that when I was in his home, there had been occasions when I caught him staring at me, and he would tell me then that I was beautiful, although never in earshot of anyone else. Once, he even told me that if the world were different, he would make me his wife. This was clearly inappropriate from a man in his forties, and perhaps it should have repelled me, but I was 13 years old, an outsider hungry for the world's notice, and his words gave me a secret thrill. I was so naïve, I never fathomed their implications.

The afternoon of my follow-up visit, I found myself alone with the doctor in his office. I don't know where his nurse had gone, but she wasn't in the outer reception area where she usually sat. I undressed from the waist down and climbed onto the examination table, as the doctor instructed. I placed my heels in the metal stirrups, knees in the air. The doctor explained that I was growing up, and this was part of how he was now required to examine me. I felt embarrassed, exposed, but I took him at his word.

"All right, Ellamae," he murmured, his voice soothing as he moved toward me, "I want you to relax, let your knees fall to the side and close your eyes." I did as I was told. A moment later, I felt the rough cloth of his suit brush against my legs and then suddenly, a terrible pain. I whimpered and squirmed. "Shhh," the doctor said, his fingers rooting into the flesh of my thighs. "You're doing fine, Ellamae." But the pain went on and on, like something tearing inside me. I gripped the sides of the exam table and prayed for it to end.

When at last the doctor stepped away from me, there was a sticky wetness between my legs. I looked down and realized I was bleeding. As the doctor buttoned his suit pants and refastened his belt, I was filled with shame. Yet I still didn't understand what he had done. I didn't know what sex was. My mother hadn't explained it to me, because I had not yet begun to menstruate. I didn't know what a hymen was, much less the significance of a ruptured one. When the doctor saw that I was bleeding, he said, "Oh, I must have penetrated you more deeply than I thought." He handed me a wad of tissues to wipe myself and then left so that I could get dressed.

I have spent my entire life since wondering how many girls this doctor forced himself on before he did the same thing to me. How many after me had endured what I had, and had continued to go to him as their doctor because so few physicians in the area would treat blacks? He did not caution me never to tell anyone what he had done; he knew he didn't have to. Who would have believed me, a colored girl accusing one of the town's most prominent white citizens of rape—because make no mistake, that is what he had done, although I didn't understand this at the time.

Many years later, when I was in medical school, I began to realize the degree to which I was not alone in this harrowing experience. By then I had met many young black and Latina women who told me how they, too, had been violated during routine pelvic exams, and that it had happened to their sisters and mothers too. Most male doctors never abused their professional position in this way, of course, but it was clear that there were many who had. And in the first half of the twentieth century, at least anecdotally, it happened with distressing regularity to black and brown women, who were seen as powerless to do anything about it. It's no coincidence that many of the African American and Latina medical students I would later encounter had been motivated to go into women's healthcare so as to provide an alternative to physicians such as the one who had forced himself on me.

How to explain that for many years after, I continued to babysit for this man's son, and even to discuss his medical cases when he brought them to me? He continued to compliment my intelligence, and to tell me he thought I had what it took to become a nurse, but I no longer felt a flush of pride when he said these things. I knew what he was, what he had done. The doctor is long dead now, and I have refrained from using his name out of consideration for his descendants, some of whom still live in my hometown. But it haunts me to this day that I remained as silent as a tomb about the unspeakable thing that was done to me in the office of a physician I had once respected. As is typical in sexually abusive encounters involving minors, for a long time I thought I was at fault. Even though I was a mere child, I feared that I had somehow entertained the doctor's attentions and led him on. For many years after, this misguided idea filled me with deep shame. And so I did not reveal to my parents, or even to my adored music teacher, what had happened. Sadly, until I began writing this story, I did not tell a single soul.

At 17, I had never met a black college graduate but was determined to become one myself.

CHAPTER 4

Higher Learning

In the 1930s it was monumental for a poor black girl to dream of a college education. Nevertheless I did. I heard white students in my high school graduating class speaking of going away to various colleges—Ohio State, Western Reserve, Denison, Kenyon, Oberlin and others—and I knew I wanted to go to college too. The fact that black children were not expected to pursue higher education was unacceptable to me. Why should my future horizons be set any lower than that of classmates who were not nearly as academically motivated as I was?

My local high school offered vocational guidance but not as it might pertain to an aspiring black student. The education of Negro children was intended to end with high school graduation. It was expected that the young men would get service or laborer jobs after that, and the young women would work as domestics or hairdressers. I can recall clearly that our high school principal told one black mother that her son did not need to go to college because he would just end up working in the local foundry. This student went on to become an electrical engineer with a Ph.D., and he eventually taught in the College of Engineering at Ohio State University. Imagine if he or his mother had listened to that principal, what a loss that would have been to the world! There were numerous such stories of Negro students defying the odds. I intended to be one of them.

I had indicated to several of my high school teachers that I wished to enter a school of nursing. Some of them showed interest and encouraged me, but they wondered aloud where I could get such training. Certainly they had never heard of the scores of Historically Black Colleges and Universities (HBCUs) that might

37

welcome a student like me. The first of these schools were funded by states under the Senator Justin Morrill Land-Grant Act of 1890, which ruled that states receiving federal land-grant funds were required either to open their colleges and universities to black students or to set aside money for the creation of all-black colleges to serve as a "separate but equal" alternative.

Between 1890 and 1910, sixteen exclusively black colleges were established with the land-grant funds. The black church had also opened schools; the Quakers had built others; and still others had been established through a joint effort of the American Missionary Association and the Freedmen's Bureau, which had a mandate to create a path to higher education for people of African descent.[11]

Prominent and influential black leaders—from Booker T. Washington, who had graduated from Hampton Normal and Agricultural Institute in Virginia in 1875, to W. E. B. Du Bois, who graduated from Fisk University in Tennessee in 1888 and went on to earn a master's degree in history from Harvard—were trained by these fine institutions. In a nation whose mainstream colleges routinely excluded blacks, HBCUs contributed greatly to the progress being made by Negroes at the time. Unfortunately, none of my teachers had ever heard of these schools, and so I remained ignorant of the fact that in states across the country, institutions of higher learning had been established for the express purpose of educating and creating opportunities for black people.[12]

I was exactly the kind of student who should have known about these schools, too. I graduated in the top 3 percent of my high school class in 1936, with a numerical point average of 96 percent. In a class of 140 graduates, I had been one of a few students selected to the National Honor Society. My academic credentials were impeccable and my ambition unwavering—I still wanted to be a nurse like my mother. And so I took the only course that seemed open to me: I applied to my tax-supported state university for admission to their school of nursing. I reasoned that as a citizen of the state with stellar grades and whose parents paid taxes like everyone else, I was not asking for anything to which I was not entitled. Besides, Ohio State University, located in nearby Columbus, had enrolled a few black students in its undergraduate college in recent years. Admittedly, almost all of them were male and most of them were involved in varsity sports.

The most prominent was Alabama-born and Cleveland-raised athlete Jesse Owens, who in NCAA competitions had brought home a raft of medals for Ohio State, and who had gone on to earn four gold medals in the Berlin Olympics in 1936, the year in which I applied. I was innocently excited by the prospect of attending the same college as this home-grown hero, whose victories in the 100- and 200-meter sprints, the long jump and the 4 x 400-meter relay race had crushed Nazi dictator Adolf Hitler's goal of demonstrating Aryan racial supremacy at the Berlin games.[13] Better yet, Jesse Owens had cast the Negro race in a triumphant international spotlight. I suppose I assumed that I could bask in his reflected glory; surely Ohio State's admissions officials had all the proof they needed of black commitment and accomplishment in this star of track and field.

What I did not know was that Owens had not been exactly welcomed at Ohio State, despite the fact that he brought such accolades to their door. As a student, he had been obliged to live off campus with the handful of other black athletes, and when he traveled with his team, he and the other black athletes had to order carryout while the white students dined in local restaurants. Although he had been elected the first black captain of Ohio State's varsity track and field team, Owens also could not stay in the same hotels where his white teammates were housed; he had to find black rooming houses or seek lodging with a local colored family. Nor had the school offered him any sort of scholarship, which meant he had to work a series of part-time jobs to pay for his education.[14] His academics suffered and he eventually left Ohio State without earning his degree.

It had been a bitter pill for him to discover that despite the honors he had brought to his country, America remained hardly more hospitable to him than Hitler's Germany had been. As Owens said when he returned from the Berlin games, "When I came back to my native country, after all the stories about Hitler, I couldn't ride in the front of the bus. I had to go to the back door. I couldn't live where I wanted. I wasn't invited to shake hands with Hitler, but I wasn't invited to the White House to shake hands with the president, either."[15]

Had I realized the degree to which this international superstar was treated as a second-class citizen at his own state university, I might have anticipated the school's response to my application to train as a nurse. Perhaps on some level I did expect it, because when a thin, white envelope arrived at our home about a month after I had applied, I went to my room to open it, wanting to be alone with the news.

My fingers were shaking as I tore into the envelope and extracted the single, folded sheet of onionskin paper. I thought my whole future depended on the words typed on that page, which rustled loudly in my hands.

The language was terse and impersonal: "We have no facilities for training colored girls in our school of nursing," the letter said. I stared at that single line of black type for a very long time.

I realized I was not truly surprised.

And yet I was devastated.

I will never forget that stark sentence—thirteen words that seemed to erase my very future. I had never understood more clearly than in that moment how completely the cruel calculus of race controlled my life. My parents had insisted that I could be anything I put my mind to, but the world was trying to tell me a different story. It was saying that I didn't need to go to college, because I was not expected to pursue—much less attain—the level of professional success that white college graduates do. More than anything, this made me angry, because the country had built its ivory towers on the backs of black labor, and whites had watered their paths to prosperity with the blood, sweat and tears of black slaves.

Some of my friends said, "Ellamae, you knew you would not get into that university. You knew they hardly ever admit colored. Why would you even apply?" In fact, I had applied there because I had no knowledge of any other schools of nursing. I applied because Jesse Owens' attendance at the school had given me hope. I hadn't understood that as a world-class athlete, Owens was the exception that proved a painful and long-standing rule. I imagined the hundreds of thousands of Negro youth who had graduated from high schools across the country in the same year as me and who now had no prospects for a brighter future than that of their parents. Everything in me rebelled at the idea that my potential should be shut away in a box that America had constructed for dreamers who looked like me. I refused to accept that rejection letter with its thirteen pitiless words as the end of the road for me. As much as it felt like a door slamming shut in my face, I immediately began looking for a different door. I resolved that I would not let myself be defined by the culture's deep-rooted prejudices about who I was and who I could be. I would not carry that burden!

Of course, I had no clue yet where the different door to my future lay. Biding my time, I went to work after graduation as a domestic—cooking, washing and cleaning for a white family in town. Sometimes wealthy white women also hired me to style their hair. Occasionally, I made a few additional cents pulling weeds and digging up plantains in the gardens of friends, and I continued babysitting for the family of the doctor who had abused me. I earned about five dollars weekly, which I carefully set aside in a postal savings account for my education. The lingering trauma of the Great Depression, the 1929 stock market crash, and widespread bank failures had instilled a fear of bank safety in my parents, who guided us to deposit our earnings in an account with the post office instead. That year, I saved over $600 in my postal savings account. In the ratio of dollars earned to dollars saved, I have not equaled such a savings record since.

Even though I was working in the kitchens of two different families and doing babysitting and farming jobs as well, I also enrolled in shorthand and typing courses at my local high school. I thought these would be useful when I entered college the following year. I enjoyed my classes, as indeed I have always enjoyed any form of school. I was even selected to compete in the state's competitive typing contest in Bowling Green, Ohio. I did not win, but it hardly mattered. My steadfast goal of entering the medical field remained uppermost in my mind. I still did not know where I would find a school of nursing that would admit me, but I believed the answer was on its way.

And it was.

The solution came to me from, of all places, my mother's Seventh-day Adventist church, which I had recently abandoned. On graduating from high school, I had declared to my mother that I wanted to find my own house of worship. For several months, I went from church to church, looking for a spiritual home that would accept me and that I could accept. I had finally become a Unitarian, attracted by the fact that, while it was a Christian congregation, it held as a central belief that spiritual truth and meaning can be found in all faiths, and it welcomed everyone into its pews. I tried to explain to my mother that the Adventist church had not been a good fit for me, because I did not see myself reflected anywhere in the three hundred or so members of its congregation. Furthermore, the church felt too restrictive. To my mind, it was all *thou shalt not* and not enough *thou shalt*. My poor mother was heartbroken. But that did not stop her from advocating for her youngest within the congregation when an opportunity to do so arose.

A professor from Virginia, a black man, was visiting the church. After the service, he and my mother began talking. She told him about her daughter who wanted to be a nurse, and who was more than capable of fulfilling that ambition, but the state school of nursing would not admit her. The professor turned out to be a member of the faculty at Hampton Institute in the city of Hampton, Virginia. He explained to Ella that the Institute had been one of several historically black colleges founded after Reconstruction for the express purpose of educating Negroes. He told my mother that there was an excellent school of nursing at Hampton, and that her daughter should consider applying there. He felt sure that with my grades I would be accepted, and he went so far as to offer to write me a letter of referral, which he did that very afternoon.

Oh happy day! I could hardly take in what my mother was telling me when she arrived home from church with the Hampton professor's letter of recommendation in her gloved hands. I immediately wrote to the school and made my formal application that summer. As the professor had predicted, I was accepted. I was even awarded a small scholarship of $200, which was very respectable in those days.

And so in September of 1937, I stood with both my parents on the platform of the Baltimore & Ohio (B&O) station in my hometown, waiting for the train bound for Newport News, Virginia. A bus would take me the rest of the way to the Hampton campus, which was a thirty-minute ride from Newport News. The B&O was the first and oldest passenger railway in the country, but even though it had been a background fixture my entire life, I had never before boarded one of its cars. Mother was sobbing as the train pulled into the station, and I was crying, too. My father stood stone-faced, his large brown hands absently smoothing the hem of his suit jacket, his broad-brimmed fedora shadowing his eyes. I knew he was afraid for me, and holding back his own tears. He patted my back as my mother embraced me. When I lingered, still crying, they both gave me a gentle push toward the train. I felt so alone as I boarded and found a seat from which I could look out at my parents, the two of them united for once in apprehension and pride as my train pulled away.

I was 19, an unsophisticated, frightened, but eager small-town girl who had not been raised around many other black people, and now I was going to a school where almost all the other students would be black. The only people of color I had known growing up had been my cousins, aunts and uncles, my music teacher, and the few other black families in my town. I wanted more than anything to go to this nursing school in Virginia where I would for the first time be in the majority, but now that the day had arrived, I was possessed by a wild desire to stay amid familiar surroundings. This was my first trip away from home, except for when I had attended the typing competition in Bowling Green and the occasions in childhood when I had been to Barnesville in Belmont County with my father and siblings for the annual Simmons family reunion. Now I was headed for an entirely new world. What would it be like to sit in class and look around me, I wondered, and see eager brown faces that reflected my own?

That afternoon on the B&O, my thrill at this prospect was mixed with fear. There was a queasy fluttering sensation in my midsection, like hundreds of loosed butterflies. I could barely sit still in my seat, my rising excitement tempered by a looming reckoning with the unknown. I was heading to the South, where my parents had warned the most virulent forms of discrimination played out. They had cautioned me to be aware of my surroundings always, and they had tried to prepare me for the reality of Jim Crow segregation laws: As soon as the train crossed the Ohio border into Kentucky, they explained, the Jim Crow curtain would come down and all Negroes would be obliged to move to the segregated section behind that partition. My parents advised me that I was to obey the conductor's instructions and not to cause any trouble. And so when I crossed into the South for the first time in my young life, I gathered up my brown cardboard suitcase and held fast to my dignity as I moved with the rest of the black passengers to the back of the train.

Members of my nursing school class, circa 1938, on the steps of Dixie Hospital, where we were trained. I am third from left in the second row.

CHAPTER 5

Balm in Gilead

Hampton! The school and the town were a revelation! I saw black people functioning in ways I had only dared to dream—black college professors, black doctors and nurses, black businessmen, blacks managing the campus bookstore and post office, blacks in military uniform. I had never seen so many black people together in one place in my life. I thought I had died and gone to heaven—and heaven was full of black people! And everything was run efficiently and professionally. There were also white teachers and administrators at the school, but they seemed comfortably integrated into the environment, and I grew to consider the Hampton community as a sort of mixed-race extended family.

Recently, I encountered a description of the campus by a former student, Tamara Jeffries, a journalist who is now a professor at another HBCU, Bennett College in Greensboro, North Carolina. Jeffries attended Hampton in the 1980s, and yet her recollection of what it felt like to be on that campus is timeless. Her words say beautifully what I wish to convey, and so with her permission I quote them here:

Hampton's campus is in a word, romantic. It's the water that makes it so. A peninsula on a peninsula, the school is bordered on two sides by the Hampton River; Jonas Creek branches off along the southern edge of campus. It is the water encircling it that makes Hampton its own private place. It is the lapping water that beckons first as you enter the campus gates: See me first, the river whispers. The rest of the campus can wait.

When you turn away from the water, four-story Virginia-Cleveland Hall commands the view. The Hampton Singers "sang up" the oldest girl's dormitory in 1874; at the turn of the century another section was added to its sprawl. The brick building features a tower capped with a High Victorian roof like a witch's hat. When the sun sets on her front façade, the building becomes imposing in the darkness and reminds students of the story that a ghost roams the halls.

Near the water, but nestled in the privacy of flowering shrubs and stately trees, stands the Mansion House, the pristine white building where the president's family lives and guests are entertained. Look a little farther along to see a redbrick clock tower, 150 feet high. On Sundays the bells chime, calling students to worship in the chapel at its foot below. The interior of Memorial Church is cool and dim on Sunday morning, a little light filtering in through leaded glass windows. The pews arc so that students can get a view of the pulpit—and the chaplain can get a good view of them.

Back at the center of campus, Ogden Circle—which superstition says students should not walk across—makes a circular drive in front of Ogden Hall, where students come to watch performances or hear speakers deliver inspiring words.

The library sits along the circle, too, its white stone columns speaking of the purpose of the college: education for life. Walking in the heavy doors, the ceiling soars above you. You choose staircases on the left and right that circle up to the stacks and the familiar dusty smell of books.

There is a powerful sense of history here. One can imagine students emerging from an event at Ogden or an evening studying at the library in years past. The young men would escort young ladies to women's dormitories on the northern side of campus before crossing back to the men's halls on the other side.

The pride of Hampton Institute is the Emancipation Oak. The history of its massive trunk and broad-spreading boughs is explained proudly to visitors: It was under this tree that the Emancipation Proclamation was read for the first time in the South. Later, former slaves, eager for an education to complete their freedom, came to this same spot for lessons taught in its shade. Thus, the tree is where the seeds of what would be Hampton Institute were planted. The tree became a symbol of what Hampton was to become.[16]

My own Hampton story was set five decades earlier, and began in 1936. My room was in the famed Virginia Hall, a sprawling Victorian mansion that had once been the main building of the school, housing not just the women's dormitory but also classrooms, a dining room and the chapel. I felt welcome in this place from my very first day. When I got off the bus from Newport News, upperclassmen were there to greet me. They gave me directions to the dorm, and one young man even helped me carry my suitcase. My roommate had already moved in, her bed neatly spread on one side of the room. Ena Rita Shillingford was from a family of some wealth in the U.S. Virgin Islands, and her older brother was also a student at Hampton. She planned to study English literature and become a teacher back home. Ena and I became fast friends. Up to that point in my life, I had formed so few friendships with black girls my own age. I realized happily that all that was about to change.

Hampton Institute's president at the time, Dr. Arthur Howe, was a white man. He was married to Margaret Armstrong Howe, the daughter of General Samuel Chapman Armstrong, a former Union solider who had been appointed superintendent of the Freedmen's Bureau of the Ninth District of Virginia. In this capacity, Armstrong had secured funding from the American Missionary Association to establish a school for coloreds in a plantation area known as Little Scotland. Built on what was formerly Wood Farm, the original building overlooked the northern peninsula of the harbor of Hampton Roads. The college I would attend more than half a century later opened its doors on April 1, 1868, as the Hampton Normal and Agricultural Institute.[17] Its stated purpose remains a guiding principle and is still quoted in the university's catalogue today:

> *The thing to be done was clear: to train selected Negro youth who should go out and teach and lead their people first by example, by getting land and homes; to give them not a dollar that they could earn for themselves; to teach respect for labor, to replace stupid drudgery with skilled hands, and in this way to build up an industrial system for the sake not only of self-support and intelligent labor, but also for the sake of character.*[18]

Given this founding mission, the school naturally emphasized the teaching of industrial trades and skills. The goal was to ensure its graduates would be financially able to support their families in vocations secure enough to give the generations after them a running start. Hampton trained hundreds of teachers, farmers and skilled craftsmen in the years before it became a fully accredited college in 1926.[19] Its excellent nursing school diploma program was added in 1931, six years before I enrolled as a student there.[20] Just the fact that such an institution of learning existed was a source of wonder to me. I wanted to discover everything I could about its history, and to understand my humble place on its storied landscape.

I learned how in 1861, shortly after the Civil War began, the North had taken control of Fort Monroe near Hampton, and a Union general named Benjamin Butler had declared that any enslaved Negroes who reached the fort would not be returned to their Southern plantations; they would henceforth be considered free men and women, or as he put it, "the contraband of war." Soon fugitive blacks were pouring into the area in a desperate bid for freedom. So many of them came that the Union army had to build a camp to house the refugees. Called The Grand Contraband Camp in a nod to Butler's bold decree, it was effectively the first free African American community in the South.[21]

That summer, a black Hamptonian, Mary Smith Peake, was engaged by the American Missionary Association to teach the newly freed blacks the skills and knowledge they would need to establish themselves outside of slavery. Peake, the daughter of a free black mother and an English father, had attended school in Washington, DC, as a child. A passionate believer in the power of education to uplift the race, she had made her living as a dressmaker while secretly teaching blacks out of her home. When the Confederate army torched her family home in Hampton shortly after the fall of Fort Monroe, she and other displaced Negroes found refuge at Contraband Camp. There, she jumped at the chance to openly establish a formal curriculum for the education of Negroes. With more than fifty children during the day and twenty adult students in the evenings, she initially held classes under a massive oak that stood on the camp property. Two years later, that magnificent oak would be the site of the first reading of President Lincoln's Emancipation Proclamation in the South. The tree, which still stands on what is now the campus of Hampton University, became known as the Emancipation Oak, an enduring symbol of freedom, educational equality and justice for all.

Sadly, Mary Peake would not live to see the date, January 1, 1863, when all enslaved men and women were declared free. She died of tuberculosis the February before, but her contributions to the founding of the school that would one day become my haven were inestimable. [22]

Hampton was also the alma mater of Booker T. Washington, one of the foremost African American authors and educators of our time. Although Washington had died three years before I was born, he had been a powerful icon of black intellectual life to me, and a hero of my former music teacher, Mrs. Gertrude Jones. Now here I was, a student carrying my books through the same hallowed halls of learning where he had walked. I was sure that it had been God's plan all along for me to be here. I was grateful now, that this was the door that had opened for me, because as a black girl who had been raised in a 98 percent-white Ohio town, what I needed even more than an education was a way to see myself whole. Hampton held up the mirror in which I could do just that. I had the privilege of going to class in a setting where I could be steeped in the history of my people and be encouraged in my endeavors by teachers, black and white, who had not just my interests at heart but also the interests of my entire race. My perspective on what was possible for my life was expanding by leaps and bounds. Little did I realize that returning to my small town in the Midwest would never feel quite the same.

I did sometimes experience pangs of homesickness, but my mother penned messages to me daily and mailed them in a letter at the end of each week. In this way, I was kept informed of what was happening at home, and with my dog Jan, whom I adored. My music teacher also wrote to me often, and occasionally my siblings wrote too. Mother regularly baked cookies, fruit-filled tarts and chocolate fudge, which she meticulously wrapped and packed for shipping. I was always overjoyed to receive these sweets, which arrived from her like clockwork every six weeks. Everyone on my floor of the dorm seemed to know when the box would be arriving, and they would crowd into my room to share in it.

Even though I missed my family, I was enthralled with my life at Hampton. I was a diligent student, resolved as always to do well in my classes. Schoolwork had long been an area of mastery for me, a sure refuge from a world that had managed in ways both overt and veiled to diminish me based on nothing more than skin color. But there was so much more at Hampton to engage me than my courses. On weekdays, for example, attendance was mandatory at evening vespers held in the grand auditorium of Ogden Hall, named for Robert Curtis Ogden, chairman of the Board of Trustees from 1894 to 1913 and a benefactor of the school.[23] Evening vespers was a pleasurable experience for me. Each person had an assigned seat, and somebody better be sitting in it at the appointed hour or have a good excuse why it was empty, otherwise you would have to visit the office of the Dean of Women or Dean of Men for a stern reprimand. Or so I heard; I never missed evening vespers unless I had been expressly excused for a good reason, such as being sick, or doing clinic rotations as part of my nursing program.

Vespers began with music, usually a Negro spiritual, followed by the reading of a scripture and a lecture by a speaker from the faculty or the surrounding community. After the lecture, the beautiful voice of a soloist would fill the air, and I always got chills as the chorus of student voices in the audience joined the refrain:

Oh, freedom! Oh, freedom! Oh, freedom over me!
And before I'd be a slave I'll be buried in my grave
And go home to my Lord and be free.

One Negro spiritual in particular never failed to resonate in the deepest, most yearning part of my soul:

Sometimes I feel discouraged and think my work's in vain,
But then the Holy Spirit revives my soul again.
There is a balm in Gilead to make the wounded whole;
There is a balm in Gilead to heal the sin sick soul.

I am sure that the spiritual held such meaning for me because Hampton was nothing less than my balm in Gilead. After my application had been rejected by Ohio State, I had been discouraged, afraid all my hard work had been in vain. Sitting in that auditorium, singing that haunting hymn, I saw how profoundly I had been wounded in my small Ohio hometown. Although I had been blessed with good and caring parents and had known some attentive teachers, I had been deprived of the full knowledge and experience of my heritage, and I now saw that this deprivation had been destabilizing to my developing self. There was also the secret that I had carried since my thirteenth year, which continued to weigh me down with shame, as I did not yet understand that the sin of that abusive encounter was never mine. But now, in evening vespers, the exquisite music of a Negro spiritual promised to "make the wounded whole." This particular music fed a deep hunger in me, then and now. For me, Negro spirituals are still among the most beautiful and treasured melodies ever composed, an alchemy of hope and healing, and the sweet assurance that no matter what our troubles, we will rise above.

I cannot describe the joy I felt at being able to hear and be a part of these musical devotions daily. Despite a fairly extensive musical background in piano, spanning more than fifteen years, I had certainly never experienced Negro spirituals as they were sung at Hampton. Where had all of my classmates learned this music? I was to discover the enormous role that the black church had played in their lives, and the advantages they had gained from the care and dedication of the black teachers who had guided them in their schools. I understood now why my music teacher, Mrs. Jones, had been so intent on having me play recitals in the African Methodist Episcopal church back home. She had tried in whatever small ways she could to expose me to as much black culture as was possible in that place. But it had never been enough. There were too few of us, and we had been too oppressed, often without our even recognizing the true extent of our subjugation. I realized that I was never able to feel the pride in my race or the sense of belonging to a rich and enduring culture because I had no real understanding of who I was and how I fit into the larger context of the black American experience—until now.

Already, I was beginning to develop a different sense of myself. I saw new beauty in dark skin, and in the features, bodies and speech patterns of my fellow students. This allowed me to become conscious of the beauty in my own blackness, to which I had been blind. And not only had I been blind, I had also seen blackness as a negative quality in myself and in others. How could there be pride in being born black when it alone could exclude one from the full rights and privileges of citizenship? This is how I had thought about my race as a lonely and disillusioned adolescent. I was now starting to grasp that it was up to me to stake my own claim to the rights and privileges that were due to me and every other citizen, no matter how much trickier that might be for me than for the white children who had once been my playmates.

In Mount Vernon when I was growing up, white people would often say to my mother, "But Mrs. Simmons, your children are different," as if we were somehow better than the regular class of Negroes. *We were not different!* I wanted to scream now. I was surely no different from hundreds of my fellow Hamptonians, people of all shades and personalities and abilities and complex sensibilities and dreams. Most white people had never experienced the opportunity to know and interact with such a diverse and talented community of black people, with the result that most whites in America did not know us, would never know us, and even more than that, did not care to know us.

It seemed to me that as long as whites could maintain us in a dependent status, we would continue to meet their economic, emotional and opportunistic needs. But now I was beginning to understand my true history and to be justly proud of it, and I was feeling equal to white society for the first time in my life. Most of my Hampton fellow students were better prepared for the realities of life as a black person in America than I was. Students from Alabama, Georgia, Mississippi and Virginia challenged me socially and scholastically and often outperformed me. They possessed a more positive self-image than I did. They knew how to live in one accord with other black people and how to stand firm in the truth of who they were when interacting with white people. In this, I was playing catch-up.

It helped that my life was being enriched daily by the visits of so many outstanding dignitaries, both black and white, who came to the campus and addressed the student body. Among the nationally celebrated people I was privileged to hear at Hampton were the brilliant agriculturalist from Tuskegee Institute, Dr. George Washington Carver; the renowned singer Marian Anderson; the Harvard-trained composer and pianist Dr. R. Nathaniel Dett; and concert tenor Roland Hayes. When Roland Hayes sang the anthem, "Were You There When They Crucified My Lord?" he took us with him to the crucifixion. When he reached the phrase, "Were you there when they pierced Him in the side?" his voice echoed with such suffering and pathos that I could almost feel the sword slicing into the side of Christ and see it dripping with His blood.

I also met the First Lady of the United States, Eleanor Roosevelt, while I was a nursing student at Hampton. After her lecture in Ogden Hall, she asked to be shown around the campus by students, and I was fortunate enough to be a part of the chosen group. As we walked, Mrs. Roosevelt inquired about our lives and our studies, asking specific questions about our future goals. She exuded intelligence, sincerity and optimism, and her smile was unforgettable for its warmth and humor. *What a lady,* I remember thinking. We beamed in return, proudly showing off our little corner of a nation that had been built by black labor yet was spun by mostly white fingers. It occurred to me that the First Lady's presence on our campus was both a challenge and an exception to America's rules of social intercourse between blacks and whites; I had the sense these rules were meaningless to her. On our campus, her graciousness and humility commanded such a level of respect that race seemed totally transcended.

The students in particular admired her, so much so that some of the pilots from the school's Civilian Pilot Training Program (CPTP) invited her to take a private flight with them. The First Lady had reason to be impressed with the pilot program: Founded by her husband's administration in 1938, the CPTP included a landmark antidiscrimination clause that would eventually allow the training of 2,000 black pilots at six black colleges and universities, including Hampton, during World War II, as well as 2,500 women pilots at four women's colleges during the same period.[24] Perhaps this was the reason that she immediately accepted the young pilots' invitation to fly with them. This caused a minor uproar and brought some criticism down on Mrs. Roosevelt, as the pilots were not yet licensed. As I recall, Mrs. Roosevelt enjoyed her sightseeing flight over the campus and let her critics have their say.

Another especially memorable occasion took place toward the end of my first year. In Ogden Hall on a warm Spring afternoon, Harlem Renaissance author and activist James Weldon Johnson, NAACP leader Walter White, Howard University president Mordecai Johnson, and Bethune-Cookman University founder and president Mary McLeod Bethune all occupied the dais along with Hampton's president, Dr. Arthur Howe. James Weldon Johnson, Walter White and Mordecai Johnson were all of light complexion, which prompted Mary McLeod Bethune to comment wryly, "When you look at the faces on this podium you don't know what races these other folks are, but with my rich mahogany brown there's no mistaking me!"

The entire auditorium erupted into knowing laughter. A few weeks later on June 26, 1938, James Weldon Johnson was tragically killed in an automobile accident while vacationing in Wiscasset, Maine.[25] In my sorrow at this news, I was glad to have been present in the audience that day when he and other prominent educators spoke to the student body at my school. It had felt to me like a family gathering where everyone was chosen and in on the jokes. It is a cherished memory.

As I began my second year as a nursing student, I remained as impressed and elated with Hampton as I had been when I first arrived. I decided to write to my sister Rowena back in Mount Vernon and encourage her to apply. I believed that she was as trapped as I had been by the uncompromising narrative of our small town, which held that good black girls should find jobs working in white folks' kitchens once they had completed high school. Indeed, as soon as Rowena graduated, a white family in town had hired her as a domestic servant.

She complained to me that she could not afford college on the limited wages of a domestic. I explained to her that Hampton offered a work-year program. Students with insufficient tuition funds could work for a complete year off campus, then attend classes at the school with guaranteed work hours during subsequent years, graduating with a bachelor's degree in five years. I also wrote to my mother, urging her to encourage Rowena to enroll in Hampton's work-year program. I even mailed my sister the application to register. I wanted her to feel the rush of pride and sense of possibility that I had found since arriving at Hampton. I wanted her to have the awareness, as I now did, that her life was hers to direct. I wanted her to start visualizing whatever exciting challenges she might imagine for her future, knowing that she was giving herself the education she would need to meet them.

But my sister resisted my pleas. My mother wrote to say that Rowena had received the application papers I had sent her, but she had shown them to her employer Mrs. Tyler, whose comment had been, "You don't need to go to college. You stay here with me. I'll pay you six dollars a week. At the end of ten years we'll see where you are and where Ellamae is. I bet you'll be just as well off as Ellamae." And her employer had added, "Those Southern colored schools are no good anyway."

Oh, I was furious! Clearly Mrs. Tyler was exerting a strong influence over my sister, and Rowena was allowing that to drown out the advice and good intentions of her own blood. To this day, the memory of Mrs. Tyler's comments pains me. Rowena could not seem to appreciate that Mrs. Tyler simply did not wish to lose her domestic servant. Not only was Rowena responsible for her housework, she also shampooed and set Mrs. Tyler's hair and regularly gave her manicures and pedicures. Now this woman was baiting my sister with an additional dollar or two per week in an effort to maintain control over her.

Mrs. Tyler, whom I had previously met, had always been bitterly opposed to me. She was a neighbor of the doctor's family that had previously employed me as a domestic, and she believed I was dreaming above my station. Sadly, my sister fell prey to this woman's selfish beguilement. It was the age-old story of white dominance over the economic fate of the black family, with Northern whites disparaging Southern black colleges, of which they were totally ignorant. All across America, this story was being repeated again and again. It was another form of divide-and-conquer—Mrs. Tyler had divided my sister and me and thus conquered (wrested control of) her future. She had sowed dissension and doubt between us and manipulated a deep-seated master-slave mentality that had many blacks believing we needed the benevolence of whites to survive. To my utter frustration, my sister continued to work for this woman throughout my years at Hampton. In my final year, she became pregnant by a young man named Robert Ellis Harris, and she married him. Gus and Ella disliked Rowena's new husband intensely, especially after their middle daughter moved away with him to his hometown of Newark, Ohio. Rowena had finally escaped Mrs. Tyler, but she would not escape domestic work altogether.

Rowena and Ellis went on to have three children together—Robert, Cheri and Melvin—but their union broke down and they were divorced while their children were still young. I was distressed to learn that Ellis had gained custody of the children, mainly because my sister had no viable means of taking care of them. She was qualified only for domestic work, and she could not pursue such work with three children in tow. And so my nephews and niece went to live with Ellis' sisters and their families, while Rowena became a domestic for a well-to-do family in Newark, the Ruggs, who were lawnmower manufacturers. She lived on the Rugg estate even after she met and married her second husband, Robert Edward Rutland, a chauffeur for the Rugg family who also lived on the premises.

I could not help thinking how different Rowena's life might have turned out had she entertained my plea that she enroll at Hampton. I have since had to make a hard peace with the fact that my dreams for my sister were not hers. Although life was hard for Rowena at times, in fact the Ruggs were good to her and Eddie, even building them a small house on the black side of town. In her will, Rowena was able to pass on that house to her daughter.

My frustration with what I saw as my sister's lack of imagination about her life was reflected everywhere in my hometown. For decades after I found Hampton, the reality for young black men and women in Mount Vernon remained virtually unchanged. Black high school graduates who were college material found white tax-supported state colleges closed to them, no matter how faithfully their families had paid their taxes year after year. Too many would become convinced that menial positions such as foundry workers, domestic servants and day laborers were the only jobs open to them. Those who rejected this script and pursued an education had to bang and kick down doors and wedge their way inside.

Fortunately, white academia's effort to deny us an education was one of the first institutional obstacles dismantled by the civil rights movement of the early 1960s. Today people of all races look at me in slack-jawed disbelief when I recount the story of Ohio State telling me, "We have no facilities for training colored girls." They say to me, "Why did you take it? Why didn't you report them? Why didn't you sue?" They don't understand the dusty, winding trail we have traveled to this moment, or the perseverance and courage of those who came before, and the powerful shoulders that held steady the ladder on which we climbed. Among the sturdy shoulders that bore me up on my journey were those of my parents. At Hampton, I found a multitude more.

I found lifelong friends among my fellow students at Hampton. I also had a memorable encounter with the chief of surgery at Dixie Hospital, Dr. Rupert Alstyne Binet Lloyd, the first black physician I ever met.

CHAPTER 6

Dare to Dream

When I attended, Hampton's nursing program lasted three years and included summers. At the school, we were taught that a nurse is the most important spoke in the medical wheel. She—in those days nurses were almost invariably female—was to medicine what a good wife and mother was to the family unit: She held the medical effort together, was a master at improvising, and could competently carry on for the doctor, pharmacist, physical therapist or occupational therapist should any member of the team be unavailable or, worse, inept or uninformed. It was drilled into us from day one: A nurse could never afford to be inept or uninformed.

I took this edict to heart, immersing myself in my course work and vigilantly studying my patients' medical charts during clinical rounds. Every medical case fascinated me, each one a unique story with something important to teach me. During my pre-clinical study in 1938, for example, I had my first encounter with sickle cell syndrome, a condition that affected the Negro race almost exclusively. This particular case was in a black infant whom we referred to as Baby Franklin. He had been admitted to the hospital nursery in an apparent sickle cell crisis. I can still see the projection of the microscopic slide that had been made from a blood smear from this infant. The scattered sickling of the red blood cells was easily visible to the eye. Because of their sickled shape, these cells tended to clump together and block the vessels, thus interfering with the flow of oxygenated blood to an organ and often starving it entirely.

Sickle cell syndrome raised so many questions for me, especially because it was not yet entirely understood. Researchers did not yet know, for example, that the disease was hereditary, and that if one had inherited only a single copy of the sickle cell gene, one could live a relatively normal life, but if one had inherited a double dose of the same abnormal hemoglobin gene (one from the mother and one from the father), the result was full-blown sickle cell disease, which in those days almost certainly meant an early death.[26]

Nor was it yet well known that in parts of Africa where malaria was widespread, those who had been born with the sickle cell trait—one copy of the abnormal gene—demonstrated a superior resistance to the high fevers, muscle pain, enlarged spleen, headaches and anemia that were the rigors of malaria, because the parasite could not survive the sickling of the red blood cells. As a result, those with the trait were more likely to survive and pass on their genes, which was perhaps one reason that sickle cell was so prevalent in people of African descent.[27]

In a letter to my mother, I described sickle cell disease and asked her if any member of our family had ever been afflicted with the symptoms. Of course, my mother had never heard of the disease, and I marveled that a condition so critical to the health of black people was so unknown to those who were most susceptible. Sickle cell was just one of the many medical mysteries that occupied me and convinced me I was on the right path.

When I finally began hospital ward duty in 1939, I loved clinic days. While textbook medical cases had challenged my analytical brain, I now found that patients and their human stories interested me even more. When I was a student nurse, one of my all-time favorite patients was Dr. Robert Russa Moton, a Hampton graduate who had served as the second president of Tuskegee Normal and Industrial Institute in Macon County, Alabama, after his friend and founding president Booker T. Washington had died of congestive heart failure in 1915.[28] I met Dr. Moton in 1938 when he was being treated at Dixie Hospital, where Hampton's student nurses were trained. I knew that he was a great scholar, and that he subscribed to Washington's ideas about advancing the Negro race through industrial and technical training, superior character and the acquisition of economic means. This, Washington believed, would demonstrate to whites that blacks deserved to be equal members of society, accorded their full rights as contributing citizens.[29]

Booker T. Washington's approach had been famously criticized by another towering black figure, W. E. B. Du Bois. The prominent scholar, intellectual and political strategist felt that Washington and later Moton needed to agitate for more lasting social change by also seeking political and legislative solutions to the problem of racial inequality. Du Bois considered the notion of building up the black community solely through education, character and commerce to be shortsighted. He argued that financial success, no matter how great, was not sustainable without legal enforcement of African Americans' equal rights under the law. Until the law codified the equality of Negroes, he argued, black capital would always be at risk. [30]

By the time Dr. Moton became my patient, this fundamental difference in approach between the two camps had simmered to a mutual recognition of the need for cooperation on all fronts in the struggle for civil rights. Indeed, Du Bois and Moton had great respect for one another, as was evident from letters they exchanged throughout their lifetimes.[31] In one letter, Du Bois wrote to Moton: "I think you know I have the deepest personal regard for you and share thoroughly your feeling that we are both aiming at the same things. I do think your methods are often dangerous for the accomplishment of those things just as you may think the same about mine, but I trust we are going to find much common ground."[32]

Even Du Bois could not help but acknowledge that Dr. Moton had spent his life fighting for equal opportunity for students like me. If his approach was intentionally concrete and measurable, the result was that during his twenty-year tenure at Tuskegee, the school grew and flourished. In addition to increasing the endowment by some $6 million, Dr. Moton added new buildings and oversaw the renovation of existing facilities, including the installation of the beautiful stained-glass "singing windows" in the chapel, which portrayed eleven well-loved Negro spirituals. Dr. Moton also expanded academic programs leading to bachelor's degrees in agriculture, mechanical industries, home economics, teaching and aeronautical training, even as he recruited eminent scholars to join the school's faculty. [33]

In 1923, Dr. Moton also presided over the construction of the Tuskegee Veterans Administration Hospital on 300 acres donated by the school. The hospital was to be devoted entirely to the treatment of black World War I veterans, of which there were an estimated three hundred thousand in the South.[34] Having served their country during the war, once back home, these black soldiers were having trouble accessing the same level of medical care as their white counterparts. Dr. Moton was determined to remedy this. With the help of the NAACP, he had secured the endorsement of President Warren G. Harding to have the new facility be entirely staffed by black doctors, nurses and administrators. When news of this got out, the local Ku Klux Klan was outraged. They argued that the budgeted $2.5 million in salaries should go to qualified white medical personnel, and they stormed the Tuskegee campus, threatening Moton's life if he did not capitulate. Dr. Moton was unmoved. "You can wipe me out; you can take my life; but you can't take my character," he is reported to have told the white mob gathered at his door. "So far as I am concerned, gentlemen, I have only one life to give, but I would gladly give a dozen for this cause." [35]

In the end, both the school's president and the hospital escaped the confrontation unscathed. For years after, black doctors and nurses traveled from all corners of the country to work at the Tuskegee Veterans Administration Hospital.[36]

I had heard all the stories of Dr. Moton's commitment and courage throughout his tenure at Tuskegee, but as I attended to him during his later years, it was not his public stature that most impressed me. I was moved by his dignity and refinement in the face of his own looming mortality, and by the graciousness with which he treated all those with whom he came in contact. Dr. Moton faced the end of a distinguished life with a serenity I have seldom witnessed. I considered it my supreme privilege to make this former Hamptonian as comfortable as possible while I had the chance, and it angered me when some of the white nurses at Dixie Hospital treated this giant of a man with less than the esteem he deserved.

In that era at Dixie, black nurses were referred to as "Nurse" while white nurses were called "Miss." All black patients were called by their first name regardless of their station in life. Oh, that used to burn me! One day a white nurse, in speaking to Dr. Moton, called him Robert. His private physician, a white man by the name of Dr. Harold Howe, overheard her. With firmness and not a little annoyance in his voice, he addressed the young nurse. "Miss Jones, that man's name is Dr. Moton. You may call him President Moton or Dr. Moton or Mr. Moton, but don't you ever let me hear you refer to him again as Robert." I silently cheered Dr. Howe's defense of his patient, recognizing anew how different Hampton was from what I had been used to back home.

Dr. Moton died two years after this exchange and is buried on the campus of his alma mater, and mine.

Hampton would continue to shape my view of what was achievable for black people in ways I could not have anticipated. Perhaps the most significant exchange of my entire life occurred one day when I was accompanying a physician and nursing supervisor on ward rounds as part of my clinical rotation. On that cool spring afternoon in 1938, a tall, thin, distinguished-looking doctor whom I recognized as my anatomy professor walked by, stopped, turned back to me and said, "Young lady, what are *you* doing in our school of nursing?"

I was stunned, alarmed and expected a reprimand, even though I wasn't sure what I had done wrong. In the medical hierarchy of the time, nurses lived in fear of doctors, and especially of surgeons. We stood at attention whenever a physician entered the room and remained standing until told, "Be seated." When a doctor spoke to a nurse, she was expected to respond, "Yes, doctor" or "No, doctor" and to make only oblique eye contact. This was ostensibly in recognition of the doctors' superior knowledge, education and ability, or so we were taught. No doubt our submissive behavior was reinforced by the fact that most of the doctors we interacted with were white and male, and a de facto racial and gender code was in operation. Despite this unspoken code, or perhaps because of it, I thought most doctors to be unreasonably cocky and holier than thou, and I tried to avoid them as much as a nurse in training could.

But on that day, the doctor who addressed me was black, although he was so light-skinned that had I not already known his race, I might have thought him a white man. I later learned that his father had been a white Frenchman, and his mother an American mulatto, but of course just one drop of Negro blood was enough to define him as a black man. He was, in fact, the first black doctor I had ever met and the first who had ever spoken to me directly. His name was Dr. Rupert Alstyne Binet Lloyd and he was one of two chiefs of surgery at Dixie Hospital. It was one of the idiosyncrasies of segregation that there was a black chief of surgery and a white chief of surgery, a black chief of medicine and a white chief of medicine, and so on. At hospitals throughout the South, each chief dealt with patients and staff of his own race exclusively, although at Dixie, the nurses treated both black and white patients, white doctors might admit patients of color (such as Dr. Moton, whose primary physician was white), and black doctors might consult medically across racial lines.

Now, in response to Dr. Lloyd's question, I stammered, "I want to be a nurse like my mother. She is a practical nurse, and I want to help people. Like her."

"Well, you can be a good nurse, or you can go on and be a good physician," Dr. Lloyd said. "I've been watching you, young lady, and you have what it takes. I've observed your intellect and your innate ability, and I believe you are wasting your time in nursing school. So you just get on out of here and go to medical school."

I hesitated, not sure how to answer. The truth was I had secretly wondered what it would be like to be a doctor, but I had never been able to see a path to it. Becoming a nurse had been a distant-enough horizon. But now this surgeon, who was black like me, was telling me to dream a little bigger.

"I don't have any money," I said finally. "My parents are poor. They can't afford to send me to medical school."

Dr. Lloyd snorted. "That's no excuse!" he said sternly. "You can work. You get out of here and get a job and put yourself through medical school."

No one had ever spoken to me like this before. I was 19, an impressionable freshman from a town where very few black residents lived and where there were certainly no doctors who were black and female. My parents had continuously stressed, "You can be anything you want to be, but whatever it is, you must be the best. If you clean houses, be the best house cleaner. If you teach, be the best teacher there is. If you sweep streets, be the best street sweeper there is!" Gus and Ella had emphasized the quality of effort, as well as the quality of the end-product of effort, which was achievement. I realized that in his way, Dr. Lloyd was saying much the same thing: If you want to do medicine, then go all the way—reach for the very pinnacle of the mountain you have decided to climb. The thought was both frightening and exhilarating. Me! Ellamae Simmons—a doctor!

Dr. Lloyd's belief in me was such that he did not confine his encouragement to that one conversation. He told his wife Blanche about me, apparently describing me as one of the most gifted students he had ever encountered, and a natural for the field of medicine. A few days later, Mrs. Lloyd sent me a note inviting me to dinner at the family home. I was thoroughly intimidated, and I'm embarrassed to admit that I simply ignored the note. What on earth would I talk to my anatomy professor and his wife about for the hour it took for us to consume a meal together? I assumed my silence would be the end of it, but I had not counted on Mrs. Lloyd's resolve. When she didn't hear back from me, she simply got into her car and drove to campus to find me.

As I exited my anatomy class one afternoon, she was standing at the door, a squat, rounded figure in a tailored, floral silk dress and a church hat on her head. Her smile was both indulgent and no-nonsense, and her eyes were alight with purpose. Although she was short and plump, she cut an imposing figure, because she held herself regally erect, and walked as if she were twenty feet tall. Under her straw hat, her long, wavy brown hair was twisted into a braid and wrapped around the crown of her head. (When I got to know her better, I would learn that when she took down and washed her waist-length hair, inherited from her Native American grandmother and white father, she would sit out in the backyard and hang it like a sheet over a chair to dry.) She took my hand in hers and told me graciously and firmly that I would be joining her and Dr. Lloyd for dinner that evening.

I knew better than to ignore her second invitation, and so that evening I presented myself at the Lloyd home as I had been commanded. How fortuitous it was that Dr. Lloyd had noticed me at all. He and his wife became surrogate parents to me at Hampton, treating me like their fifth child, a younger sibling to their four grown sons, all of whom were already married or betrothed. Dr. and Mrs. Lloyd saw something in me, a hunger for more, a willingness to work hard, and perhaps a sense of awe and gratitude at the support that was suddenly available to me in a predominantly black academic environment. They became my second family, doling out advice, and keeping me close throughout my years at Hampton by including me in regular dinners and social gatherings at their home. I grew particularly close to their third son, Blanchard, who had been one of the first black students to study engineering at Rensselaer Polytechnic Institute in Troy, New York. Blanchard was the life of any party; we both liked to laugh, which made us instantly compatible. When he became engaged soon after to Lucille Louise Ford, a beautiful and vivacious chestnut-brown schoolteacher from Washington, DC, she and I became devoted allies as well. I also developed a warm lifelong friendship with two young women around my age who were the Lloyd's neighbors, Frida and Judy Nervers, daughters of the Jewish couple who ran the country store next door to the Lloyd's home.

My association with all these Hamptonians would last for the rest of my life, surviving into subsequent generations, with Blanchard and Lucille honoring me by naming me godmother of their three adored children, Linda, Brian and Carol. I would be forever grateful to Dr. and Mrs. Lloyd for the way they folded me close and made sure I understood the full measure of my potential. Their belief in me planted and watered the seed that flourished and became a powerful belief in myself, a dawning confidence in my ability to achieve what had once seemed an impossible dream.

My new goal of eventually attending medical school and becoming a physician in no way diminished my respect and admiration for the field of nursing, however. Nurses were utterly necessary to the medical profession, I knew, but then so were doctors, especially black female doctors in a world that had seen far too few of them. Dr. Lloyd's comments to me on that afternoon when I was doing my clinical rounds at Dixie Hospital would completely alter the course of my professional life. His words fanned a secret ember into a burning fire of ambition, but I spoke of it to no one. Not yet, because I didn't have a clue about how I would find my way to medical school. All the same, I redoubled my efforts to learn all I could about medicine and to be the most outstanding registered nurse I could be.

At my graduation from Hampton's nursing school in 1940.

CHAPTER 7

Student Nurse

I remember the morning I was permitted into the operating room to observe my first surgical procedure. I donned the customary cap, mask and gown and stood in line along the OR wall with several other student nurses. The patient that day was a middle-aged white woman who had been diagnosed with breast cancer and was scheduled for radical mastectomy. After she was sedated, the surgeon and his assistant began to cleanse the skin of the operative site and to cover the area around it with sterile drapes. The anesthetist, already in position at the head of the OR table, proceeded to put the patient more deeply under.

I watched as the surgeon placed his scalpel and sliced through skin, making a neat incision that exposed the underlying fascia and muscles. His assistant quickly moved to clamp off the vessels that were bleeders, but not before I caught sight of what appeared to me as a pulsing mass of bloody red meat. Suddenly, despite the bright floodlights in the OR, everything around me grew dim. The room was spinning; the doctors' green scrubs were fading into a watery gray mist; I felt dizzy and clammy. A moment later, my limbs gave way. I saw the white linoleum floor rising to meet me. Someone called out, "Catch her! She's falling!" They were the last words I heard.

I recall little else of the surgical procedure. I do know that on regaining consciousness minutes later, I was mortified. "I don't know what happened to me," I mumbled, but the OR supervisor only smiled. He knew that what I had experienced was a typical bout of vasovagal fainting, an involuntary nervous system reflex that causes the heart to pump less blood and the blood pressure to fall, thus depriving the brain of oxygen. It was more common than I knew among student nurses and medical students who were watching their first surgery. Even so, I silently vowed that never again would I repeat this embarrassing experience, no matter how little sleep I might have had the night before or how many hours I had been on duty.

I quickly realized that I was entering the medical field at an auspicious time. The antibiotic era had dawned, and with it great advances in the treatment of infectious diseases. After the accidental discovery in 1928 of the antibacterial properties of the common fungus *Penicillium notatum*, bacteriologist Sir Alexander Fleming of St. Mary's Hospital in London had been able to formulate a substance that could destroy the growth of the Staphylococcus bacteria. He called it penicillin.[37] Before this, infectious diseases had been treated experimentally with aspirin, hydrotherapy, physiotherapy, bed rest, incision and drainage, and other such congeners. These measures joined with the body's innate immunologic forces to relieve the symptoms of illness, but the underlying bacterial cause of infection remained unaddressed by any specific therapy. Now, with the arrival of penicillin, patients with such conditions as syphilis, gangrene, rheumatic fever and tuberculosis were being dramatically healed. Around the same time, other classes of antibiotics were being tested, including a sulfa derivative marketed under the name Prontosil, which had been developed by the German scientist Gerhard Domagk just five years before I arrived at Hampton.[38]

In 1938, Prontosil was the first antibiotic I ever saw administered. A young white female patient had been admitted to the hospital with a diagnosis of acute bacterial endocarditis. In the past, this inflammation of the heart membrane had inevitably been fatal, but the patient's family had consented to her physician trying an experimental new treatment. I was one of the nurses assigned to care for the ailing woman, who was suffering greatly with painful joints, high fevers, skin rashes and splinter hemorrhages on her nail beds, which indicated embolization, or the blockage of small blood vessels. I stood at her bedside as her doctor administered the drug Prontosil, the first time any antibiotic had ever been used at Dixie Hospital. I sensed the apprehension in the usually calm and stoic physician, whose brow was creased with concern. Fearing some problematic reaction or an acute emergent change in the woman's condition due to the Prontosil, the doctor slept in the hospital for two nights, hardly leaving his patient's side. By the third day, the woman began to recover, and by the tenth she was virtually back to full health.

The experience served to further stimulate my interest in becoming a doctor. Even though I found the nursing profession fascinating, the idea of being able to pull patients back from the brink of death by selecting the right treatment protocol seemed a thrilling prospect. Of course I still had absolutely no idea how I would ever be able to pay my way through medical school. Besides, I still had to master the nursing profession.

At Dixie Hospital, student nurses were normally assigned twelve-hour clinical rotations. The same was true at Piedmont Hospital in Burkeville, Virginia, where I was assigned to complete an affiliation in pulmonary tuberculosis, and at St. Philip Hospital in Richmond, Virginia, where I did a stint in pediatrics. Perhaps what was most remarkable to me about these clinical rotations was the way in which caring for gravely ill patients forced me to rise above issues of class, race and gender. Between patient and student nurse, the connection was stripped down to its most elemental state, becoming a relationship between two human beings in need of one another, one for the learning and the other for the healing. To this fragile connection, physicians brought their knowledge, diagnostic skill, experience and goodwill, as well as trust in the patient's fighting spirit. On all sides, there also needed to be faith, perseverance and hope. I soon grasped that if any of these ingredients was missing from the therapeutic bond, the patient's outcome could be severely jeopardized.

In early 1939, for example, a young married white female was admitted to Dixie Hospital diagnosed with an overwhelming sepsis infection that was secondary to a self-induced abortion. This was my clinical introduction to the pregnancy intervention process that in those days was considered a criminal act. This woman might as well have been marked with a scarlet letter as her medical chart bore a large red stamped inscription "Criminal Abortion." A mother of two children, the patient had conceived a third pregnancy. Her husband was opposed to a third child, distraught that the family could not afford another mouth to feed. Feeling the weight of her husband's distress, the woman had attempted to terminate the pregnancy using a wire coat hanger inserted through her vagina into her uterus. The result was a raging septicemia, or blood poisoning, that threatened to cut short her life.

Antibiotics of the sulfonamide group were available for use on this patient, and she needed them desperately. But the doctor overseeing her case withheld the medicine, deciding that the woman was not worthy of such a high-value treatment. The scorn that the medical establishment heaped upon this wife and mother for trying to end her pregnancy was horrifying to me. The woman remained hospitalized and critically ill for several weeks. Her immune system eventually rallied enough for her to be sent home, but she was chronically ill with various infections for months afterwards, requiring several more hospital admissions. She lost weight to the point of cachexia, a wasting syndrome marked by muscular atrophy, weakness and debilitating fatigue. With each new hospitalization, I wondered about the patient's children, and how they were coping without her. After eight or ten months, the uterine sepsis had cleared, but the woman's body was left ravaged and immune deficient, and she developed pulmonary tuberculosis soon after. This was before the advent of tuberculosis-fighting chemotherapy. At the time, bed rest and nutrition were the primary treatment modalities. For this mother of two, it was not enough. This woman, whom I had followed for so long, finally died from pulmonary tuberculosis, leaving two small children without a mother, a husband without a wife, and a family fractured by loss.

Even as a young student nurse, I found the long-smoldering

infection, prolonged suffering and untimely death of this patient hard to accept. It was impossible to ignore the fact that had she been treated with antibiotics when she was first admitted, she could easily have been saved. Instead she had been subjected to ongoing derision and blame that I considered mean and unwarranted. While I looked forward to becoming a registered nurse upon my graduation from Hampton, this woman's experience made me even more determined to find my way to medical school. Had I been the doctor in charge of her treatment, she would have received the sulfa drugs, and her children would never have been forced to grow up without their mother.

I knew that a long and circuitous road lay ahead of me as I sought the door that would help me to afford medical school. It seemed clear that in this endeavor, I would have to start by earning my way as a nurse and saving as much as I could. Fortunately, I thoroughly enjoyed bedside nursing. I knew by then that hospitals could be places of great trauma and sorrow, but when the right treatment was given, they also offered the incomparable satisfaction of helping patients recover from illness and return to healthy and productive lives.

The day of my graduation from Hampton nursing school, September 23, 1940, dawned cool and overcast, but by noon the sun had burned off the last of the morning mist, so that the campus lay like a sparkling jewel, showing off its pristinely manicured lawns and stately buildings in a crisp blue afternoon. As the university brass band played a rousing rendition of "Pomp and Circumstance," a procession of thirteen radiant black nurses marched into Ogden Hall to receive their diplomas. Initially there had been thirty-nine of us, but deficiencies in finances and other circumstances had reduced our number by more than half.

My mother had taken the train from Ohio to be in the audience as I walked up on stage. Scholastically, I was at the top of my class, and I had also passed the Virginia state board licensing examination, making me officially an RN. As the school's dean handed me my ribbon-wrapped scroll, I heard my mother's voice cry out, "She's mine! She's mine!" When I looked out into the auditorium, I saw that she had jumped up from her seat next to Dr. and Mrs. Lloyd and was bobbing excitedly up and down in the aisle, clapping jubilantly and pointing toward me, making sure everyone knew I was her child. I could hardly contain my own happiness in that moment, especially at my mother's uncharacteristically exuberant display. The woman whose intellect I had held as the standard my entire life was cheering for me, her smile like a thousand suns.

To this day, my graduation from Hampton Institute's School of Nursing represents the most cherished milestone of my life. There would be future graduations and future milestones, but none would equal the personal satisfaction and euphoria that were mine at this graduation. I took great pleasure in shepherding my mother around, showing off my dorm and my classrooms, telling her the story of the great Emancipation Oak, and introducing her to my teachers and friends. Later that evening, after we had dined with the Lloyd family, I sat with my mother in the soft grass down by the river. I remember feeling keenly that I belonged to Hampton, and that Hampton belonged to me. I tried to explain how, for the first time in my life, I had experienced total and complete acceptance unencumbered by any shadow of prejudice. I think, being there with me on graduation day, Ella felt some measure of it too.

In a very deep sense, Hampton had been my renaissance. It had given me pride in my blackness and showed me that I could do with my life as I wished—it was up to me to shape the clay God had given me. Hampton accepted me fully for who I was while challenging me to become more completely myself. The school and those associated with it would never fail to celebrate my successes, both small and large, not just during the three years I was in nursing school there, but throughout my entire life.

Today, I carry in my heart not the institution of Hampton so much as its vision of an America that could be enjoyed by all, a place where I could become the most excellent expression of myself. At Hampton I had learned to love the woman I was becoming, as I had never been able to love her before. Here, on this pastoral campus at the mouth of the blue Chesapeake, I found not just my life's calling but also the courage to pursue it with all that I had, all that I was, and all that I might ever be.

*Hampton's director of nursing, Clara Lewis (front row, center)
encouraged graduating nurses to join the American Red Cross and
serve our country. For me (second row, left), this advice would prove to
be life changing.*

CHAPTER 8

Mental Hospital

At Hampton, our chief of nursing, Clara Lewis, had urged all her graduates to join the American Red Cross, which was responsible for recruiting nurses to serve with the United States Public Health Service (USPHS), as well as the Army or Navy. Our chief emphasized that if ever we were asked to serve in the event of a local or national emergency, we should not hesitate to do so. I saw no reason to doubt her guidance, and so upon my graduation at the age of 22, I joined.

Emergency medicine was not my primary focus, however. Human behavior and mental disorders had captured my interest as a student nurse, even though my schooling had not addressed the range of psychological conditions in any depth. I surmised that specialization in an area of nursing would make me more desirable to an employer, so I decided to enroll in a twelve-month post-graduate course in psychiatric nursing. The certification program was offered by Central State Hospital, a segregated facility in Petersburg, Virginia. There I was introduced to the nursing care of patients with various neuroses and psychoses. I quickly noted that regardless of my patients' mental illness diagnoses, many of them could function quite normally for long intervals. They were not "crazy" in all spheres; rather, some seemed calculating and "crazy like a fox." Most compelling to me, though, were those patients who had been institutionalized as a result of being unable to manage the weight of racial animus, the accumulation of slights and insults to psyche that came with being born black in America. I had not a doubt in my mind that had these patients been born white, with all the protections and privileges that entailed, their mental functioning would not have become so fractured.

It was at Central State that I first observed electroconvulsive therapy being used in some schizophrenic and manic-depressive patients who were cycling through the depressed phase. I attended procedures in which seizures were induced electrically or pharmacologically using the central nervous system-stimulating drug metrazol. The seizures would then be modified or effectively terminated with the use of the muscle relaxant succinylcholine. Many patients were terrified of such treatment, and they would fight the attendants with superhuman strength. As a nurse in post-graduate training, I found electroconvulsive therapy, at least as it was practiced at the time, to verge on the barbaric. I felt as if I had to leave my humanity at the door in order to watch these convulsive episodes, with patients jerking wildly and uncontrollably as attendants held them down in bed. And yet I could not deny that some patients showed noticeable improvement in their ability to function after the treatments.

It was also as an RN at Central State Hospital that I was first introduced to homosexuality. It says much about the state of psychiatry in that era that my first encounter with a gay person was in a mental hospital. In fact, homosexuality was considered a psychiatric disorder until 1974,[39] and there were laws in almost every state criminalizing homosexual interaction. Even after these laws were struck down by the U.S. Supreme Court in 2003, twelve states still refused to decriminalize same-gender sexual behavior.[40] Unsurprisingly, back in the 1940s, most gay people kept themselves all but invisible to mainstream America, so it was perhaps unremarkable that a sheltered young woman from a small town in Middle America had never heard of such a thing.

The patient at Central State was an effeminate 17-year-old black male who had been admitted for marijuana addiction. He had long, lye-straightened hair, earrings in both ears, thin tapered fingers adorned with rings and bright-red-polished nails. He had a high-pitched voice and a feminine gait and was reported to be hermaphroditic, although I suspect that he simply preferred to dress as a woman. At night, he was locked in a separate area for fear he would try to initiate sexual relations with other patients. He told me he had come from New York, where he had worked in the Come What May club. I was never sure whether this was an actual club or a metaphor for the uncertainties of his life.

This man's flamboyant dress and mannerisms were baffling to

me at first, but the more I conversed with him, the stronger my conviction grew that he did not belong in a mental hospital. I was quite sure he had been committed to the institution only because he refused to tone down his exaggerated expression of a sexual orientation that was not widely understood, much less accepted, in the 1940s. Indeed, the words used in this man's chart to document his condition included such descriptors as "degenerate," "evil sodomite," "extreme medical disorder," "perverted," "immoral" and "sex criminal." I came to believe that my patient's open expression of his sexuality, as well as his race, had hindered his ability to provide for himself in a world that discriminated against him at every turn. Eventually, I counted him among those patients who seemed to be at the hospital for no reason other than their need for custodial care. They had no means of survival, and no family or other person who could be responsible for them on the outside.

This being the early 1940s, another condition commonly seen at the state hospital was central nervous system syphilis, which caused the progressive loss of mind and body. I became familiar with its symptoms, diagnosis and treatment, which was complicated by the fact that the tertiary stage of the disease usually occurred some twenty years following the original infection. Contracted through intimate sexual contact or via congenital transmission from an infected mother, syphilis initially presents with a chancre sore at the site of infection. The sore can last for several weeks but will eventually heal. In its secondary stage, the patient may develop fever and rashes on the hands and feet that can mimic other diseases. These also disappear spontaneously, and the infection can advance silently for decades. Following a long latent period in which there might be virtually no symptoms, patients experience tertiary onset of the disease. At this point, they present with an array of psychiatric symptoms, including slurred speech, decreased memory, diminished judgment, full-blown dementia and delusions of grandeur.[41]

The mental impairments caused by late-stage syphilis often led to infected patients being institutionalized. At any stage after initial infection, syphilis could enter the nervous system, causing altered behavior that mimicked mental illness, and neuromuscular degeneration that resembled Parkinson's or Huntington disease.[42] Most heartrending to me were the congenital victims of the condition, children whose lives were stunted before they ever began. I can recall two cases of congenital juvenile paresis in pre-teen boys whose symptoms corresponded to those seen in adult neurosyphilis. But juvenile paretics also presented with Hutchinson's teeth (peg-shaped central incisors with notching), a saddle-nose (nose with a sunken bridge) and frontal bossing (a marked rounded protrusion of the forehead).

During the year I was at Central State, there was no proven cure for syphilis, although penicillin trials around the country had begun to show promise. But in most hospitals, the nursing protocol for central nervous system syphilis was pyrotherapy, which included placing the patient in a fever cabinet, a device resembling an iron lung, and raising the body temperature to 105-107 degrees Fahrenheit. The idea was that the fever would "cook" the syphilis spirochete to its thermal death point, allowing the patient to recover. The elevated body temperature would be maintained for approximately four to six hours, causing profuse sweating and tremors and leaving the patient exhausted. The usual prescription was twenty such courses of treatment. Fever paroxysms were also sometimes achieved by introducing the malaria parasite (protozoa of the genus Plasmodium) into the body through infusions of diseased blood, fighting fire with fire, so to speak. At the end of the series of treatments, the malaria would be brought under control with antimalarial drugs such as quinine.[43]

All this to say, the options for the treatment of syphilis during my training as a psychiatric nurse were bleak and unproven, even if a small percentage of patients had in fact been known to recover after these rather alarming treatments.

I mention these encounters with syphilis so as to offer some context for my anguish and outrage when I later learned of the "Tuskegee Study of Untreated Syphilis in the Negro Male." Conducted by the USPHS on the campus of Tuskegee Institute from 1932 through 1972, the study followed 600 black males in order to track the progression of untreated syphilis in the late stages. The men were mostly poor, illiterate sharecroppers from

Macon County, Alabama, who could not afford healthcare for their families. Lured by the promise of family medical care for minor ailments, rides to and from the clinic, free meals on testing days, and money paid to their families in the event they died, hundreds of black men eagerly signed up; 399 of them were ultimately diagnosed with syphilis, and the rest were studied as a control group.[44]

Investigators did not inform any of the study participants that they had syphilis. They were told they were being treated for "bad blood," which in those parts was used to refer to conditions as varied as syphilis, anemia and even general fatigue. None of the men were informed of the true nature of the study, nor of the risks involved in the diagnostic spinal tap, which was billed as a "special free treatment." The men did not know enough about what they were getting into to give any sort of informed consent. They didn't know, for example, that their doctors would withhold treatment of their condition in the name of medical research, and that they would continue to do this for forty years. Even after penicillin became established as a proven cure for the disease in 1947, the USPHS doctors refused to administer the drug to the men and even prevented them from seeking effective treatment that was easily available to them anywhere. Not until whistleblower Peter Buxton, himself a USPHS employee, passed information on the troubling and deeply unethical methodology of the research to a reporter in 1972 did the study finally come to an end.[45] By then, 28 of the original participants had died of syphilis; 100 more had died of complications related to the infection; 40 wives had contracted the disease from their husbands; and 19 children were congenitally infected as a result.[46]

To my mind, the Tuskegee syphilis study was the height of medical malpractice. Certainly the USPHS would not have perpetrated such a travesty against poor white sharecroppers who needed treatment for syphilis. It was clear to me that poor, rural black lives had been seen as somehow less valuable to those who conducted the research; otherwise they would not have been content to stand by and watch so many men die when their deaths could have been prevented. It was personally heartbreaking to me that Dr. Robert Moton, who had been a favorite patient of mine at Dixie Hospital, had been president of Tuskegee in 1932 when the study began. It is not clear whether Dr. Moton was aware of the methodology of the research when he retired three years later. What is clear is that the project should have been shut down and all the participants given life-saving penicillin treatment as soon as it was understood in 1947 that late-stage syphilis could be entirely and completely cured.[47] The only good thing to come out of this criminally racist study was the subsequent passing of federal guidelines governing how human subjects were to be treated in future medical research.

I was recruited by the American Red Cross to work for the USPHS myself after completing my training at Central State, long before I knew anything of the horrors of the Tuskegee syphilis study. In preparation for my first job as an RN, I took the required civil service examination in November 1941. My score was high enough to qualify me for an appointment to one of the Public Health Service's member hospitals. I soon learned that I was being sent to New York City: I was to report to the U.S. Marine Hospital at 67 Hudson Street, on the corner of Jay Street, on January 3, 1942. I was pleased with the appointment. For the time, the salary of eighty-five dollars a month was excellent. My plan was to register for classes in a premedical curriculum at a New York college. I would then work during the day and attend classes in the evening, all while living in the nurses' quarters, as I had done at Central State. It did not occur to me that not all hospitals provided living quarters for its nurses.

I was just finishing up my year of training at Central State and preparing myself for the move to New York City when the Japanese bombed Pearl Harbor near Honolulu, Hawaii. The naval base attack was in retaliation for sanctions and trade embargoes the U.S. had imposed after Japan had gone to war with China four years before.[48]

The date of the Pearl Harbor bombing, December 7, 1941, is as indelibly marked in my memory as another air attack, carried out on September 11, 2001, would be etched in the nation's consciousness. Both these attacks would draw the country into the fray of war. Although I didn't yet know it, World War II would turn out to have a profound effect on the future course of my life, eventually becoming my ticket to affording medical school. But when the bombs fell that December day, I knew only that the two-hour barrage had wiped out almost the entire Pacific fleet, destroying some twenty ships and two hundred airplanes, killing more than two thousand soldiers and wounding a thousand more. I can still hear the booming voice of President Franklin D. Roosevelt pronouncing the attack "a date which will live in infamy" as he asked Congress for a declaration of war.[49]

This was the cloud under which I made my way to New York less than a month later to accept my USPHS appointment. Carrying all of my worldly possessions in a steamer trunk and a small suitcase, I boarded the Greyhound bus in Petersburg, Virginia, on the Friday morning of January 2, 1942. En route, I stopped in Washington, DC, for several hours to visit with my friends Blanchard and Lucille Lloyd. Blanchard's parents, Dr. R.A.B. Lloyd and his wife Blanche Lloyd, had continued to be cherished mentors to me, and indeed, Dr. Lloyd never ceased from prodding me toward medical school. As he was visiting with his son in DC at the time I was passing through, I wanted to share with him and his wife, and my dear friends Blanchard and Lucille, my successful completion of the psychiatric nursing certificate from Central State and my appointment to the U.S. Marine Hospital in New York.

Lucille seemed concerned when I told her where I was headed. "Ellamae, I don't think there are any black nurses or physicians at that hospital," she said. "Do they know that you are black? Did you send them a picture?"

"They know that I graduated from Hampton, and they must know that Hampton is a black college," I responded.

This did not allay her worry for me. She continued to believe a mistake had been made by the USPHS in hiring me, and she worried that I would arrive in New York and find that no blacks were on staff at the U.S. Marine Hospital. If that happened, she told me, I should get on a bus and come right back to them in Washington to figure out my next move. I was nervous, but I saw no alternative at that point but to proceed to New York as planned.

At 23, while living in Harlem, I enjoyed taking out-of-town friends (such as my college roommate, Ena Shillingford, pictured here) to Sunday services at the world-famous Abyssinian Baptist Church, which was so close I could hear choir rehearsals from my rented room.

CHAPTER 9

Harlem Song

When I arrived at New York City's Port Authority that Friday night, it was freezing cold out. Cursing my lack of foresight in packing away my good wool cape, I stepped out into the street and hailed a checkered taxi as I had watched other bus passengers do. After loading my steamer trunk and suitcase into the taxi, I asked the driver to take me to the corner of Hudson and Jay streets. I watched the towering skyscrapers of the city sweep by outside my window, and I marveled at how alive the streets of the avenues were, even at this late hour. As we pulled up to 67 Hudson Street, a neon clock in a store window flashed 11 P.M. I saw that the hospital building was dark, a five-story brick-and-stone edifice silhouetted against the ambient glow of the evening sky. I thought surely I must be in the wrong place, but the sign on the building read "U.S. Marine Hospital," so I exited the cab, asking the driver to wait for me, my steamer trunk and suitcase still in his car. I climbed the two-sided staircase to the stately wooden front door, which was set off by grand sandstone columns on either side. I found a doorbell and rang it, then stepped back against the wrought-iron railing, peering up at the dark building for signs of life. A grizzled old night watchman appeared at the door. He said nothing, just stood and stared at me, scratching his beard. My apprehension mounted.

I explained to the watchman that I had a letter directing me to report for duty as a nurse at the hospital the following morning, and I asked him to show me to the nurses' quarters. The man tugged at the white strands of his beard and explained that the building was an outpatient clinic facility only, and there was no place for nurses to live on the premises. The main hospital with inpatient beds was located on Staten Island. There might be nurses' quarters there, he said, but he didn't rightly know.

Fear and dismay knotted my insides. I asked with more calm than I felt, "Well, where do the nurses live who work here?"

The night watchman shrugged. "Around in the city," he said.

I stood there for several minutes, not knowing what to do. What must the watchman have thought of this naïve 23-year-old brown-skinned woman, standing uncertainly before him in a beige knee-length skirt and matching belted jacket over a thin cotton blouse. I had tried for my most stylish attire, a small-town girl eager to impress, but all I had achieved was being chilled to the bone. The hospital was closed for the night and I was alone in the city, shivering in the cold, with nowhere to go. The man merely stood in the dimly lit vestibule, his colorless eyes bored and incurious. I prayed fervently that God was looking down on me that evening, and that guardian angels were at my side.

Both the watchman and the cab driver were white; I realized that my fate at that moment lay completely in the hands of these two men. I decided to return to the cab driver, leaving the night watchman to lock up behind me. I asked the cabbie if he knew of a residence hotel for women nearby. I told him that I had been hired by the U.S. Marine Hospital but had just learned there were no living quarters on the premises. He thought for a moment, and then suggested I try the YWCA a few blocks away. He offered to drive me there.

It was near midnight by the time we pulled up in front of the downtown YWCA. Displaying more confidence than I felt, I went inside and explained my plight to the night clerk at the front desk. A pale, bird-faced woman, she hesitated for a moment, then pushed a key across the desk to me. I could stay for one night only, she told me. In the morning, I would have to move uptown to the Emma Ransom House, which was the residence of the Harlem YWCA. Although she didn't expressly say why, I understood this had to do with my race. As a black person, I was being directed to accommodations among my own kind. The clerk was matter-of-fact and even quite pleasant as she pointed me toward the stairway that led to my room on the second floor.

And so I went back outside and paid the cab driver, dragged my trunk and my suitcase up a steep flight of stairs, and deposited my belongings and myself in a tiny green room furnished with a narrow cot, a brass lamp atop a scuffed desk, a small dresser and a straight-back chair. The bath was down the hall, but there was a small sink in one corner of my room. I washed up there tiredly and climbed into bed, falling asleep as soon as my head hit the pillow. This was how I spent my first night in the city.

The following morning, still feeling some trepidation as to whether there had been a mistake made in my USPHS assignment, I reported for duty at the U.S. Marine Hospital. The chief nurse was white. And yes, they were expecting me. They did not seem at all put out by the fact that I was black. In fact, I soon saw another black face, another nurse! And then I met five other black nurses, all of whom had been hired within the previous year. My apprehension began to dissipate. It was my first day at my first job as a registered nurse. I was in New York City, still an unsophisticated Midwestern girl, but in my immediate surroundings everyone seemed to be friendly and helpful.

I still faced the task of moving my belongings from the downtown YWCA to the Emma Ransom House on 137th Street in Harlem. I planned to accomplish this after work, but I knew no one in the city who I could ask to drive me, and I was ignorant of the public transportation system. I had no idea how to read the tangle of lines that was the city bus and train map; and I had never been in Harlem. I decided I would take a cab, but one of my fellow black nurses, upon hearing of my plan to move my belongings by taxi, very kindly phoned her husband to meet us with his car. And thus I was moved to the Harlem YWCA with the help of this generous couple.

I soon learned that the YWCAs in the city were still segregated, and it was only the benevolence of the front desk attendant at the downtown facility that had allowed me to stay my first night there. I was to live at the Emma Ransom House of the Harlem YWCA for the rest of the time I was in New York,

paying a reasonable rent of $8.50 a week for a private room and
an adjoining private bath.[50]

Harlem at that time offered a wealth of new experiences for me.
In the 1940s, many great African American writers, artists, politi-
cians and entertainers called Harlem home. A decade and a half
before I arrived there, Harlem Renaissance writer Alain Locke
had described the vibrant mix of the neighborhood thus:

> *Here in Manhattan is not merely the largest Negro community
> in the world, but the first concentration in history of so many
> diverse elements of Negro life. It has attracted the African, the
> West Indian, the Negro American; has brought together the
> Negro of the North and the Negro of the South; the man from
> the city and the man from the town and village; the peasant,
> the student, the business man, the professional man, artist,
> poet, musician, adventurer and worker, preacher and criminal,
> exploiter and social outcast. Each group has come with its own
> separate motives and for its own special ends, but their greatest
> experience has been the finding of one another.[51]*

The Harlem I came to in January 1942 was not much changed
from this hustling, bustling oasis of black life. It was the heyday
of Smalls Paradise, the Savoy Ballroom, the Apollo Theater, and
Sugar Hill, with its famed living quarters on Edgecombe Avenue
and St. Nicholas, where bold-faced names such as Thurgood
Marshall, Cab Calloway and Walter White tasted "the sweet life"
in elegantly appointed row houses. In Harlem, one could drop
names endlessly. Bill "Bojangles" Robinson was there, as were
Duke Ellington and Louis Armstrong and their orchestras, and
Jackie "Moms" Mabley and others. On any given day, one might
run into Zora Neale Hurston or a young Malcolm X on 125th Street
or hear Count Basie on stage at the Cotton Club. Black sailors and
soldiers on leave from the war swarmed the avenues and poured

into the clubs and speakeasies, eager to find the artistic pulse of the neighborhood. Twenty years after the height of its Renaissance, Harlem's heart still beat with stubborn optimism, despite the economic losses of the Great Depression and the long shadow of the Second World War.[52]

The year before, FDR had signed an executive order outlawing racial discrimination in shipbuilding, weapons manufacturing and other defense industries related to the war effort. The boom in factory jobs newly open to blacks had helped to pull Harlem out of its post-Depression slump.[53] For me, this resurgence was nowhere more visible than on Sunday mornings, when Harlemites decked out in their finest filled the pews of the magnificent Abyssinian Baptist Church, which stood just behind the Emma Ransom House. Founded in 1808 by a group of twelve women and four men—a mix of black Americans and Ethiopian immigrants who had objected to the racially segregated seating in the Baptist Church of New York—Abyssinian's original home had been in lower Manhattan. Its current sanctuary, a massive Gothic Revival and Tudor style construction at 132 West 138th Street, had been completed in 1923 under the visionary leadership of its seventeenth pastor, the Rev. Dr. Adam Clayton Powell Sr.[54]

The interior of the church was breathtaking, with stained-glass windows imported from Europe and a pulpit carved of Italian marble. By the time I walked through its heavy wooden doors in 1942, the Rev. Adam Clayton Powell Jr. had succeeded his father at the helm of the church, and membership had swelled to more than fifteen thousand souls, making Abyssinian one of the largest black houses of worship in America. With a broad base of social justice initiatives, such as its kitchen and relief program to feed and clothe Harlem's poor, it was also one of the most influential churches, not just in Harlem but also in the nation, especially after Rev. Powell became the first black congressman from New York in 1937. Powell went on to serve fourteen terms in the U.S. House of Representatives. He also welcomed black political agitators and luminaries such as Malcolm X, Nat King Cole,

Martin Luther King Jr. and Marian Wright Edelman to speak from Abyssinian's pulpit.[55]

On Sunday mornings, when the church choir's glorious voices rang out in hymns and spirituals and gospel songs, it seemed that the very gates of heaven opened wide. It was impossible for me to remain in bed on Sunday mornings, no matter how arduous my week at the Marine Hospital had been. One had to arrive early to get a seat in the sanctuary, especially in 1942 when, as I recall, some five hundred seats were regularly reserved for a Columbia University class in race relations. Abyssinian encouraged its members to become active in politics, and its Community House program was dedicated to addressing homelessness, joblessness, adult education, elder care, early childhood education and other community needs. To this day, when I am asked about my time in New York City, it is not the glitzy Harlem nightlife or the lively artistic scene or the proximity to black power and wealth that I remember most keenly; it is my time spent in the architectural and musical splendor of that historic church.

Other than Abyssinian, I did not love New York. It was not my natural habitat. I ventured into clubs like the Savoy and the Cotton Club when my friends Blanchard and Lucille, or my sisters Georgeanna and Rowena, came to visit me, but in general I found the city too big, too fast, too hectic, too impersonal, with too many people crammed together in small spaces. Sometimes I felt that I couldn't breathe, and that there was such a cacophony of voices I couldn't hear my own. I knew from the beginning that the city would never be my permanent home. Still, my work at the U.S. Marine Hospital was satisfying. I had been assigned to the EENT (eyes, ears, nose, throat) clinic, and my beginning salary was enough that I could pay my rent and still bank every second check toward medical school. Mostly, I assisted the staff ophthalmologist in treating eye diseases and injuries, and I prepared the patients' case histories. Between my hours on duty at the hospital and my Sunday mornings in the pews of Abyssinian, I bided my time, looking, always looking for the door that would lead me to my ultimate goal of becoming a physician. It was never out of my mind.

Although I didn't know it then, I was one step closer when I began receiving mailings from the American Red Cross, urging me to consider joining the Army Nurse Corps. The letters explained that with war raging overseas, there was a critical shortage of military nurses, and all RNs who were "not engaged in an essential industry" were urged to enlist. Nurses were needed to serve in station hospitals and field evacuation units, on hospital trains and ships, and on medical transport planes. After receiving the third such letter, I discussed the opportunity with my chief nurse. I wanted to better understand the function of the American Red Cross and to assess whether it was worth giving up my very good USPHS salary to become an Army nurse. I feared that my reduced income upon joining the Army Nurse Corps would hinder my efforts to save, thereby interfering with my plan to study medicine.

The chief nurse pointed out that even with a reduced beginning salary, as an Army nurse I would probably be able to save more money because the majority of my living expenses would be covered. She assured me that if I were to become an Army nurse, I could be on military leave for as long as necessary; my job with USPHS would be assured upon my return to civilian life. I thanked her for her advice. But for several weeks more, I was in a quandary. My family back home was stiffly opposed to my joining the military and going off to war, making my decision that much more difficult. But at last, I decided to enlist.

The choice would have been far easier to make had I known that the GI Bill of Rights—which among other benefits would pay for the further education of military veterans—would be signed into law by President Roosevelt just two years later. For me, the GI Bill would be the real jewel in the crown of military service, opening up a path to my personal holy grail, a medical degree.

Camp Livingston, Louisiana, offered a brutal education in the daily realities of Jim Crow. I am on the left in the photo, taken in 1943.

CHAPTER 10

Camp Livingston

I was inducted into the Army Nurse Corps as a second lieutenant on December 15, 1942, assigned to duty at Camp Livingston Station Hospital in Louisiana. Just a few weeks later, all doctors and nurses in the USPHS received U.S. Coast Guard commissions. Had I known the Public Health Service would be militarized, I could have elected to continue working at the U.S. Marine Hospital while still serving my country.

At the time I enlisted, there were only 150 African Americans in the corps, among some fifty-nine thousand Army nurses. By the time the war ended, there would be a total of 479 black Army nurses, a number that was kept low by Army quota systems.[56] In leaving New York, I had wished for an overseas assignment, but I was sent instead to the deepest South. To say I was disappointed with the location of my assignment would have been an understatement. I had no experience living in the Deep South, which always stirred in me visions of black men swinging from trees, Negro settlements burned to ashes, and other racial horrors that my parents had told me were indigenous to the former slave-owning states. It did not dawn on me that the Midwest possessed its own share of terrors. Indeed, I had grown up right next door to members of the Ku Klux Klan, a family that had held cross-burning rallies in the parkland right across the street from our front yards. Yet to my mind, Mount Vernon and the South were worlds apart, so when friends inquired if the Army Nurse Corps had given me a foreign assignment, I responded archly, "Yes, Louisiana. That's foreign to me."

Located near the town of Alexandria, Camp Livingston was entirely segregated, which meant there were two of everything, from living quarters and mess halls to hospitals and dispensaries, one for whites, another for blacks. I remember one cold winter day watching as hired civilians who were working on the military post built fires to keep warm. All the white workers were standing around one fire, while about fifty feet away, all the black workers were standing around another fire. It seemed to me that black soldiers were at war on two fronts: At home and overseas, we were fighting and dying for a country that considered us second- or even third-class citizens. Every day black soldiers put their lives on the line to protect the freedom of a country in which they were not free.

At Camp Livingston, Japanese and German POWs were confined in the post's stockade, along with a number of American soldiers who had been accused of committing some breach of Army protocol. Many of them were black. By law, all prisoners were allowed routine outdoor exercise on post. I had observed that when the German, Japanese or white American prisoners were in the yard, there might be ten or more of them under the guard of one or two military police. However, if three or four black prisoners were in the yard, there would be one MP on guard for every soldier, rifles trained.

There were so many such examples of racism within the armed forces that I had to consciously choose again and again not to become bitter. Some Southern whites became inflamed at the very sight of a black military officer in uniform. Indeed, it often seemed to me that whites in Louisiana did not know there was a world war going on, for they were still engaged in the Civil War. Most black citizens in the rest of the country naïvely thought that race relations would improve once the war was over. My father, for one, believed this with all his heart. In Louisiana, I saw that he was mistaken.

Before writing this part of my story, I pored through a box of old letters I had written to my parents, especially to my mother, during my Army Nurse Corps service, which lasted from December 1942 through April 1946. I had complained frequently to my mother of vicious racial incidents I had encountered, witnessed or heard about, but until I read them again in my letters, I had forgotten many of them. Being fully reminded of those incidents was painful indeed, but the letters were a valuable historical record.

My complaints to my mother were interrupted briefly when I was transferred from the Station Hospital at Camp Livingston, Louisiana, to the Station Hospital at Fort Clark, Texas, in November 1943. The black 761st Tank Battalion was stationed at Fort Clark, which was just seven miles from the Mexican border. On an all-black base, the atmosphere was completely different from Louisiana. The prejudice against non-whites from local civilians was more muted, with the main focus directed toward Mexican border patrols. My fellow nurses and I made several visits to the Mexican border towns of Villa Acuña and Piedras Negras, where we dined in restaurants that served delicious entrées of T-bone steaks, squab, pheasant and venison at very reasonable prices. We even attended bullfights on a couple of our visits across the border, and I came to view this new assignment by the Army as not so bad after all. On reviewing letters to my mother while I was in Texas, I note a distinct change in mood. I was more cheerful, full of stories of grand adventures, and even my penmanship seemed to have improved.

But just three months later, I was transferred back to Camp Livingston. My only consolation was that I wouldn't be there for long, because I already had orders for yet another transfer, this time to Fort Des Moines, Iowa. I was happy I would be leaving Camp Livingston for good and hoped for an uneventful few weeks until my new assignment came through. A few nights before my departure, however, a Negro soldier was shot and killed by a white bus driver on the road into town. Later that same evening, another Negro soldier was beaten senseless by local whites, who then dragged his body to the gates of the camp and dumped him there. The MP on gate duty phoned the Station Hospital for an ambulance, and I was there when the severely battered soldier was brought in. Why didn't the MP detain the men who had dumped the body? Had they beaten and dumped the body of a white soldier, I can guarantee you those men would have been rounded up and prosecuted to the fullest extent of the law. But a black soldier—well, at least the MP had called the ambulance for him. I wasn't sure he would survive the night, and when he did, I had no hope that he would survive the next. In fact, he died of his injuries that afternoon.

These and many other such atrocities never reached the media. But as black nurses in the Station Hospital, we witnessed the constant, cruel, unprovoked brutalization of black soldiers by white civilians. As I wrote in one letter to my mother, "These injustices could be visited at any time on my own brother, or my father, or some dear friend, or even on me; any one of us could be in the wrong place at the wrong time to incite these vile attacks based on nothing more than the skin we were born into."

My experience at Camp Livingston confirmed ten times over the stories of the South that had been told to me by my parents. As I saw it, my presence in that part of the country only made encounters with such horrors more likely, and I could hardly wait to put as much distance as possible between me and Louisiana. "I would say this is the closest I have come to hell on earth," I wrote to my mother. "In my 25 years I have never witnessed such hatefulness as I have seen here and I hope never to meet with ever again."

My transfer from Camp Livingston to Fort Des Moines Provisional Army Officer Training School in Iowa became official in early March 1944. I was one of eight black nurses assigned to travel to Iowa in uniform under military orders. We would drive across the country to Fort Des Moines in cars that belonged to two of the nurses in our group. We were expected to average 200 miles a day and were allotted four-and-a-half days of travel time. Our commanding officer stressed that we were not to disclose to any person where our final destination might be.

I didn't think much about the secrecy. I was used to the Army keeping its strategic actions strictly confidential. We piled into the two cars, four of us in each vehicle, and departed early on a Saturday morning. We had decided to stop in Shreveport, Louisiana, for breakfast, because one of the nurses in our group had an uncle who owned a restaurant there. The first car reached the restaurant a few minutes ahead of the second. I was traveling in the second car that morning, and when we pulled into the parking lot of the restaurant, we immediately noticed three white policemen standing around our friends' parked car. The four nurses who had been in that car had already gone into the restaurant and apparently did not yet know their car was a source of trouble outside.

And what was the trouble? It was nothing more than that the car's left rear wheel was outside of the yellow line that marked off the parking space. But this was enough to cause one of the policemen to bark in a very nasty tone, "Whose car is this? This car is parked illegally! Where is the driver of this car?" He was so loud and antagonistic that a crowd of civilians had gathered at the edge of the parking lot, waiting to see what would transpire. The situation was becoming more volatile by the minute.

The four of us exited our car, but we knew better than to make a move toward the restaurant. The police officer saw we were all in military uniform and demanded to know who we were and where we were going. His tone continued to be unpleasant. As the highest-ranking member of the group, I stepped forward and told him that we were from Louisiana and we were traveling as Army nurses to take up a new assignment. I explained that we were under strict orders not to discuss where we were going or what our assignment would be once we got there. On hearing this, the police officer's face grew beet-red. How dare we not respond to a direct question, he shouted. He didn't give a damn who we were or what uniform we were wearing, he had asked us a question and we better give him an answer. He then accused us of lying about being from Louisiana, saying he could tell from our accents that we were not from these parts. The four of us looked at each other nervously and remained silent.

We could see the other nurses in our group peering out from the restaurant now, drawn by the commotion. To say we felt terror in that moment does not begin to capture it. There was no telling what this white policeman stalking angrily up and down the parking lot with his hand on his pistol might do. He demanded again to know who owned the car. The nurse whose car it was, as well as her three passengers, hurried across the parking lot to claim the vehicle. At the officer's request, she produced her insurance card and driver's license. Squinting at the paperwork, the policeman snarled, "I don't care where you're from, as long as you're down here in my territory, you're going to do as we say, whether you like it or not. If you talk back, I'll take every one of you and throw you in the basement of the jail and wear out a tug on you. We have a place in the back of the jail for people like you. No matter how loud you holler, no one can hear you!"

All eight of us nurses stayed silent. Along with the fear of being thrown in jail was a needle of shame at how this white man was treating eight black women in Army uniform, in front of white and black civilians. Would he really prevent us from carrying out our commission, and what would the Army do about that? I was afraid to find out. We were still in the South, where I'd seen injustice after injustice against black people go unanswered. One of the other policemen stepped forward at that point and suggested that they call the chief on us, meaning the chief of police of the town. And that's what the angry cop did—called the chief from his squad car radio and told him that he had "eight nigger nurses" here who had broken the law.

The chief arrived minutes later, pulling up in an officially marked car. He walked toward us with his thumbs looped into his belt, cowboy style, and addressed his officers.

"So what did these girls do?"

The policeman who'd been doing most of the talking pointed to the parked car with the left rear wheel outside the yellow line.

The chief walked over, removed his sunglasses, and looked down at the wheel, his expression unreadable.

"What else did they do?" he asked the officer.

"One of them gave me a lot of lip," the policeman stated. That, of course, was me, as I was the one who had insisted we weren't at liberty to say where we were headed.

The chief asked the policeman what he wanted to do with us. The policeman shrugged. "Well, that's up to you, Chief."

The chief looked us over, eight frightened and trembling nurses in Army uniform. "Well, if that's all they did, I guess you could let them go," he said finally, and with that he replaced his sunglasses, got back in his car and drove off.

We could feel the glare of the policemen boring through us as we scrambled to get back into our cars. Our appetites had deserted us. We could not flee the scene fast enough. We wanted nothing more than to drive until we were clear of the Louisiana border and never look back. No one spoke a word in either car until we reached Texarkana on the Arkansas side. We pulled over then, and made a prayer circle in a storefront parking lot to thank our Creator that we had not been beaten or incarcerated, and that we were still alive. Then we stocked up on sodas and sandwiches for the trip and got right back on the road.

I had heard numerous stories about police overreach of authority and outright brutality, especially against blacks and especially in the South, but this was my first direct brush with a hostile force of law, in or out of the Army. I had never before felt so completely helpless to defend myself, and so at the mercy of a blistering hate that threatened to do me lasting harm. Once, I had believed that if you just "behaved yourself" in such situations, nothing bad would happen to you. I saw now how sorely misguided I had been.

Taking turns driving and sleeping, we did not stop again until we reached Fort Des Moines, Iowa, on the evening of March 14, 1944. Much the worse for wear, the eight of us reported to the chief nurse of the Station Hospital and were shown to our sleeping quarters. I noted we were in a barracks that also housed white nurses. This was highly unusual, but I was exhausted from our travel and still deeply unsettled by our encounter with the Louisiana police, so I simply set down my trunk, washed up and fell into my bunk as soon as I could. I slept dreamlessly.

On the following morning, we reported again to the chief nurse, as we had been instructed. She escorted us to meet the colonel who was the commanding officer of the Station Hospital. First, he welcomed us and told us a bit about the Station Hospital, which was small, with only 400 beds compared to the 1,750 beds at Camp Livingston. He told us the Army had intentionally selected this small hospital for an experiment in racial integration. The eight of us would be housed in the same quarters as white nurses, and even more significantly, we would care for white soldiers as well as black, and all patients would be together in the same wing. Never before had Negro nurses attended white wounded, but now, with our presence at Fort Des Moines, the base would be considered officially integrated.

The commander looked at each of us in turn, emphasizing again that it was the first time in history that Negro nurses had been allowed to care for white soldiers. But this was something we all already knew. We had only ever cared for Negro troops in the South. The commander went on speaking. Because of this experiment, he said, we should be very aware that "the eyes of the Army are upon you here." And then he added: "Upon your behavior rests the success or failure of this trial at integration. So there are some protocols you must observe. I do not want you to give orders to the corpsmen; I want you to give suggestions. If problems arise, I do not want you to try to handle them. I want you to tell me and let me handle them. I do not ever want you to pull rank."

We nurses stole fleeting glances at one another during this briefing. We were all thinking back to Shreveport and how the incident with the police there could so easily have derailed the Army's integration experiment. We could visualize the newspaper headlines: "Eight Negro Army Nurses Arrested" on whatever trumped-up charges the harassing cop might have used against us. What an embarrassment we would have been to the Army had the subjects of its grand experiment ended up in jail.

We would later learn that the integration of the Army Nurse Corps in Iowa was the first step toward dismantling segregation in the armed forces as a whole, which would be achieved with the stroke of a pen on July 26, 1948, when President Harry Truman enacted executive order 9981.[57] At the time, however, we were totally ignorant of the government's intent to integrate its entire military operation. We were preoccupied only with the day-to-day problems of coping with, as we ironically referred to it among ourselves, "this man's Army."

First Lieutenant Ellamae Simmons, Army Nurse Corps, 1945.

CHAPTER 11

This Woman's Army

It soon became apparent to us that Fort Des Moines was occupied mostly by women, most of them in officer training with the Women's Army Corps (WAC). When we arrived, there were some fifteen hundred WAC recruits on the base. They were continually being deployed to other assignments, with new recruits moving in just as quickly to take their place. Women serving in the U.S. military was brand new. A year before, faced with a severe shortage of soldiers to man the frontlines in both Germany and Japan, the federal government had approved the creation of an all-women's volunteer corps as an auxiliary to the Army. Dubbed the Women's Army Auxiliary Corps (WAAC), the new troops were led by Oveta Culp Hobby, chief of the women's interest section in the public relations bureau of the U.S. War Department. Hobby, a prominent Texas socialite, was very well connected politically, and she lobbied tirelessly for the women to be recognized not merely as civilian volunteers but as full-fledged soldiers. Her efforts were rewarded in July 1943 when Congress passed a bill that gave the sixty thousand or so WAAC volunteers formal military status. The women would henceforth be recognized as soldiers of the Women's Army Corps.[58]

Less than a year before I arrived at Fort Des Moines, the first class of WAC officer candidates had begun training at the base, under the direction of Oveta Culp Hobby herself. Of the original 440 officer candidates, 40 were black. Although their basic training was the same as that of male soldiers, candidates did not undergo weapons and tactical instruction, because they were not expected to be under fire on the front lines. They were trained instead for "safe" military jobs, such as switchboard operators, mechanics, cooks, postal clerks, drivers, seamstresses and stenographers. Later, the WAC would also train women to repair small arms and heavy weaponry,[59] but women in the armed forces would not be allowed to carry firearms until the 1980s.[60]

The conditions for women at Fort Des Moines were hardly ideal. In records from that time, one soldier recalled "falling out for reveille at 6:00 AM in the dark, below-zero weather in deep snow ... the oversized man's GI overcoat which I wore over a thin fatigue dress ... a typical sad sack GI shivering with a coat dragging in the snow...."[61] Another wrote, "We went through Officer Candidate School in tennis shoes, foundation garments, seersucker dresses with bloomers and gas masks. Apparently there was a supply mix-up somewhere in the pipeline. The over concern with underwear by the male planners paid dividends. But they were not pink with lace. They were tannish and awful. Foundation garments, such as even our grandmothers would not have worn, did give us moments of hilarious parading in our barracks after the 'study hour.'"[62]

As Army nurses, we were somewhat better equipped, with a good field overcoat, leather and woolen gloves, and a military-issue cape that we could don over our nurses whites. I thought it singularly interesting that the Army would initiate its experiment in racial integration with women in the military rather than with men. In letters to my mother from Fort Des Moines, I wrote that I enjoyed my hospital work very much. People were mostly friendly, I told her, and despite my former ardent desire to be sent overseas, I now expressed the wish that I might remain on this base for the duration of my military duty.

Of course there were still plenty of daily reminders that we were seen as second-class citizens, but the bigotry here was not nearly as vicious as we'd endured in Louisiana. It generally amounted to being frequently called "nigger" by some of the white nurses. I remember, for example, during a gas mask drill when a black nurse was having trouble adjusting her mask, a white nurse casually commented for everyone to hear, "Nigger nurses never do anything right." Highly offended, I reported the incident to our chief nurse, suggesting strongly that the white nurse owed the black nurses an apology. The chief looked at me over her glasses and commented, "Oh, you think so, do you?" With that, she walked away.

Despite such indignities, the experience at Fort Des Moines turned out to be a rewarding one. For the first time since enlisting, I was assigned a nursing service in which my postgraduate training was utilized. I was put in charge of the neuropsychiatric wards, which was pure serendipity, because in the Army at the time, medical and nursing specialties were generally ignored. One might have specialized in pediatric nursing and be assigned to the genitourinary service. A physician might be a hematologist by training and yet be assigned to emergency room duty. In short, we were sent where the Army needed us. As it happened, there was a great need for neuropsychiatric nurses, as one in twelve patients in Station Hospitals was in need of psychiatric care, and during the course of the war, some four hundred thousand soldiers would be discharged from the service due to a diagnosis of mental illness.[63]

The neuropsychiatric nursing service at Fort Des Moines offered opportunities for travel, sometimes to escort a mental patient to another facility or to accompany a troop train of Women's Army Corps personnel. I never stopped hoping for a trip that would pass near to my home; however, the train routes were never publicized. In fact, the trains never traveled the direct route, but instead zigzagged between bases, picking up more troops on the way. Several times I accompanied WAC personnel from Iowa to the East Coast, which gave me some insight into troop movements in general, as well as opportunities to get to know some of the women.

Interestingly enough, whenever I crossed the Mason-Dixon line into the South on a WAC troop train, I was not subject to Jim Crow laws. The same lack of Jim Crow visibility obtained when I escorted a group of female mental patients from the neuro-psychiatric service of the Station Hospital at Fort Des Moines to other mental facilities in the South or to their homes. Such travel was always by regular civilian train, with Pullman car accommodations of a bedroom or roomette in the white section of the transport. Following regular protocol, I would report to the MP on the train at the start of the journey, making him aware that I was traveling with mental patients. Always on these trips, the MPs and the Pullman car attendants treated me courteously and professionally. Most of the Pullman car attendants were Negro, and they were particularly protective and solicitous of me, clearly pleased to see a Negro Army officer serving in my capacity.

In one letter to my mother, I described a trip from Fort Des Moines, Iowa, to Bushnell General Military Hospital in Brigham City, Utah. I had accompanied two female mental patients for further treatment there. These usually calm patients had become agitated during the journey and required sedation and my unceasing supervision. I was unable to sleep for four straight days on this trip, and I complained bitterly to my mother. How patiently and reassuringly my mother read and responded to all of my grumblings about the Army!

It was as a psychiatric nurse at Fort Des Moines that homosexuality in the military, as a diagnostic entity, entered my vocabulary. In 1944, the chief psychiatrist on the base discussed homosexuality with me, and the problem it had become for the Army, especially among the Women's Army Corps. At that time, when a person had committed an overt homosexual act or had been so accused, separation from military service was the only option considered. This fell under Section 8 of the military code, which referred to various "undesirable habits and traits of character" that would require immediate discharge. The code was meant to apply to psychiatric conditions that would render a recruit unfit to serve—depression, suicidal tendencies, hypochondria, various forms of psychosis—but during my time at Fort Des Moines in 1944 and 1945, a number of female soldiers were evaluated as "Section 8s" based on findings of homosexuality, and were dishonorably released from service.

Many of these women were admitted to the neuropsychiatric ward while awaiting the disposition of their cases. Relieved thus of the pressures of war, they relished one another's company and often paired off in opportunistic relationships. Some of them would tease me as I took their histories, asking, for instance, if I liked men and telling me that if I did, it was only because I'd never tried women. Their teasing aside, it was clear to me that most of them had been good soldiers, and that they had found a refuge of sorts in the military, where many of the women officers were known to be lesbians. I suspected that some who were from small towns had been drawn to the military as a way to escape restrictive attitudes and expectations back home. Perhaps they had joined with the hope of finding other women like themselves. From my purely anecdotal experience at Fort Des Moines, they found one another in numbers far exceeding the 33 percent that the armed forces officially reported.[64]

In October 1944, four Negro nurses from our original group of eight were transferred to Fort Francis E. Warren in Cheyenne, Wyoming, leaving only four of us to cover the Station Hospital at Fort Des Moines. I missed my friends, with whom I had shared so much. I was further disheartened when a former colleague from my time at the U.S. Marine Hospital, who had been commissioned as a Navy nurse, visited me, and I learned that her starting salary had been higher than my Army salary of not quite $900 per year.[65] In letters to my mother, I began to gripe more and more about inequities in the armed forces as I saw or imagined them. In November, I wrote that this, hopefully, would be my last Thanksgiving in the Army. It wasn't. There had been rumors that Fort Des Moines would be closed and turned into a convalescent hospital for casualties from overseas. That did not happen. Once again my hopes for an imminent discharge were dashed.

The following March, just three days before my twenty-seventh birthday, the eight nurses who had integrated the Army

Nurse Corps together were appointed to the rank of first lieutenant. Only days after bestowing this honor, President Franklin
D. Roosevelt suffered a massive cerebral hemorrhage and died
on April 12, 1945.[66] Gloom settled over the military base at Fort
Des Moines. The end of the war was in sight, but the president
who had led the nation through its darkest days would not live
to see it. A month later, V-E Day (Victory in Europe) was celebrated when German forces signed their unconditional surrender
at Rheims on May 7, 1945. Three months later, after the United
States dropped atomic bombs on Hiroshima and Nagasaki, V-J
Day (Victory in Japan) was achieved on August 14, 1945. The war
was over, and our troops were coming home, but my longed-for
separation from duty would not be issued for another several
months. I would not leave Fort Des Moines until March 3, 1946,
and even then I remained on terminal military leave through
April 3, 1946.

I began to feel that my service was just dragging on and that
I was wasting valuable time that could be better spent studying
my pre-med course. I chafed to return to school. The whole time
I was in the Army, I had diligently saved toward my pre-medical education, sending checks to my mother that she regularly
deposited in my postal savings account. During this time, the
letters I received from my mother telling me of the mundane
details of family life had been my lifeline. The decades since
have altered my memory, so that much of what was worthy of
remembering has been forgotten, and some events worthy of
forgetting are etched in memory. But the boxes of old letters
between my mother and me tell the truth of how my time in the
Army actually unfolded.

During my final months in Iowa, as I waited for my discharge
to come through, one event was definitely worth remembering. In
July of 1945, I had the distinct pleasure of meeting the renowned
psychiatrist from Topeka, Kansas, Dr. Karl Menninger, author
of the 1930 bestselling classic, *The Human Mind*. The eminent
psychiatrist had come to Fort Des Moines to interview me for

possible employment as a psychiatric nurse. The Army doctor in charge of the neuropsychiatric service on the base had previously been a Menninger fellow, and he had recommended me to his former boss when he learned that Dr. Menninger was recruiting black professionals to staff Winter Veterans Administration Hospital in Topeka.

Dr. Menninger explained to me that he needed assistance to deal with the mental and emotional problems of returning black veterans at the close of the war. I remember him saying during our interview, "Being black in America by itself creates problems, and being a black soldier returned from combat with mental illness only compounds that problem." He added a statement so profound I have never forgotten it. "The phenomenon of being black in America is so complex that no white person can ever understand it," he told me. "And that is why I need you." This brilliant psychiatrist, researcher and author, whose understanding of human behavior was far ahead of his time, had grasped a truth I had despaired of any white person ever discerning. I knew then that Dr. Menninger had his finger on the pulse of America, and on the pulse of America's sickness—racism.

But as grateful as I was to be courted for employment by this famous and unusually socially aware psychiatrist, my plans had been made. As soon as my honorable discharge from the Army Nurse Corps was issued, I would embark on my pre-medical studies. I explained my goal of becoming a physician to Dr. Menninger and expressed my regret that I would not be able to take up his job offer. He remarked that he hoped I would indeed pursue my goal because my expertise in the field of medicine was greatly needed. With all sincerity, I promised him I would not get turned aside. Indeed, I had never been more filled with optimism about what came next. It was as Dr. Menninger himself once said: "Hope is an adventure, a going forward, a confident search for a rewarding life."[67]

Two decades after I enrolled at Ohio State, my grandniece Shawna Wilson (the baby in my niece Varian's arms) was born. She would one day live in the same residence hall that I integrated in 1946.

CHAPTER 12

Baker Hall

While in the Army, I had written away for my high school transcripts and nursing school records and I had quietly forwarded them to Ohio State. This time, the university accepted me into their pre-medical program. It helped greatly that I was a war veteran and covered by the Servicemen's Readjustment Act of 1944, or as it was more commonly known, the GI Bill of Rights.

With millions of soldiers returning to civilian life, Congress hoped the GI Bill would stave off another Great Depression by encouraging veterans to go back to school rather than flood the job market all at once. Signed into law by President Roosevelt on June 22, 1944, the bill promised to pay the full cost of education of war veterans; guaranteed loans for the purchase of homes, farms and businesses; and provided unemployment pay for veterans who for whatever reason could not be absorbed by the workforce. Unlike after World War I, when many returning soldiers were given sixty dollars and a train ticket back home, the federal government hoped to secure the future of America's war veterans by creating a path to education and home ownership. [68]

In practice, the GI Bill was an uneven proposition for black veterans, especially when it came to home ownership in the nation's segregated housing market. While whites were able to secure loans to purchase homes that over the next two decades would skyrocket in value, banks refused to extend similar loans to blacks. As a result, black families were shut out of the nation's key wealth-building equation—home ownership—for generations to come. In this context, home ownership among white veterans outstripped that of blacks, giving whites a way to become middle class and create a nest egg for their children. With black veterans unable to take advantage of the home loans promised them under the GI Bill, they and their families lagged behind economically, contributing to a racial wealth chasm that persists to this day.[69]

The nation's housing disparity based on race was an issue I would one day do my part to redress, but that was still many years down the road. First, I had to further my education. In this, the GI Bill was far more democratic. As economic policy analyst David Callahan has observed in his essay, "How The GI Bill Left Out African Americans," published by Demos, a think tank to promote economic equality, "The one big upside of the GI Bill is that it did pay for many black veterans to go to college and graduate school … [T]he influx of subsidized black students forced many white universities to open their doors to nonwhites, helping begin the great integration of higher education." [70]

Exactly ten years after Ohio State had turned me away from their school of nursing, I was a fully trained, licensed and experienced RN about to enroll as a pre-medical student majoring in biological sciences. Ohio State's academic year was on the quarter system, and I was to begin my course of study in the spring quarter, with a plan to continue through summer and fall, going to school year-round. I was one of 7.8 million veterans opting for colleges, trade schools and training centers after the war. By 1947, the height of college enrollment under the GI Bill, veterans represented 49 percent of college enrollment across the nation.[71] The pressure on U.S. universities to accommodate the influx of war veterans was so intense that classes were scheduled from seven in the morning until ten at night, with the latest sessions letting out at midnight, and some classes enrolling as many as three hundred students. Ohio State alone was host to some thirty thousand students after the war, an overwhelming statistic for me, who had been raised in a town of just ten thousand souls.

I knew that I would face difficulties as a student at Ohio State. The land of my birth had not changed *that* much. But I firmly believed that if others could do it, I could too, and more than that, I *would* do it. In this regard, the GI Bill felt like a lifesaver. In my wildest imagination, I could not have conceived that the government would actually pay me to better myself by going to college. I had been taught that you alone are the master of your fate and you advance in this world by paying your own way. I couldn't quite believe that not only would my tuition be paid for up to forty-eight months of study, but I would also receive a small living stipend during that time.[72] Sure enough, checks in my name began arriving regularly from the government. Four years prior, I had been skeptical about enlisting for U.S. Army duty for fear it would prevent my saving enough money and thereby interfere with my plan to study medicine. Now, I could not be happier to have served my country!

So it was with a great sense of anticipation that I went to register at Ohio State University in the biological sciences program in March 1946. I was still on terminal military leave and was wearing my first lieutenant Army Nurse Corps full dress uniform with my branch insignia pin and rank plainly visible. I wanted there to be no mistake that I had the power of the U.S. armed forces behind me, just in case any university administrator tried to equivocate about my right to register.

The young white clerk sitting behind the desk was less than enthusiastic about my presence, but I refused to let her unfriendly demeanor bring me down. She frowned at my transcripts and allowed that my grades were "okay." I knew my high school average had been 96 percent; that I had been on the national honor roll; and that in nursing school, I had received the highest scholastic honor, but I only smiled at her assessment and let it pass. Then the young woman commented that I had gone to a Southern school that was not as good as Ohio State. I could not let that pass. I drew myself up to my full five-feet-two-inches in height and told the clerk that I had applied to my tax-supported state university upon graduating high school, but I had been denied admission despite my outstanding record because, as Ohio State had put it, there were "no facilities for training colored girls" in their school of nursing. I added that I had then enrolled at Hampton Institute, where I had received superior training as a nurse, followed by extensive practical experience in hospitals both as a civilian and as a soldier. My tone was polite but firm, and perhaps a bit haughty. I wanted the clerk to be clear: I had every right to be there, and if she wasn't convinced of that, I certainly was.

The clerk looked up from my papers then and met my gaze. I could tell she was taken aback that I had spoken up for myself, and that she wasn't quite sure exactly who she might be dealing with. She noted that at least my school of nursing was accredited, so I could receive elective credit for my nursing courses. She signed my registration card and filed it in a box with hundreds of other cards, and with that, I was registered. The hurdle had been cleared.

My next challenge was to find housing. I was staying with my sister Georgeanna, who lived across town from the Ohio State campus in Columbus. We had agreed only to a temporary arrangement. I was sleeping on her couch, and with her friends coming and going at all hours from her small apartment, it was not conducive to study. I had gone to the Office of the Dean of Women in person to make a formal request for dormitory residence on campus. One of the dean's assistants interviewed me. She was a dark-haired woman in her forties, with a nervous manner. Her voice was apologetic as she informed me that colored girls had never lived on campus.

"Where do they live?" I inquired.

"They live on the East End of town," she said.

I pointed out that I was currently living with my sister on the East End, and the commute was untenable. As I was undertaking a fairly demanding pre-med curriculum, which I planned to complete in two calendar years, I could not afford to waste at least two hours daily in transit between the East End and campus. The assistant then referred me to "a colored lady on Eleventh Street," who housed students. Eleventh Street was adjacent to campus, so this might have worked nicely, but when I investigated, I discovered the woman had no vacancies.

As I pondered my next move, I remembered a friend from

Hampton whose brother had studied pre-med at Ohio State. The family was from Columbus, and my friend's mother, Mrs. Calloway, still lived in town, although both her children had moved away. I decided to go and see Mrs. Calloway and seek her advice, as she had had some experience in dealing with the white administrators at the university. As luck would have it, the Dean of Women, Christine Yerges Conway, had been Mrs. Calloway's son's faculty advisor before becoming the dean. Mrs. Calloway had met her son's advisor on several occasions, and their interactions had always been pleasant. She immediately placed a call to Dean Conway and explained my need to live on campus. Dean Conway told Mrs. Calloway that I should present myself at her office the following day, and she would see what she could do. I hugged Mrs. Calloway warmly, marveling that God had once again provided an angel to smooth the way.

As instructed, I returned to the Office of the Dean of Women the next day and again was seen by her assistant. The woman was even more nervous this time, stammering as she repeated the same refrain as before, that no colored women had ever lived in the dorms. I appreciated that she found difficulty in expressing the discriminatory practices that governed campus housing. I replied simply that I understood her predicament, but that the world had changed, and I was capable of living on campus among white students and causing no trouble. She noted that a colored female graduate student might have lived on campus once, during a summer session, "but it has never happened during the regular academic year."

I sat patiently as she leafed through sheets of paper in a fat manila file—looking, I presumed, for a suitable arrangement. I was hopeful now that I would be accommodated, thanks to Mrs. Calloway's intervention with the dean. But after a moment, the assistant closed her file and suggested I check back with her in a few days. Deflated but not deterred, I spent the rest of that week going from one administrative office to the other, trying to find a dean or faculty member who would support my campaign to live on campus. I dressed myself in full military uniform, thinking the fact that I had served my country might help sway people in favor of my cause. But everyone told me the same thing: It had never been done before. Even Jesse Owens, the greatest athlete the school had ever seen, had not been given a room on campus. They were sorry, they said, but what I was asking was impossible.

Finally, I went back to the Office of the Dean of Women and again met with her assistant. This time, the woman advised that in one of the campus dormitories there was a single room I could have. The dormitory was Baker Hall, and it housed 750 women. She added carefully that I could not have a roommate—the Dean of Women had been very clear on that point. I informed her that I did not want a roommate: I had been in the Army and was several years older than the average freshman. I then thanked her and took the key to my new room as inwardly I breathed a gigantic sigh of relief.

I moved into Baker Hall that weekend—and became the first black woman in the history of Ohio State to live in campus housing during the academic year. It was March 1946, and I was 28 years old. I confess I felt some pride at being the first black woman allowed to live in the dorms, but when I visited home a few weekends later, full of airs over finally securing campus housing, my sainted father with his eighth-grade education quickly put things in perspective.

We were out on the side porch, where he still slept most nights. I remember he gently took my hands into his big, calloused brown ones and asked me to sit with him for a moment. He sat on the old chaise lounge that was his bed, and I perched opposite him on a stack of old newspapers and magazines, piled high. My father reminded me that white people and especially white institutions had long played the game of divide and conquer when it came to black people. Those Negroes who were allowed *inside*—whether it was inside the big house during slavery days or the dorms of my big state university now—were told they were somehow "better" than other blacks, and they were encouraged to look down on the rest of their race as lacking the necessary gifts of character, intellect or personal presentation to get ahead.

"It's mighty fine that you got yourself in the dorms at that white school," my father told me, his voice gentle as always. "But you don't ever want to do anything that would keep another colored girl from doing what you're doing if she wants to do it. You're not better than other colored girls just because they let you inside their dorm. There are many good colored people you must take along with you, so you need to be a good leader, show them they did the right thing. Because, remember, you didn't do this alone; a lot of people helped prepare the way for you, and everyone is watching you now. God is using you to show what's possible." I felt humbled by his words.

I had no idea what it would be like to be the sole black woman in the dorms at Ohio State, or how I would be received as an older veteran in a residence with 749 other students, almost all of them seven years younger than I was. I knew it was possible that the women would not welcome my presence, but the reality was much different than I had anticipated. In Baker Hall, instead of the other women on my floor shunning me, most were very friendly, and a good number of them were always in my room. Perhaps because I was already a nurse and had been to war, the young women seemed to think I had answers to all their questions and concerns. Many of them looked to me as a sort of den mother or advisor, and their personal problems landed squarely in my lap. If there were girls who did not want me there, I never knew about it. In fact, my room was the most popular on my floor. I could hardly find a moment of solitude there, and I had to escape to the library to study. It became apparent to me that many of the other girls did not need or elect to study as much as did I, so I had to be careful about how much time I spent with them. Even so, some of these girls became my friends, and they made my living situation in Baker Hall surprisingly congenial.

Unpleasant incidents did occur in our dormitory cafeteria, however. I would fill my tray and sit wherever there might be space at a table. But on many occasions, when I sat down, a girl would pick up her tray and move to another table. No matter how often this sort of thing had happened, it always stung. Outwardly, I tried to project an equanimity that I did not always feel by keeping my expression carefully benign. After one such incident, a white male student who was dining at the time picked up his tray and walked across the room to me. "I saw what she did," he said of the girl who had just vacated my table. He pulled out a chair and settled down to eat with me. "She may try to pretend that you're not here," he added, "but believe me, by your presence in this room, you're doing more for this university than she ever will." After that, whenever this young man saw me eating in the cafeteria, he would make of point of joining me at my table. In this way we became friends.

Throughout my life, I've noted that the primary strongholds of racial prejudice seem to be associated with where we live and where we dine. There were several restaurants adjacent to the campus, for example, and the girls from my dormitory frequented them for Sunday evening dinners. On a couple of occasions, they invited me to join them. I was the only black student with three or four white girls, and both times, at two different restaurants, we were refused service. At both, the waiter said, "We will serve you"—referring to my white friends—"but not as long as she's with you"—referring of course to me. I remember on each occasion I felt deeply humiliated, but I held my head high as I apologized to my friends, who looked down at their shoes with embarrassment on my behalf. We did not discuss the episodes any further at the time. In fact, we never discussed it. We merely surrendered to bigotry and went home to the dorm. I stopped trying to eat out after that, except at a Chinese restaurant near campus where I was assured of being welcomed. I knew that the other restaurants were merely reflecting the policies of the university that was their landlord, and that made me angry. I was a student at the university after all. Why should I not be served, too? Why wouldn't the university protect *my* rights? I was starting to understand that the racial climate at Ohio State in 1946 was little different from that of the Deep South. Although there was less violence, the overall message was the same: If you were black, a few progressive individuals might tolerate your presence, but at the level of institutions, you were certainly not wanted.

The discrimination that prevailed in professional schools was particularly alarming to those of us who were not white but who nevertheless aspired to gain entry to these programs. At Ohio State, most of our professors actively discouraged us from trying to pursue medicine, engineering and even business administration. These schools would simply deny admission to non-white applicants or, in the case of Ohio State's medical school, limit enrollment to a single non-white student in each academic year. Jewish candidates fared little better; in a class of about one hundred and fifty students, only five or so Jewish students were admitted in any given year. But in the post-war years, people whose families had been marginalized for generations were becoming less willing to accept that lot. So many of us had served our country, and it was unconscionable that our country should now refuse to acknowledge our equal rights as citizens. And so we kept pushing and pushing at the gates that were meant to keep us out, and every now and then the locks gave way.

In 1946, for instance, one of my friends at Ohio State received his degree in business administration with a major in foreign commerce and a minor in banking. While in school he had been told by his advisor that he should drop out of the program and get a job because he was wasting his time and would "just end up as a Red Cap." This young man was later appointed by President John F. Kennedy as the first black postmaster of Los Angeles, serving from 1963 to 1969; he was also the first black postmaster of any major city in the United States. He went on to become vice president for community affairs of Great Western Financial Corporation, a holding company for all the savings and loan firms owned by Great Western. My friend who had been so ill advised died on Thursday, March 7, 1985.[73] Three years later, the $151 million Los Angeles General Mail Facility was named in his honor. It is the largest one-story post office in the nation. The gentleman's name: Leslie Nelson Shaw, Sr.[74]

I can cite examples of other black students who were discouraged or even turned away from Ohio State and other Big Ten colleges. These young men and women would triumph in spite of the discrimination playing out in the Midwest, and indeed everywhere in the country, not just the South. Our enslaved forebears who made it through on the Underground Railroad had dreamed of a better day for their grandchildren. We, the Big Ten college students of the 1940s and '50s, lived the everyday struggle encoded in the anthem "We Shall Overcome" before it was popularized during the movement for civil rights.

One of my best friends on campus was my housemother, Dean Margaret Dunaway, who was a white woman from Little Rock, Arkansas. One day as we were talking, she revealed to me that I had been more highly screened than any other girl on campus. "There was a lot of discussion about you," she told me. "Sometimes you just have to do things that are right to promote understanding, and not do so much talking about them. So many people said you couldn't do what you are doing, but you have just quietly done it."

I understood then that behind the scenes, she had lobbied for me to be able to live in Baker Hall. I'd had an ally I hadn't even known about. Margaret spoke of growing up in Little Rock, where there was great racial and gender discrimination. Her family had not wanted her to get a Ph.D., but she had persisted. Now, she wanted to see more Negro girls in campus dormitories and pursuing graduate degrees, and she believed my success at living with white students would support her argument that it was time for the racial and gender barriers to come down.

The following semester, another Negro girl, Jean Branche, moved into Baker Hall. Jean was the second black woman to live on the campus, and she and I would become lifelong friends. The next year, in other dorms on campus, more Negro girls were given rooms. The walls of prejudice were starting to show cracks, and a little light was at last getting through. It was perhaps fitting that among the young black women who moved into the dorms that year was Gloria Owens, daughter of Jesse Owens.

At the end of my first year, I was required to sit for what was then termed the Ohio State Psychological Test. When I went to collect my results from the registrar, a clerk approached me and told me I was being asked to repeat the test. When I inquired as to the reason, she told me that I had received a very high score on the initial test and they thought there must be some mistake. "How high?" I asked. "Well," she replied, "You received an A rating, but you're only doing B work, so we want you to do the test over." I considered this strange, but I didn't question her. I could see the request was coming not from her, but from some faceless power behind the scenes. I was starting to realize that whenever a student was to be confronted with a questionable endeavor or outright act of discrimination, the bearer of the news was always a subordinate and usually a white female—a secretary or clerk or assistant. It was never a male department head or other person of authority. Sexism, like racism, was endemic.

The next day I repeated the test as requested, and again I received an A rating. I was not surprised. I knew quite clearly that because this test was graded anonymously, its result was likely a truer reflection of my academic ranking than were the grades my professors handed out. I had already suspected that my color was responsible for my grades at Ohio State being lower than at Hampton or any other school I had ever attended, although I am sure the school's administrators would have argued that Hampton, being a Southern Negro college, was not in their league. I knew this to be completely untrue. At Hampton, I had received a first-rate education, more thorough in many respects than I was getting at Ohio State, but I refused to get rattled by the fact that my grades didn't seem to reflect the effort I was putting in. Instead, I made sure my work was of such quality that, regardless of how my professors felt about my presence in their classes, they could not fail to promote me.

One faculty member who endeared himself to me was my comparative anatomy professor, Dr. Hugh Setterfield. I enjoyed anatomy and I was good at it. Academically, it was one course that was said to approach the level of difficulty of medical school. Dr. Setterfield spoke of the challenges in studying medicine in general, but with me he also addressed the racial and gender bias I would most certainly face. Wherever else I might apply for medical school, he said, I should be sure to also apply to the university's College of Medicine. He noted that since opening its doors in 1914, the school had admitted only one black woman, Clotilde Dent Bowen. She was set to graduate in 1947, the year before I would be awarded my pre-med Bachelor of Science degree. Dr. Bowen would go on to become the first black female physician in the U.S. Army, and the first black woman to attain the rank of colonel.[75]

Inspired by Coltilde Dent Bowen's success, Dr. Setterfield wanted me to become the second black woman admitted to Ohio State's medical school, and he wrote glowing recommendations for me. At the same time, he reminded me that the College of Medicine had a non-white admissions quota of one. He emphasized that he did not say a Negro quota but a non-*white* quota, which meant I would be competing against the many colors of humanity for that single spot. In many years, no non-white person had been admitted at all. Dr. Setterfield added that the Jewish quota was no more than 6 percent of the class, and that there was also a female quota, but so few women ever applied to medical school that he had forgotten what it was. I realized that while assuring me I had the ability to become an outstanding physician, Dr. Setterfield was simultaneously preparing me to be turned down for admission. It didn't help my chances that there were tens of thousands of qualified male veterans also seeking medical school admission that year.

In 1947, any black woman who wanted to enter the sacred halls of medicine at a large white university had to maintain an unfailing belief in her own resources—her talent, determination, preparation and especially her refusal to quit trying. In fact, Ohio State's College of Medicine did reject my application for entry upon my graduation the following year. A young Japanese man filled the single non-white spot. I would complete the four-year biological sciences degree program within two calendar years with a high B average, but even with Dr. Setterfield's endorsement, that was not enough to ensure my admission. *They didn't want me to live on their campus, so of course they don't want to teach me in their ivory tower of medicine,* I remember thinking when I got the disappointing news.

I should note that during my undergraduate studies, I had paid a large portion of my school expenses from my post office savings account, banking most of my GI Bill checks for medical school, which I knew would be far more costly than my pre-med program. Such was my certainty of one day attending medical school. I just didn't know where that would be—or when.

John Williams as a medical student at Ohio State, circa 1947.

CHAPTER 13

First Love

On any college dormitory floor, there is an anticipated degree of activity and noise, and Baker Hall on South Campus was no exception. To find a corner of quiet, I often escaped to the medical library a few blocks away. It was less crowded than the main campus library and the students there seemed more serious. It was there that I first encountered a second-year medical student named John Williams in the fall semester of my senior year.

I noticed him because he was black. He was in fact the only non-white member of his class. He was also extraordinarily handsome: tall and lean, with curly dark hair in need of a haircut. He had brooding eyes, I saw that right away, and his long, thick eyelashes had the effect of making him seem vaguely dreamy and a little sad. His brow was perpetually knitted in concentration, and his full and sensitively shaped lips were pressed together determinedly. Most days, he was also in need of a shave, his shirt and slacks rumpled, but the effect was rather appealing to me. He seemed like a man in need of a woman's touch, an idea that I probably nursed hopefully.

I had observed that he habitually kicked off his shoes before settling himself at a table to study. I thought this strange, and one day, as I walked by him, I stopped and turned back.

"Why do you always remove your shoes when you're studying?" I asked him.

He looked up from a thick medical text as if surprised to see me standing there.

"What did you say?"

I repeated my question, at which point he launched into a long and complicated explanation about people neglecting the health of their feet. Feet needed to breathe, he told me. When kept hot and covered, they perspired and siphoned off energy one needed to put toward studying. Feet required exposure to oxygen to prevent fungal infections and to keep the rest of the body comfortable, he continued. There was more, but I don't remember everything he said. I just recall being fascinated by what I saw as his vast knowledge of the human body and by the fact that he was a medical student, black like me, and here we were actually talking.

After that first day, we began to look out for each other at the library and to study together. We would eat in the cafeteria together and take long walks all over the campus, just talking about our lives. As time went on, John and I offered each other a safe and responsive friendship in a place where few others understood the unrelieved stress of being a black person striving for academic excellence in a sea of white privilege and entitlement. Because of my own interest in medicine and my lifelong attraction to people of high intellect, I was vulnerable to falling in love with this handsome and brilliant medical student. But I kept my growing feelings to myself, because John was somewhat stoic and undemonstrative by nature. Initially, our relationship was strictly platonic. We needed each other. In each other's company we could breathe easily, letting down our guard against the ever-present possibility of racial hostility.

I was soon to learn that despite John's clearly superior intelligence, he suffered from severe and long-standing emotional problems for which he needed treatment. When he took me to his parents' home in Columbus for dinner one weekend, I realized that, as the youngest and darkest-skinned child in a family of people who were so light-skinned they could have passed for white, John had grown up feeling like an outcast. Never mind that he himself could not be considered as anything other than light-skinned. I began to suspect that John's interest in me was fueled by a deep need for affirmation and support. He was doing well in his courses, but he was often overwhelmed by his enormous insecurities and deep-seated fear of not measuring up. And he was a very lonely boy. I fell into the pattern of constantly soothing John's anxieties and assuring him that he was smart and worthy and capable of achieving anything he set his mind to. Looking back now, I realize that doling out this sort of comfort came naturally to me, perhaps because of my previous training as a psychiatric nurse but also because John's happiness had begun to matter to me deeply. John drank in my reassurances like a man who had been wandering alone in a parched wilderness for a long time. Now that his thirst for affirmation was being regularly slaked, he grew increasingly dependent on our friendship.

In 1948 within the United States, white academia's attitude was indifferent at best to the unmet psychosocial needs of Negro students. Most white colleges, if they admitted Negroes at all, offered them only academics. Not even housing was provided. If a Negro student exhibited emotional problems and sought therapy through his educational institution, he inevitably found that white therapists were apathetic or ignorant in diagnosing and treating him. But for white students, college life was more than academics. An entire social world was set up to support the students' transition from protected adolescence to an empowered adult existence.

In their defense, administrators of white institutions knew nothing of the Negro's experience as a person excluded for centuries from civic engagement in America. How could they fathom the constant vigilance required of those who walked through the world in dark skin, aware that hatred and violence could assail them at any moment, from any quarter. How could white therapists know such things? How could they grasp the erosion of confidence that might result from being "the dark one" in a family of people so light-skinned that white society accorded them privileges denied their darker-skinned brethren? How could they understand the rampant colorism that arose in black families as a result of the white world's centuries-old divide-and-conquer tactics, where to be darker-skinned was to be deemed less attractive, less intelligent, less worthy of social inclusion? Who in a white therapeutic environment would recognize these undercurrents of Negro life as lived in a thoroughly racist society? The fact was that John's mental distress was not likely to be effectively treated until society not only admitted but also addressed its sickness.

As John and I grew closer, I was reminded of my interview with Dr. Karl Menninger three years before in Iowa. "The phenomenon of being black in America is so complex that no white person can understand it," he had told me. Now, as John struggled emotionally, I shared Dr. Menninger's words with him. I hoped they would help him see that, as the only non-white student in a highly pressurized medical school class, he was suffering with an internal reality that was nowhere reflected in his external circumstance—other than in his friendship with me.

In time, our relationship deepened to a sincere and tender romance, and in the spring of 1948, I took John home to meet my family for the first time. Mount Vernon was just 45 minutes from the Ohio State campus, an easy bus ride from Columbus. My brother was already married and living in his own home down the street, so John stayed in Lawrence's former bedroom overlooking the barn. My mother and sister immediately adored John, charmed by his refined manner and his incredible good looks. My sister Rowena, who was visiting from Newark at the time, teased me that if I didn't snap up this young man quickly, she would happily steal him from me.

But it was my dear, unschooled father's reaction that would resonate most strongly in the coming years. When I took him aside on the side porch and asked him what he thought of John, he was silent for a long moment, as if choosing his words. "Well, baby," he said at last, "I think he's a mighty fine fella, but he hasn't grown up yet. You're going to have to help him grow up." My keenly perceptive father had always been masterful at finding the good in people. If his evaluation of a person was negative, he became reticent. So I recognized in his response that he had some reservations about John, but his comment that afternoon unsettled me, so for a long time, I put it out of my mind.

My graduation from Ohio State on September 3, 1948, held little significance for me, perhaps because my pride had recently been dented by the rejection from its medical school. I did not want to walk in the graduation ceremony but was advised that marching was mandatory. Still, I did not invite my family to watch as I received my pre-med degree. The whole experience was anticlimactic. There was certainly none of the joy and sense of accomplishment that had infused me on the day of my graduation from Hampton a decade before. John and a few of my Baker Hall dorm mates were the only persons applauding me from the audience.

To my mind, the ceremony was a formality, a mere signpost on the road to a far greater destination. My dream of medical school had been deferred, but not abandoned, although I now had to face the reality of my age. I was 30 years old. Could a person my age hope to gain admission to *any* medical school? And what work would I do in the interim? What professional positions were available to a black woman who was a registered psychiatric nurse with a bachelor's degree in biological science? I knew the answer well enough: routine bedside nursing.

It wasn't that I didn't enjoy bedside nursing, but I knew it would never fulfill my career aspirations. It was suggested to me that I pursue a Ph.D. in nursing. Nothing disinterested me more! I had no desire to become a nursing supervisor. I wanted to work closely with patients on a one-on-one basis in a medical setting, but even more than that, I wanted to be the one on the medical team setting the treatment protocols. For me, returning to bedside nursing was just a means to an end.

That summer of 1948, I began looking for work. As a discharged Army nurse and an RN, I had anticipated no problem in finding employment, but when I applied for a position at the University Hospital of Ohio State, where John was being trained, I was advised that they had "no place for Negro nurses." The very wording reminded me of that first rejection I had received so many years before. Once again, my tax-supported state institution had slammed the door shut in my face. In angry defiance, I applied to the State of Ohio for unemployment benefits because I was being told that, as a Negro, I could not be hired for work as a registered nurse. I did not expect my application to be approved and was surprised when checks began arriving in my name. I never told my parents of this. They considered unemployment benefits to be synonymous with welfare, and they would have been deeply ashamed of their daughter's acceptance of government assistance.

Unsure of where to turn next, I had lunch with a former Army acquaintance who had become a medical social worker. I no longer recall the specifics of our discussion; I only know that the very next day, I applied for admission to the master's program of the School of Social Work at Ohio State. The director of the medical social work department interviewed me himself. He told me he had reviewed my transcripts and was puzzled that I had been turned down by the College of Medicine. "Why did they not admit you?" he asked me, although I suspect he knew the answer to that question as well as I did. He continued: "Our course is a two-year program leading to a master's degree. The first year will consist largely of casework theory; the second year will involve fieldwork placement and writing a thesis. I know you are interested in medicine, and I believe that you will ultimately be admitted to a medical school somewhere. But if we are to admit you here, you must agree to remain here to complete the entire two-year degree program. You can't drop out after one year."

I assured him I would most certainly complete the program and would be pleased to be admitted to the school. I received my letter of acceptance a week later.

Social casework proved to be a rewarding experience that absorbed my time and energy totally for two years. I had requested a medical or psychiatric fieldwork placement and had been assigned to the VA Hospital in Dayton, Ohio. It was there that I understood for the first time how the wearing of a cap, mask, gloves and gown in a tuberculosis unit could interfere with patient relationships, undermining the communication needed to ensure proper treatment. As a nurse, I had seen the protective wear only as a means of disease control. I had not considered that it effectively blocked the human connection otherwise conveyed by facial expressions and the touch of skin on skin. Now I saw that a social worker on the team could help bridge the alienation that patients felt from medical professionals encased in what they experienced as a barrier of clothing.

The essential role of social workers in medical, industrial and social endeavors became clear to me during my graduate studies. It was also during this period, in 1949, that I first heard the term "pre-paid health plan." In my course of study, two such medical plans were discussed. One was the Ross-Loos plan of Southern California; the other was the Kaiser Permanente plan of Northern Carolina, which was based on the Ross-Loos plan but went one step further: Instead of treating patients only in doctors' offices, Kaiser built neighborhood hospitals and medical clinics throughout the state.[76] For a small monthly premium, workers and their dependents could now receive the same medical care as those with deeper pockets; it no longer mattered where they were located or whether they had any means of transportation to get to a doctor's office. And because Kaiser employed industrial workers of all races, many black families were also receiving an elevated level of medical care.

It sounded almost too good to be true, and in fact, many medical doctors at the time were staunchly opposed to Kaiser's pre-paid plans and clinic expansion. They argued that not only did pre-paid medical insurance plans limit how much they could charge for their services, but it also reeked of socialism. They wanted nothing to do with it and went so far as to ban from the state medical associations any physician who dared to work for Kaiser Permanente.[77] This was the late 1940s: Senator Joe McCarthy and his "red scare" communist hysteria was building to a fever pitch, which led conservatives to believe that all they had to do to discredit pre-paid medical plans like Kaiser's was to brand them as socialistic and un-American. But the pre-paid plans were ultimately so successful that workers and labor unions signed up in droves. It became clear that the Kaiser Permanente healthcare model was here to stay.

To my mind, the pre-payment of a small monthly insurance premium that would provide a worker and his dependents with comprehensive medical care made so much sense. It made medical care more truly democratic and not just the province of a moneyed few. I remember saying to a classmate, "If I ever gain the privilege of studying medicine, I hope I can work in a place like Kaiser."

I planted that seed of possibility on the thinnest shred of hope, because there was little indication back then that both opportunities lay in my future.

My friendship with John, who was now a senior medical student, had continued quietly. For me, it was a comfortable, undemanding relationship in which I felt needed. But some of John's behavior confused me. It was difficult for me to comprehend how such a brilliant medical student with so much obvious potential could be a victim of such overpowering doubt and anxiety about his future. He was constantly fearful of flunking out, and yet he consistently posted strong grades. His self-image was flawed, his sense of self-worth negative to the point of trauma. There were days when I would miss seeing him at the library, and I would go to the boarding house where he lived only to find him curled up under the bed covers in an almost catatonic state. He might not have shaved or bathed or eaten for days, and I would have to get him up and showered and out the door to class or to the library. And yet he was on the way to achieving membership in the profession to which I aspired daily, even as he struggled to overcome emotional barriers.

I understood that many of those barriers had been fostered by the particular social atmosphere within his family, which had left him with a crushing sense of inferiority, and an inability to see how attractive and capable he truly was. I also knew that John's parents and siblings were less than pleased that he had become romantically involved with a woman of my much darker hue. John tried to protect me from the mumblings about this within his family, but I sensed it anyway in their cool reception of me whenever John brought me around.

John was also poor. It was true that financial insufficiency plagued many medical students, but it was much worse for black students. My mentor back at Hampton, Dr. Lloyd, used to say, "Medical students are always hungry," and so they were. Any money they could scrape together was directed toward their education. John's father was a Presbyterian minister, and his siblings were all on a professional track. One was studying law and another medicine. There were also an aspiring teacher and another aspiring doctor among them. Perhaps John could have reached out to his father for financial help, but he absolutely refused to do this, reasoning that he was just one of many mouths his parents had to feed. And so his meals often consisted of a hot dog and a glass of water once a day, unless friends in town or on campus invited him over for dinner.

I had by this time decided that I would help John in his professional pursuits in whatever way I could. I had absolute confidence in his ability to finish medical school and to practice medicine, but I was worried about his mental state. Some days John was so depressed, he threatened to quit the whole enterprise and go home. I did everything I could think of to shore him up, convinced that if he could just make it to the point of graduation, he would finally be past the worst. I knew his services as a doctor were sorely needed. There was a great dearth of physicians in general, and particularly of physicians who would serve the black community. I reasoned with John that once he finished medical school, he would be in demand wherever he decided to practice, and his worries about the future would dissipate.

By his senior year, John was suffering almost daily with severe, incapacitating headaches, which signaled to me that his need for professional care was urgent. John seemed locked within himself, struggling with inner demons he was loath to put into words. Through my brother, I got the name of a white psychiatrist who was on staff at University Hospital, and I made an appointment for John. On the day of his appointment, John asked me to go with him, and I agreed. John shaved and dressed himself in a suit for this meeting. He looked handsome and urbane, all visible evidence of the troubled young medical student I so often encountered almost completely erased.

The kindly psychiatrist was Dr. George Harding, an older white man who had been brought up in the Seventh-day Adventist faith, whose brother, Warren G. Harding, had served as the nation's president from 1921 until his death in 1923. Dr. Harding immediately recognized John's immense intellect and was clearly impressed by his courteous and well-spoken manner. I could see that he liked John and sincerely wished to help him, but his critical evaluation of John was flawed. After asking him several questions about his upbringing, and about how he was doing in medical school, Dr. Harding gave him a clean bill of health and sent him on his way with an admonishment to get more sleep and eat more regular meals.

I have often thought that John must have been an enigma to this doctor, who had no way of penetrating the everyday realities of being a young black man in America. It is human nature to feel a heightened personal interest in those who physically resemble us, and John looked nothing like Dr. Harding or any of his kin, and so perhaps he could not see deeply enough into John's psyche. I knew beyond any shadow of doubt that John was struggling, but Dr. Harding missed the signs completely. At least his optimistic evaluation had a palliative effect. It was enough to help John pull himself together and get through the last months of medical school, and his final exams.

John was awarded his degree in the summer of 1950, the

same year I received my master's in social work. I thought that certainly my graduate degree would make me more attractive to medical schools, and I once again dutifully sent out my application, this time not just to Ohio State but also to a number of other programs. But once again, I was not accepted. I kept my disappointment to myself, even as I quietly determined that I would continue to pursue my ambition to become a physician until my thirty-fifth birthday.

In the meantime, as John had been accepted for an internship at Harlem Hospital in New York City, I elected to pursue employment in the New York area so that we could continue our relationship. John was reasonably functional at this point, but he continued to be distressingly insecure, and he wanted me with him. The two of us had come to care deeply for each other, and our mutual expectation was that when the time was right and John was established in his own medical practice, we would marry.

On visits home to Mount Vernon, I wore my nurse's whites proudly.

CHAPTER 14

Caseworker

John was already in New York and living in a studio apartment on 135th Street when I arrived back in Harlem in October of 1950. I had spent the summer after graduate school in my old room at home in Mount Vernon, poring over job postings in social work journals. I'd found an opening in the social service department of a hospital affiliated with a prestigious Eastern medical school. I would be counseling patients and referring them to needed services. The school was located close enough to metropolitan New York that John and I could visit each other on weekends.

That October, I traveled by train to the Northeast for an interview. The director of the department, a tall, angular woman dressed in a man's suit and tie, looked to be in her mid-forties. She asked me about my trip and welcomed me more effusively than the severity of her demeanor would have suggested. She then offered me a tour of the social service department, which looked like every other hospital floor I had ever walked through. When at last we sat down to talk in her office, a small room with a window overlooking a leafy quad, our conversation was pleasant. The director assured me that as an RN with a master's degree and a certificate in psychiatric nursing, I was well qualified for the opening that had been advertised. She questioned me about my time in the Army and was particularly interested in how I had managed as the first black woman to live on campus at Ohio State. But just as I began to feel hopeful about my chances, her tone changed.

"Well, Ellamae," she said in an almost tearful voice, "I would love to hire you. I believe you'd do good work here." She hesitated then, distractedly fingering a thick stack of accordion folders on her desk. I saw the moment when her expression grew resolved and her eyes steely. "You see, Ellamae, I'm the first female to head this department." Her tone was crisp now, more businesslike. "And quite frankly, if I were to hire you, my position would be in jeopardy." She told me candidly that racial and gender bias were prevalent in that hospital and medical school, but that gender bias was actually the more potent form of prejudice there. A Negro male would be granted admission to the medical school before a white female, she explained, and so if she were to hire me, a colored woman, no matter how qualified, she would certainly lose her job.

How many times would opportunity be yanked away right at the moment it seemed within my grasp? I pondered this as I left the interview and boarded a commuter train bound for New York City. I didn't brood on what had transpired. I had liked the director well enough and had appreciated her transparency, and besides, I was now on my way to meet John after not seeing him for some months. Sitting on the train, watching the brilliant reds and oranges of the Northeastern fall foliage rushing by, I could barely contain my excitement. Although John and I had exchanged weekly letters, I'd missed him more than I had realized.

John was waiting for me in the main arrivals hall at Pennsylvania Station. He looked gaunt, dark circles under his eyes, his suit hanging loosely on his frame. He folded me in an embrace, and I could tell he was happy to see me too. As we began walking to the stairs that exited to the street, John took my small suitcase in one hand and encircled my shoulders with his other arm. That was the moment when I decided not return to Ohio, but to look for another position while living on my savings in New York.

Later that evening, I found my way to the Emma Ransom House on 137th Street, where I once again rented a room, just as I had done when I lived in New York before the war. I knew there were social work jobs to be found in the New York area. My recent interview aside, I trusted that my race would not prevent me from being hired, given that anti-bias laws had recently been enacted in the city. Indeed, I was soon offered a position in the social service department of Bellevue Hospital, but the salary offered, $2,800 a year, was disappointing. I knew I wouldn't be able to save for medical school on that amount, so I declined the position and kept looking.

I still held a nursing license in the state of New York, and I began to realize that I could do better financially by working as a registered nurse. One of my nursing friends from my days at the U.S. Marine Hospital had explained that I could earn sixteen dollars per twelve-hour shift working as a per diem nurse. If I chose, I could work a seven-day week, which would put me at more than $5,000 per year. This was far preferable to me, so I applied and in November 1950 was hired to work in this capacity at New York Hospital's Cornell Medical Center.

I was assigned to a patient population made up of an interesting array of renowned businessmen and professional and theatrical people who, for one reason or another, required private nursing. Some were recovering from surgery. Others were emerging from addiction. Still others were aging and infirm and no longer able to do for themselves. There was no shortage of work as a private duty nurse, but the ambitious seven-days-a-week schedule I had taken on eventually began to wear on me. As John was also busy with his internship, I never saw him, nor any of the friends I had made during my first stint in New York years before. I wasn't even able to sit in the pews of my beloved Abyssinian Baptist Church on Sunday mornings. I would hear the chiming of the bells and the heavenly music of the choir pouring from the sanctuary as I rushed past on the way to my twelve-hour shift.

A year later, chafing from overwork, I saw a notice on the medical center's bulletin board that the Department of Hospitals had raised salaries for social workers with a master's degree from $2,800 to $3,200 per year. When I checked further, I saw that there continued to be openings at Bellevue Hospital, and I decided to reapply to its social service department. I was quickly hired, because there was a shortage of social workers with my particular credentials. My psychiatric training in particular made me a very attractive candidate for the assignment I was given: I would be working with unmarried mothers who had elected to give up their babies for adoption.

In the 1950s, most unmarried mothers I worked with at Bellevue were white teenage girls from corn-fed states, who had traveled to New York to have their baby in secret and put the child up for adoption. Afterward, they generally returned home with their parents, and, I suspected, the family never spoke of the experience again. Unmarried women and girls who became pregnant felt a deep shame in those days. They had broken a fundamental social contract—that women should remain virtuous until married—and society punished them cruelly. It was my role as a caseworker to guide the unmarried mother through this traumatic time by helping her establish a plan for her baby, whatever that plan might be. Occasionally, a girl would decide at the last minute to keep her child and face the repercussions. Many of these girls elected to remain in New York and raise the child there, rather than go back to whispers and pointed fingers in the unforgiving heartland.

The birth mothers who were resolved to go through with adoption often did not wish to see the baby following delivery, but this was not an option. The adoptive practice at the time made it mandatory for the mother to physically remove her baby from the hospital nursery, carry the baby in her arms to the adoptive agency, and surrender her child for adoption in person. It was a heartbreaking procedure, not just for the birth mother, but also for her parents, who usually came to support her, and I imagine for the presumed father of the child, who was seldom involved in the adoption planning and had no rights in the decision-making process at all.

I found it useful to develop working relationships with family planning agencies, such as the Margaret Sanger Clinic, and with various adoptive agencies, such as Catholic Charities. A caseworker also needed to remain cognizant of how each person's place in the family constellation might influence the individual's behavior in the situation. I learned more about the ways in which family dynamics might collide in moments of stress and shame than about anything else during that first year at Bellevue.

The following year, I was promoted to the position of psychiatric social worker in the Department of Physical Medicine and Rehabilitation. The director of that department was Dr. Howard A. Rusk, founder of the world-famous Institute of Physical Medicine and Rehabilitation in New York. Dr. Rusk would later be credited as the creator of rehabilitation medicine itself. At the time I worked with him, his patient roster included people with physical disabilities from all walks of life, from the very poor to the wealthy and famous. There were a number of nationally known persons among them, such as the elder Joseph Kennedy and Roy Campanella, the famous catcher for the Brooklyn Dodgers who was the son of a Sicilian father and a black mother and who in 1969 would be inducted into the Baseball Hall of Fame.

In treating patients with physical disabilities, Dr. Rusk believed in the team approach. That team should include a physician who was a specialist in physical medicine (a physiatrist), the physical therapist, occupational therapist, registered nurse, psychiatrist, psychiatric social worker and secretary. It was the function of that team to get the physically disabled patient back to maximal functioning and gainful employment in the least amount of time. I was fulfilled by the work I did as a psychiatric social worker on Dr. Rusk's team. Looking back now, I realize that, as with Dr. Menninger at Fort Des Moines, with Dr. Rusk I had brushed shoulders with another innovative healer and maker of medical history.

Living and working in New York was a far different experience for me in 1950 than when I had worked with the Marine Hospital there in 1942. For one thing, I was more mature; I knew what to expect of the city, and besides, John was also in New York. He continued to be very occupied with his internship at Harlem

Hospital, but after I left private duty nursing, we managed to get together for Sunday morning services at Abyssinian, followed by a meal and a walk down Lenox Avenue to Central Park, where we might sit on a bench or a rock by the Harlem Meer, listening to the rustling of trees as we talked. We spent hours discussing our dreams for the future, where we would live, and the children we would have. There was no longer any question that we would be together, but John wanted to train in a medical specialty first.

He had decided to become a psychiatrist, and so when his internship ended, he moved to a hospital in Connecticut where he had been accepted to do a residency in that field. At around this time, I grew concerned about my excessive menstrual bleeding. An Army doctor had once told me that my uterus was abnormally tilted, and that my heavy flow was a sign that I was "rejecting womanhood." Baffled by this diagnosis, I'd let the matter drop, but as John and I were now moving toward marriage, I didn't want any reproductive issues to get in the way of our having children, so I consulted a white gynecologist at Bellevue. He sent me for a series of tests, which detected large and numerous fibroid tumors in my uterus. The doctor recommended a myomectomy to remove them and assured me the surgery was straightforward and routine. And so I went under his knife in the summer of 1951, with a goal of ensuring my future as a mother. But when I awoke from the anesthesia, the doctor told me he had been forced to take my whole uterus, because they had been unable to stop the bleeding.

I was shattered. Lying alone in the recovery room after the doctor gave me this news, and then left, I wept convulsively, but there was no one to hear my sobs, no one to hold me in the most extreme devastation of my life. Not before or since would I ever know such sorrow, and there was nothing I could do but bear it. For the rest of my life, what happened to me in that surgery would remain my most painful truth, all the more so because I could not help wondering whether there was another recourse my doctor might have taken. I would be forever haunted by the thought that this white doctor had simply taken my womb because it was easiest, because who needed more black babies in the world anyway? I would later hear of many such cases in Southern hospitals, where black women had gone in for routine procedures that had ended in hysterectomies. Was I one of those women? I still don't know.

Ironically, I had pursued the surgical option because of my deep desire to be a mother, and now I had to face the fact that I would never be able to bear a child. I fell into a deep depression, which complicated my recuperation and etched deep worry lines in John's brow when he came to visit me. A week after my discharge from the hospital, I suffered from an infection and new bleeding and had to be rushed to the emergency room. It was at this point that John took a leave from his residency and traveled down from Connecticut to be at my side continuously, acting as my personal physician and ministering to me as I had ministered to him during his low points.

It was now 1952. I was still employed at Bellevue, working with Dr. Rusk. John eventually returned to his residency at the hospital in Connecticut, and I sometimes traveled to see him on my days off. One Saturday afternoon in late May, John caught the train into the city and took me to lunch at a soul food cafe in Harlem that was one of our favorites. He explained he'd elected to defer further training in psychiatry so that he could open his own medical practice in the South. He had been investigating where black physicians were needed and had settled on the small farming town of Emporia, Virginia, where a cousin of his lived. The town was about 65 miles south of Richmond, and there was a sizable black population there that could support his medical practice. His cousin had told him there was only one other black doctor in town, and he was getting on in age. John reached across the table and took my hand, lacing and unlacing his fingers through mine. For a long time he didn't speak.

"Spit it out, John," I finally said, provoking a short laugh.

I suspected what was coming, and I welcomed it. I had probably fallen in love with John during our very first conversation in the Ohio State medical library, when he had given me that long, involved explanation of the chemistry of perspiration and why feet needed to breathe outside of socks and shoes. And so, when he finally found the words to ask if I would come to Emporia with him as his wife, I immediately agreed.

"Ellamae, I need you with me," is how he phrased his proposal.

"I know you do," is how I said yes.

Although I had always been wary of the racial dynamics of the South, I reasoned that Emporia was just 90 miles to the west of Hampton, Virginia, which was such a special place for me that, in a sense, I would be going home. That very afternoon we set a date and telephoned our parents. We asked John's father, a doctor of divinity, to marry us.

We had decided our wedding would be small and informal, held in the home of my cherished friends Blanchard and Lucille Lloyd in Washington, DC. And so on June 23, 1952, in a simple living room ceremony, we said our "I do's," with John's father officiating. John's mother, and three generations of the Lloyd family, were our witnesses. The oldest was the family matriarch, Blanche Lloyd, who had kindly ambushed me after anatomy class and invited me to dinner with her family all those years ago. Her husband, Dr. R.A.B. Lloyd, had died six years before of an aortic aneurysm. He was only 61 years old, and the family missed him terribly. I had never missed his presence more than that afternoon of my wedding, and I could not help wondering what he would have thought of John, and the fact that I was marrying a physician but was not yet one myself.

The youngest person present, my beautiful five-year-old goddaughter Carol, was clearly smitten with my groom, who she shyly whispered to me was the handsomest man she had ever seen. Her impression was further bolstered by the fact that he played giggling games with her and generally indulged her excitement. She was attending her first wedding ceremony, and she was perhaps the most delighted person in the room.

If memory serves, but for the three Lloyd children, the mood was not particularly festive, as John was always a little reticent in the presence of his authoritarian father. And I was missing my own parents, who were unable to travel to be with us on such short notice. Lucille had helped me shop for the dress I wore, a white satin number flared to mid-calf, with a scooped neck and long sleeves, and a thin belt cinching my waist. A single strand of pearls adorned my throat, and my hair was freshly straightened, caught at the sides in decorative combs and falling loose on the neck in the style of the day. John wore a light-gray suit, a white shirt, and a black bowtie, with a boutonniere to match my corsage pinned to his left lapel.

In photographs from our wedding day, I am unsmiling, even as John gazes down at me with evident affection, a hopeful look on his face. In the years since, I have often peered into those photographs, noting my solemn appearance, and wondering if perhaps I already had some clue that life with my handsome new husband would never be easy or serene. In retrospect, I am sure I knew.

After our June 1952 wedding in the home of our friends Blanchard and Lucille Lloyd, John and I began married life in Emporia, Virginia.

CHAPTER 15

Emporia

John traveled to Emporia a few weeks ahead of me to set up his medical office in a small wooden building just off the main street of the seven-square-mile town. He also secured lodging for us with a lovely older black couple in town, two rooms and a kitchenette on the top floor of their home. At the end of June 1952, I gave my notice at Bellevue and we moved to Emporia. It was here, in this small rural community of about five thousand, that we began our lives together.

Almost as soon as John opened his office, his practice was booming. Everyone was overjoyed to have a young new black doctor in town. With the only other black clinician recently retired, John's arrival was seen as a godsend, as it was well known that the white doctors in Emporia did not like to treat Negroes. I soon learned that the nearest hospital was some 30 miles away, which meant minor emergencies were generally handled in the office. There was no ambulance service, so when such emergencies arose, the patient might be escorted to the doctor's office, or on weekends to his home, by the local sheriff or police officer.

The black families in Emporia could not have been more welcoming to John and me. They invited us into their homes for meals, brought eggs from their chickens and vegetables from their farms, and hosted us at multigenerational backyard barbecues on Saturdays. I seldom saw the town's white citizens. Almost evenly settled by blacks and whites, Emporia was strictly segregated, with blacks at one end and whites at the other. Jim Crow laws were in full effect—this was the South after all. Even so, on the rare occasions we did encounter them, whites treated the new black doctor and his wife with a degree of professional courtesy, and where race was concerned, our time in Emporia was mercifully free of the kind of vitriol I had experienced during my last stint in the South, at Camp Livingston in Louisiana.

An early point of contention between John and me was his desire that I should not work outside the home. He felt that, as the wife of a physician, I should take care of the domestic realm and allow him to provide financially for us both. This did not sit well with me, as I could not continue to save toward medical school without a job, and besides, housework bored me silly. I had always been a rather indifferent housekeeper, preferring to occupy myself with pursuits that stimulated the mind and could further my ambition to become a doctor. I loved nothing more than to be learning something new in the field of medicine or behavioral health. I had always been a natural student, whether in a classroom or on the job, but in Emporia there was no work to be had as an RN or a social worker. I spent my days reading books or walking from room to room in our small apartment, and rousing myself enough to cook a meal for John and myself come evening.

John saw how listless I was becoming as a housewife, and he began making inquiries of townspeople about what work might be available to me. One of his patients was a public school teacher. She told John that the school system was in need of local black teachers. At that time, anyone with a master's degree in any field could qualify to teach, and so I applied for a position in elementary education and began substitute teaching in the segregated public middle school.

Elementary substitute teaching was the first non-medical job I had held in my adult life. It was a totally new experience for me and I must confess, not an enriching one. I found the students to be undisciplined, uninterested in homework assignments and resistant to my lesson plans. They seemed intent on showing me just how rowdy and defiant they could be. Classes were often reduced to a battle of wills, a test of who could stay in the classroom the longest—them or me. They often won. Looking back, I am convinced it was only the desperate shortage of black teachers that kept me from being fired in my first week on the job.

My time as a substitute teacher showed me more clearly than anything how much I needed to do work that inspired me. I was wholly and entirely cut out for medicine—I was absolutely sure of this. My unwavering desire for that life was a powerful testament, a yearning I was sure God would not have placed in my heart had it not been the path I was meant to follow. So it was perhaps not surprising that as a schoolteacher I was a dismal failure. Away from active participation in the health field for the first time, I began to feel like a displaced person. My husband's practice seemed to satisfy his own professional needs, but his practice already had an office nurse, an older woman who had worked for years with the recently retired black doctor, so he did not need my help.

I was temporarily distracted when John and I decided to build our own home on land we purchased some four miles from the edge of town. It was a beautiful spot, with thick-leaved trees and rolling green fields all around. Real estate would turn out to be another area of compelling interest for me, the result no doubt of my father's lifelong admonishment that we should never pay rent but should always own our home. I thoroughly enjoyed overseeing the details of constructing our modest, two-bedroom, one-bathroom concrete-brick house, furnishing it, and moving into it together. For a little while after that, our life in Emporia was the American dream. I even wore little white gloves with lace edges to church on Sunday mornings. On weekends and holidays we socialized with black families from the community or we traveled to nearby East Coast seaboard towns to visit friends or just take in the sights. I was the stereotypical 1950s housewife, taking care of my husband and our home, and working at an occupation that was acceptable for women—teaching children.

John had hired a woman, call her Mary Jones, to clean and cook for us, and she became a dear friend to me. It had been her idea that once a week I would drive into Emporia and collect a carload of children from the poor section of town, and bring them out to our house to play Ping-Pong on the table we had set up in the carport. Mary and I would make them sandwiches and lemonade and talk with them about their lives, and try to plant ideas for a future that they might not otherwise have dreamed for themselves. I saw myself in these children, for whom the bar of achievement had been set so low. I wanted to help them break out of the mold of low expectation that society had cast for them.

As happy as I was during this period, my own hunger to study medicine was stronger than ever, and I thought obsessively about how I could make this happen. John was generally positive about the idea, and would often say, "You'd be a better doctor than me." I assured him I had always thought him an excellent physician. His medical knowledge was superior, and he was kind and caring with his patients, listening sensitively to their concerns and hearing even their unspoken needs. His only weakness as a physician was his increasingly frequent depressive episodes.

Emporia had not changed this particular fact of our lives. John continued to suffer from crippling anxiety and bouts of desolation so severe he sometimes had to close his practice for a week. I made sure his office nurse and patients were never aware of the true cause of his intermittent absences. I supplied excuses that ranged from a family emergency back home to a medical conference up North to a bad case of the flu. During such weeks, John would stay in bed or sit in his bathrobe staring at the wall from the living room couch, unable to rouse himself even to eat. He talked about being weary of himself, feeling hopeless and incapable of taking care of his patients. He was sure he had made mistakes in treating them— this thought was an obsessive loop in his brain—and he lamented that he had ever thought he could be a good doctor. He was so filled with self-loathing in these moments that I secretly worried about him hurting himself, and yet he was never unkind to me during these breakdowns. In fact, he was more demonstrative during these emotional storms than at other times. With tears brimming, he would thank me repeatedly for standing by him. Sometimes he would draw me to him, circle my waist with his arms and rest his head against my shoulder. This seemed to comfort him.

Because I never could fathom any external reason sufficient to explain John's depressed state, I had concluded that he must suffer from an undiagnosed mental illness. We had both hoped that our marriage and a successful medical practice would have improved his mental status, but after a few months in Emporia, he grew worse than ever before. We both recognized his need for therapeutic intervention. In fact, I already suspected that the day would come when I would need to work to support us both. I did not shrink from this responsibility, but I knew that I would have to equip myself to do more than substitute teaching in a public school.

John decided to seek professional help. Because nothing of the sort was available in Emporia, we drove the sixty-five miles north to Richmond, Virginia, for consultation with a therapist who had been recommended to us by an acquaintance of my friend Blanchard Lloyd. I sat in the outer office while John met with the psychiatrist. After an hour, they emerged and the doctor told me John would have to begin intensive therapy as soon as possible because he was "a very disturbed man."

"What's the matter with my husband?" I asked, feeling a tinge of fear.

"Well, he's hearing voices, and they're telling him quite awful things about himself," the doctor replied. "I suspect some form of schizophrenia."

My hands flew to my lips. John had never mentioned anything about hearing voices. Standing beside me, he showed no response to the doctor's words.

"And there's something else," the doctor added cryptically.

"What is that?" I wanted to know. I was still trying to digest his statement that John might be schizophrenic. Surely his mental condition wasn't *that* serious?

The therapist only hinted that I did not understand the half but that he was not at liberty to discuss John's case any further until he had been able to properly diagnose his condition. He suggested that I find some endeavor that would fully occupy my time over the next two to three years or longer, as John would need to drive to Richmond for therapy several times a week, and would need to give all his spare time to getting well. The therapist emphasized that I should not be dependent upon my husband while he pursued therapy, as this would only increase his stress. As he spoke, John stood silently, his shoulders hunched, hands in his pockets, eyes downcast. I mentioned the possibility of attending medical school and the therapist agreed that such a pursuit would be acceptable, so long as it did not interfere with John's therapy. He suggested that John maintain his medical practice for the time being, but perhaps with reduced hours.

John and I walked out of the therapist's office and back to our car in the parking lot. Neither one of us spoke for the hour-long drive back to Emporia.

Several months before, I had quietly reapplied to medical school, but this time in addition to American programs, I had also applied to several foreign medical schools, including the University of Lausanne, Switzerland, where the language of tuition was French. I heard a few weeks later that I had been accepted there—this was my first acceptance ever to medical school. Studying medicine in a foreign country was not that unusual for black women in the 1940s and '50s, when admission to medical schools stateside was abysmally low for blacks in general, and black women in particular. A black woman I had gone to Hampton with had studied medicine in the Soviet Union and had returned afterward to the U.S. to practice. A black man I knew from my pre-med days, who had been rejected from American medical schools, had instead qualified in Lausanne and now had a thriving practice in Los Angeles. So I was encouraged and silently exuberant when I received my acceptance letter all the way from Switzerland. Someone, somewhere, thought I was fit to study medicine!

Of course, I recognized that the obstacles ahead of me might be almost insurmountable. For starters, I would have to become fluent in French; I had every intention of mastering the language if it came to that. But because John had recently been having such a difficult time emotionally, I had not told him of this acceptance. To pursue it right then seemed unrealistic and unfair. I could not leave John alone in the state he was in.

Fortuitously, a few months later, I was accepted to a medical school in the United States. At last my long-deferred, determinedly sought after, and cherished dream of studying medicine was beginning to come true. By this time, John was in a more stable place mentally, thanks to his weekly schedule of therapy in Richmond, and so it was with great excitement that I told him about my acceptance to Meharry Medical College in Nashville, Tennessee.

To my surprise, John was not happy for me.

He implored, "Why do you need to become a doctor, Ellamae? I need you here. You're a doctor's wife. Isn't that good enough?"

I looked at him slack-jawed. We were standing in the kitchen of our home in Emporia, my acceptance letter lying on the counter between us.

"Maybe you just need to become a mother and you'll be happier," John suggested then. But this only twisted the knife of pain inside me, because as John well knew, I could not get pregnant.

"Well, that's not going to happen," I reminded him bitterly.

But John barely heard me. He had been caught by the idea of children and was talking excitedly, his sentences tumbling over one another at a fast clip. "We'll adopt, Ellamae! We'll adopt! There's a young girl, one of my patients, who just had a baby and she's giving it up for adoption. We'll take in the baby and raise it as our own!" I sensed an edge of desperation in his voice, and I realized he could not imagine his life without me making sure all the details remained in order. He did not want me taking care of other people as a physician. He wanted me all to himself, completely focused on taking care of him. But I had been admitted to medical school. I picked up the letter from the counter where John had tossed it, and I scanned its contents for the umpteenth time, just to make sure I wasn't imagining them. I was now 36, and the grail I had pursued for so many years was not just within reach, but was actually in my hand, in the form of an acceptance letter from Meharry. I wouldn't have to get a passport and spend a year studying French! How could I let this opportunity pass me by?

"John," I said finally, "we're not adopting that child. She's going to find a good family somewhere else."

I paused to make sure he was paying attention. I wanted there to be no mistake.

"John," I said, "I'm *going* to medical school."

As a medical student in Washington, DC, 1955.

CHAPTER 16

Meharry to Howard

The weeks that followed were a flurry of preparation for my physical absence from our home. I began to pack at once, and gave notice at the public school that I would not be returning to teach in the fall. For the foreseeable future, the study of medicine was to be my life; all else would be held in abeyance. I knew that had I been born at a different time, when race and gender discrimination were not so systematically entrenched, I would have pursued medicine right out of college. By now, I might have been practicing alongside my husband. As it was, it had taken me a decade and a half to earn a spot in medical school, and nothing was going to deter me from going forward.

A week later we got the news that John's brother-in-law, the husband of John's favorite sister, had been admitted to the same medical school in the same freshman class as me. He too had been seeking medical school admission for several years. My husband and his family were overjoyed at the brother-in-law's admission. I tried not to show the stab of resentment I felt at their response to my own acceptance into medical school, which had fallen somewhere on the scale between indifference and outright disapprobation. And yet, there was no question that John's brother-in-law would take up his invitation to study medicine at Meharry, even though he and his wife were the parents of two infant girls.

In subsequent family discussions, John's family quickly determined that his sister would need financial help while her husband was in medical school. It was concluded that John's sister and her two young daughters should move into our home in Emporia, where they would live with John while his brother-in-law and I were in medical school. I should note that these "family discussions" were initiated and led by my mother-in-law, and had not involved me. They had included John and his mother and sister only, but I accepted the outcome of these deliberations, because I was focused only on the fact that at last, the privilege of studying medicine would be mine. Being left out of family consultations had been painful for me in the past, but this time, I was actually relieved that John would not be alone in Emporia and would have his favorite sister with him. Everyone seemed to agree that this living arrangement would be beneficial to the siblings while their spouses were away at medical school. We would both return home for winter holidays and summer vacations, and in the meantime, John and his sister could offer one another much needed emotional and financial support.

And so, in the fall of 1954, two very happy people went off to Nashville to medical school. Meharry Medical College was the second-oldest medical school serving students of African descent in the country. Founded in 1876 by the Methodist Episcopal Church and the Freedmen's Aid Society, it was started with a $30,000 donation from a Scots-Irish salt trader named Samuel Meharry, who wished to repay a kindness shown to him by a once-enslaved black family. The donation was made in their honor, and the program was established with the goal of giving medical training to those who had been formerly enslaved.[78] The year I entered, the school was under the leadership of a black president, Dr. Harold West, for the first time, and the college of medicine and its affiliated Hubbard Hospital were in the midst of a major building and program expansion.

My first year of study reassured me that the massive amount of material I would have to master to become a physician was not beyond my intellectual grasp. While I drew strength from this knowledge, I came to understand more intimately the pressures that John had been under at medical school at Ohio State, where he did not even have the familiar comfort of black faces around him undergoing the same trials. For a personality already fractured by a parade of personal demons, John had hewn a rough road, and yet he had prevailed; he had graduated and become a doctor, despite the voices in his head that told him he never would. The deeper I got into my studies, the more deeply I admired John's perseverance in the face of such tumultuous emotions.

My husband's family was no stranger to his psychological state, but they had a curiously aloof approach to his troubles. It was as if they thought that if they refused to acknowledge his periodic breakdowns, they would go away. In fact, with his sister's encouragement, John reduced the frequency of his counseling sessions in Richmond, which concerned me, because I thought the sessions were helping him. He also decided to permanently close his practice in the spring, so that he could complete his psychiatric residency at St. Elizabeth's Hospital in Washington, DC. Filled with renewed purpose, John drove out to Nashville to see me halfway through my second term. He had determined that I should transfer to Howard University College of Medicine in Washington DC at the end of the year, so that we might be together again. He could not continue a marriage in which we existed in separate states, he told me, and he pressed me to seriously consider the plan. In truth, his idea was delivered more like an ultimatum. Still, I thought it was a good idea for us to be closer together, and so I agreed to try to negotiate the transfer.

But John's visit to Meharry would turn out to be disastrous for my studies, and ultimately for our marriage. He stayed with me in Nashville for several weeks and was introduced to a number of my instructors. John could turn on the charm when he chose, and on that visit he was at his most buoyant and charismatic. I didn't realize what was happening at first, but it slowly dawned on me that while I studied, John was spending an inordinate amount of time with my gross anatomy professor, whose sexual orientation was whispered to be "controversial." John and this man developed a close bond, one that seemed to me to be something more than friendship. My professor seemed obsessed with my husband, inviting him out for drinks or other social dates at all hours. Ruminating on why their time together made me so uneasy, and even jealous, I understood in a flash what I had never let myself see before: John himself was unresolved about his sexual orientation, and he had been wrestling with it for years. As far as I knew, he had never acted on an attraction to men, because he had been raised to believe that to be homosexual was sick, disgusting and shameful. I did not doubt that John loved me, but now I saw that his sexuality was more fluid than the social mores of the time allowed, and this had been part of his psychological struggle all along. This, I realized, was the "something else" that his therapist in Richmond had discerned.

I think I put my head in my hands that night and wept. I felt lost, because John's sudden, intense connection with my anatomy instructor felt like as much an infidelity as if he had gone out and had an affair with a woman in our town.

At last John returned home to Emporia. It was a relief to no longer have to turn a blind eye to what I knew was happening between him and my professor, because the reality was, I had no time to indulge my sense of betrayal. Heartbreak would have to wait. My workload never stopped, and so I had to put my new insights about my husband to the back of my mind in order to stay abreast of my studies. Medical school became my refuge from having to deal with the painful questions that now assailed me about the future of my marriage, because as much as I loved John, and wanted to be with him, I had no idea what came next, or how we would begin to address what had transpired when we had not even acknowledged it was happening. But I pushed down the hurt and confusion John had left in his wake, and I buried myself in my schoolwork, more determined than ever to excel.

One day, a few weeks after John had left Nashville, the professor with whom he had been so involved stopped me in a hallway. "Mrs. Williams," he said, "what are you doing here in medical school when you have such a good husband at home?" I was stunned by the instructor's question, and distraught. Every medical student, but especially freshmen, knew that in dealing with professors, you tread carefully as if on a tightrope. You simply did not cross those who had power over your grades.

Sure enough, even though the rest of my grades were decent, at the end of the year this professor gave me a D in gross anatomy, a course I had enjoyed and in which I had expected to do well. A grade of D meant I would have to repeat the course, because it was a prerequisite for subsequent classes. At most medical schools, a course could be redone during the summer session, but my grades had been mailed too late in the summer for this to be an option. I would have no choice but to repeat the course in the following academic year. Because I could not move on to second-year coursework until I had posted a satisfactory grade in this class, I had now added a fifth year to my medical school education. I could not help but think I had been held hostage by a scheming professor who hoped to end my medical school career by effectively failing me.

That summer in Emporia, I confronted John about my anatomy grade and his relationship with the instructor of this class. I wanted to know if he had colluded with the professor since he had not wanted me to go to medical school in the first place. But John denied having any knowledge of, or influence on, the grade I'd received, and I believed him. He also denied that his relationship with the professor had been anything more than drinking buddies. This I did not believe. There was no doubt in my mind that this anatomy professor was somehow resentful of my marriage to John and wished to deter me from ever becoming a doctor. I would never allow him that satisfaction!

John still planned to enter a psychiatric residency program at a hospital in Washington, DC, the following spring, and he urged me to move forward with our plan for me to transfer from Meharry to Howard. Howard University was one of the premier institutions in the country dedicated to training people of color in the fields of medicine, dentistry, pharmacy, engineering, nursing, architecture, religion, law, music, social work and education. Founded in 1867, it was often referred to as the

Harvard of the HBCU system.[79] The idea of moving to Washington, where my dear friends Blanchard and Lucille Lloyd lived with my precious godchildren, was appealing to me. But I was now requesting to transfer with a D in gross anatomy on my transcript, a blemish that would have to be resolved. And so, I approached the dean of Howard's medical school with an unusual request—that he allow me to transfer from Meharry and repeat my entire freshman year.

I will never forget what the dean, Robert S. Jason,[80] told me at our meeting. He sat back in his large leather chair and scrutinized me over his glasses. He appeared stern, yet cordial, and seemed sympathetic to my cause. He had reviewed my record, he said, and had been impressed by my grades in everything but anatomy.

"Mrs. Williams, your grades aren't that bad," he continued, "and it is possible for your transfer to be arranged. But if you do transfer and get an MD degree, it will be the end of your marriage. If you are determined to become a doctor, then Mrs. Williams, your marriage is already over. It is said, vanity, thy name is woman, but that is not true. Vanity, thy name is man. Men are far more vain than women. The only thing your husband has which you do not have is an MD degree. If you get an MD, he'll have nothing that you don't have. That will end your marriage."

Given all that had happened between John and me in the year just past, the dean's words caused me many hours of soul-searching. I knew that John continued to be unhappy with our living situation, and he had even pleaded with me to delay going back to medical school until the spring, when we could live together in Washington. Because I thought this would jeopardize my start at Howard, I did not consider his suggestion feasible, and I told him so. But I kept thinking about what the dean had said to me in our meeting that summer. If his assessment were true, did I want to be a doctor more than I wanted to be Mrs. John Williams? The answer must have been clear to me—or else I simply chose not to believe the dean's words—because I began classes at Howard as planned in the fall of 1955 and continued my pursuit of medicine.

As far as I knew, John was still in Emporia with his sister and would join me at the start of the new year to take up his psychiatric residency at St. Elizabeth's. In the meantime, I busied myself with my studies and trusted we would work out the troubles between us when were living together once more. But four months into my first term, as I lay on my bed in my room in Wheatley Hall, medical textbooks open all around me, there came a knock on my door. I opened it to find a state marshal in full uniform standing there. He announced that he was officially serving me with divorce papers, and then he handed me a thick legal-sized envelope, turned and stalked off down the hall.

I couldn't breathe, and yet my heart was hammering in my chest.

I did not want a divorce. I still loved John, and even though I knew he was struggling, I felt he loved me too. I saw no need for a divorce and couldn't fathom why John had initiated such a cause. As I sat on the edge of my bed, motionless as a statue, the divorce petition sliding from my hands to the floor, the words the dean had spoken hung in the air. *Mrs. Williams, your marriage is already over.*

The house John and I built was located on wooded land four miles outside of Emporia. The property became a point of contention as our marriage dissolved.

CHAPTER 17

A Vacant House

This is what I learned later: In Emporia some weeks before, my husband had suffered a psychotic break—what form this took, I was never able to discover, not from him, not from his family, not from his doctors. No one would ever explain to me exactly what had happened on the night when John's symptoms so terrified his sister that she called their parents in Philadelphia, where they were now living. John's father and mother had moved from Columbus so that his father could take a position as a pastor at a Presbyterian church in nearby West Chester. The night of John's "episode," as it came to be called in his family, his father got into his car and drove without stopping to Emporia, where he collected John and a suitcase his sister had packed for him, and drove him back to Philadelphia. There, he went directly to a psychiatric hospital where John's mother met them. John was admitted to the hospital as an inpatient that same evening, and there he would stay for more than a year, undergoing intensive psychiatric treatment.

I would not lay eyes on the man I had married for many years after that, as John's father discouraged me from visiting him whenever I tried to make arrangements to do so. He insisted that John did not want to see me, and that I would be disruptive to his therapy. He said that he himself had not visited his son, who consented to seeing only his mother. "I am sure it would be better for no one to visit him against his will," his father wrote to me at one point. "It seems like we are taking an advantage of him to force ourselves on him. We should give him the privilege to get well and not upset him and hence delay his recovery."

It was, in fact, my father-in-law who had negotiated the divorce action. He had convinced John that I was no good for him, and that I was largely to blame for his mental breakdown, because he needed a wife who would stay home and attend to his

165

needs, whereas I was off pursuing my own ambitions—and not just any ambition, but medicine, which would surely consume my time and effort for years to come.

But I did not yet know any of this in early January1956 when I returned by bus and then taxi to our small home in Emporia for the winter break. I opened the front door to find a living room devoid of furniture or any other sign of habitation, which is how I discovered that my sister-in-law and her family were no longer living in the house. I stood in the doorway in shock, not quite comprehending that all the furnishings John and I had chosen together were gone. I thought I was in some kind of parallel dimension and would wake soon to hear my sister-in-law, a baby in her arms, coming down the hall to greet me. Instead a chill wind blew in through the open doorway, sending particles of dust eddying in motes of sunlight that streamed through the bare windows. Beyond them, the snow-covered fields looked barren, the trees looked frozen and bare, and I marveled that I had ever been happy in this now-desolate place.

Where were the curtains I had sewn myself? Where were the hide-a-bed couch, the kitchen dinette set, the floor lamp and desk lamp and Queen Anne-style end tables? I walked through the rooms of the house, feeling as vacant as they were. I opened closets, every one of them bare of the linens, tablecloths, towels and sheets I had folded and arranged myself. There was not a chair to sit on, not a pot or plate or fork to prepare a meal. Not even a bed remained for me to sleep on. Even the gas range and water heater had been removed. Even my Bibles and my cookbooks had been taken!

Setting my suitcase down in the middle of the empty living room, I closed the front door and walked past the porch with the missing metal glider and matching chairs, past the carport that no longer held the Ping-Pong table or our car. I was heading to the home of my friend, Mary Jones, the woman John had hired as our housekeeper. I was four miles from town, and night was already falling as I set off on foot. Ice and gravel crunched beneath my shoes, and a light snow was beginning to swirl. I think I had never felt more abandoned and confused. And I was angry, too. Who would empty a person's home of all effects and not think to mention it to the owner? I realized with a fresh pang that John's family had never considered me an appropriate partner for him, and I knew deep down that it was my darker complexion and classically Negroid features more than my medical ambition that had prejudiced them against me from the start. I could not help wondering how they might have viewed my desire to become a doctor had I been as light-skinned and straight-haired as their older married daughter, who was currently living away from her husband and child while studying law. She was all the proof I needed that John's family did not find it strange for women to pursue a profession, and yet they had failed utterly to support my dream. These were bitter thoughts on that cold evening, and yet try as I might, I could not deny them. They churned inside me as truth.

Sitting with Mary an hour later, I listened as she described how two men in a truck had come and packed up the house and carried the contents away. Mary later drove me to the house to collect my suitcase, and then to the bus depot, where I used a pay phone to call John's parents in Pennsylvania. They were businesslike on the line, assuring me that John was "doing as well as can be expected." They explained that because I now lived in the dormitory at Howard, they had arranged for "John's things" to be removed from the house in Emporia and sent to them. Evidently, they had decided the contents of the house belonged exclusively to John. They had hired movers to ship and store everything so that John would have the use of them when he was once again ready to set up house. It went unsaid, but was nevertheless clearly understood, that as far as my in-laws were concerned, John's future living arrangements would never again include me.

I did not want a divorce. I knew that my husband's emotional symptoms required professional intervention, yet I still felt that we could make it, but only if his family would stop interfering with our marriage. On the bus back to Washington that night, I stared into the darkness outside the window, and I arrived at a decision. I would not grant John a divorce, at least not yet. I felt that he had no grounds for a divorce, and besides, I was now sure the idea had been my father-in-law's and not my husband's. If I became convinced that John also wanted the divorce, I would consent, but until that time, I would fight the action and seek the return of the possessions that had been taken from our house in Emporia.

And so, the following week in Washington, I hired a lawyer. For the next two years, I would have absolutely no direct contact with my husband, who was still undergoing psychiatric treatment, first as an inpatient and later as an outpatient. All communication was channeled through our respective attorneys. I confess there were moments when I wondered if the collapse of my marriage had been of my own making. Would John have spiraled into whatever dark place he had landed if I had been with him? I was then, and am still to this day, ignorant about exactly how his psychotic episode had unfolded. I only knew that John's parents blamed me for leaving him, even though his sister and her girls had moved in with him, and he had not been alone. I had never been blind to my husband's emotional fragility, but nor had I believed that John would fall apart without me. I had married him out of love, but my desire to spend my life as his wife had not dampened for a minute my determination to study medicine. I had believed, mistakenly it turned out, that he understood this.

The more I thought about it in the weeks following my return from Emporia, the more obvious it became that given John's emotional state, there had been serious flaws in our planning around medical school, but we had dealt with our situation with all the insight we had at the time. Armed with my acceptance letter from Meharry, I had forged ahead at full speed, my jaw determinedly set. The truth was, my husband's ambivalence in "allowing" me to study medicine, and his vacillating back and forth once it was decided I would enroll, had been annoying to me. How diligently, how arduously, he had worked to gain admittance to and finish medical school. My faith in him and my love for him had been steadfast during that time; I had stood by him. I simply could not accept that he was so unwilling now to stand by me.

I had finally begun medical school after being out of graduate school for four years and out of pre-med for six years. In retrospect, I had surmounted great odds, but at the time, these obstacles had seemed par for the course for an older black woman in pursuit of a professional education. I was prepared for medical school to be challenging. I was, after all, older than the majority of my classmates, although there were a few older veterans who had embarked on the study of medicine with me. As I labored to stay abreast of my classes at Howard, it was only through prayer and the support of dear friends that I survived the heartache, the loss of self-esteem, and the financial drain that came with being a student while fighting John's family in the divorce proceedings. I had lost my husband and best friend, who, I was to learn, had been officially diagnosed as a paranoid schizophrenic.

With John undergoing psychiatric treatment, I was now financially on my own. I had one more year of eligibility left under the GI Bill, after which I would have to work to continue in medical school. My plan had always been to seek weekend and summer vacation private duty nursing jobs to finance my tuition once the GI Bill payments stopped coming. Fortunately, this plan worked adequately, despite the need for ongoing payments to the attorney I had hired to represent me in the divorce action. The case ground on for two long and emotionally wrenching years, during which John never once agreed to meet with me face to face.

The wrangling over the empty house in Emporia, and the way his father treated me during John's hospitalization, refusing to allow me to see him or to speak with his psychiatrist, was rancorous. I had requested that our furnishings be returned to Emporia so that I might rent out the house to help defray costs, because annual payments on the land had fallen to me, despite John's lawyer promising otherwise. John had sent in the first check for $347, but he had inexplicably put a stop-payment on it. Perhaps it was his father who stopped the payment—I didn't know. I only knew that unless I resumed paying off the land from my savings earmarked for school, we would lose the property.

The vacant house had quickly fallen into disrepair, the yard wild with tall grass and thick underbrush, the paint on the outer walls peeling. I wanted to go to Emporia on weekends and try to clean and paint and get the house and yard back in order, but

I needed the use of John's car to make this feasible. As far as I knew, the car was sitting unused at my in-laws' home, so I asked to borrow it for a month so I might be able to get back and forth from Washington to Emporia easily. My father-in-law refused to entertain the idea, suggesting in his return letter that I should avail myself of "the use of a bus and taxi instead."

At last, I decided that the headache and anguish needed to end. I was deeply disappointed at the way John had allowed his family and his attorney to treat me, but life had to go on. And so, as painful as the proceedings had been, I conceded to the divorce, which became final on February 28, 1958. John agreed to return the possessions and furnishings that had been taken from our marital home in Emporia, and to sign over full ownership of the house to me. By this time, I had no desire to return to Emporia anytime soon. The place held only agonizing memories for me now, so I decided to refurbish the house and rent it to a family in town. Emporia's funeral director, who had become a good friend, agreed to oversee the property for me. I was now an absentee landlord, and a woman finally free of all legal encumbrances. I poured my energies fully into becoming a physician, allowing my attention to be consumed and my hurt anesthetized in this pursuit.

Two years later, I received a letter from John dated September 3, 1960. Its contents gave me a glimpse of what the time immediately following his release from the psychiatric hospital had been like for him. In its entirety, his letter read:

> *My dear Ellamae —*
>
> *I think of you quite often. Today I got a $1000.00 raise so I'm quite happy!*
>
> *I finish my residency training is Neuropsychiatry come February 1961 and I suppose I shall go to the West Coast.*
>
> *I met a wealthy white friend in 1957 — we lived together for two and a half years and he married a prostitute and proceeded to have his fourth schizophrenic break. He will be going with me. He*

*has an independent monthly income of $360.00/ mo. We lived on
the Main Line in 1957 in an apartment for two and a half years
in Haverford. He's a complete child and of course I always wanted
one and now I have one. Incidentally he is 31 and German.*

*I have a housekeeper in Philly and my phone number is now
unlisted. PO9-6106. May I hear from you?*

*P.S. B. and I enjoyed Tanglewood, you'd like it too. What are
your immediate plans?*

I never did respond to John's letter. I had finally put myself back
together emotionally, and was beginning a new romance, so I
chose to let silence on my part be my answer. Still, I was mysti-
fied by the casual friendliness of John's tone, as if the bitterness
between us had never happened. I was also intrigued to note that
he was now living with a "wealthy white friend" whom he had
met in 1957, which would have been when he was still hospitalized. This younger friend was, like John, a schizophrenic, and
their connection was such that they had moved in together after
John's release from the hospital. They had survived the German's
ill-conceived marriage, a fresh psychotic break and his re-hospi-
talization; and they would be moving to the West Coast together
after John finished his neuropsychiatry residency.

I think now that I was glad for that letter, although I probably
didn't acknowledge it at the time. I only allowed myself to feel
bemused and somewhat irritated by its tone. But looking back,
I can see that the affability of John's letter offered me a kind of
closure, and the realization that I didn't have to be so angry and
wounded anymore. Despite the way our marriage had ended, for
the first time since our divorce, the memory of our years together
did not cause me to wince. As I slipped the letter back into its
envelope and tucked it into a drawer for safekeeping, I found
myself wishing John and his wealthy German housemate, peace.

After my father died in 1959, townspeople who rode in his hay wagon as children poured into the funeral home to pay their last respects.

CHAPTER 18

He Left His Mark

White friends often ask me, "Ellamae, have you met more prejudice in your career because you're black or because you're a woman?" I never answer this question directly. Instead, I might respond, "Are you asking me which is worse, to be born black or to be born female? Perhaps there is enough prejudice in this country to go around for both, but neither one is a cruel fate and I'm proud of both."

It was true, however, that for women and people of color who aspired to the medical field in the 1940s and '50s, the journey was made all the more arduous by the fact that every medical school in the United States was biased against female candidates, and aside from Meharry Medical College and Howard University College of Medicine, and later Morehouse School of Medicine, all were biased toward whites. Race and gender bias have been such powerful tools of oppression in American society that it is impossible to determine where they begin or know where they will end.

As a realist who had the good fortune to attend medical school at a historically black university, I was able to prioritize becoming an MD over fighting this double-barreled race and gender war. But while being in a majority black academic environment helped mitigate racial bias, as one of a handful of women in the class, I still had to contend with America's pervasive gender bias as it was expressed by some of my professors. There was also a touch of ageism, as I was among the older students, war veterans for whom the GI Bill had made a way. We had little in common with the recent college graduates that made up the majority of the class. But I refused to let any of this throw me off course as I picked my way through the all-consuming years of medical school. I had a paradoxical advantage: When I wasn't studying, all my defensive resources went to navigating the legal and emotional aspects of the breakup of my marriage to John.

During my final year of medical school, just as I was beginning to regain my equilibrium after my divorce the previous year, I faced a fresh heartbreak.

My dear father, now 82, had been scheduled for cataract surgery, but I wasn't unduly worried, because Gus had remained in relatively good health throughout his life. He had never smoked nor used alcohol in any form, and his work had always afforded him vigorous physical exercise. It was true that he no longer slept in the bracing cold of the screened side porch but had moved into the sitting room downstairs. He slept on a chaise lounge there, next to a little table on which all his salvaged collections were piled high. Lawrence had put in a bathroom next to that room, because our dad had developed arthritis and had difficulty going up and down the stairs to the only other bathroom. Yet even after he turned 80, Gus still raised a few vegetables in the yard. But his eyesight had grown poor, and his doctor had advised a cataract extraction. It was a routine and often-performed procedure, and I really hadn't given it much thought.

The day after the surgery, a student knocked on my dorm room door and told me I had a phone call. It was a Friday, and I had just returned from an afternoon lab. I walked to the far end of the hall and picked up the phone. My sister-in-law Isabelle was on the line. "You father had a heart attack," she told me. Her voice was thick with urgency. "Ellamae, you need to come home."

I could barely comprehend what she was saying. I kept repeating dully, "But nobody dies from cataract surgery." As a nurse and a medical student, I was never prepared for the death of a patient, much less a family member, much less my father. Time slowed to a crawl. I could not imagine Gus not being in this world, holding everything together back home on East Pleasant Street. For my entire life, he had been our family's moral center. I still felt pricks of guilt that it had taken me decades to see his goodness and strength and creative resolve so clearly. How could this robust farmer, who slept on the open porch in winter and had hardly been sick a day in his life, be dying? Deep in denial, I boarded the first available flight for home.

By the time I reached Mount Vernon, my father had stopped breathing. I have often wondered if, when Isabelle called me, he was already dead, and she couldn't bring herself to tell me that. Lawrence took me straight to the funeral home, where our father's body was being prepared for viewing. When at last I saw Gus in his casket, he looked like the beloved father I had always known, as if he were simply resting his eyes while stretched out in his lounge chair on the porch. I reached out to trace the lines of his weathered face, and I tried to curl my fingers into his roughened, arthritic hand. His skin was stone-cold, like frozen protoplasm; the lifelessness of it stunned me. This was my father's body. The map of lines on his face looked like him; the dark suit, starched white shirt and black bowtie belonged to him; the gnarled hands resembled the ones I had so often held. And yet this was not my father. This was a body bereft of all life, and the man I had known and loved was no longer there.

My heartbeat was a deafening roar; my legs felt like rubber; beads of perspiration dampened my forehead. I reached for the straight-backed chair next to the coffin and lowered myself to the seat. I gazed for a long time at the body of my kind and gentle father, who had asked so little of this world but who had given so much of himself in return. I had never told him how much his humble way of living had inspired me. I had never shared how much his love and goodness had been my compass. I hadn't said how much I had loved him. My brother and sisters and I all wept quietly in that parlor, knowing that the great guiding light of our lives had been extinguished.

That night, Lawrence told me that our father's cataract surgery had been successful and uneventful, and he had been progressing well. In fact, he had been scheduled for discharge from the hospital the next day when he took a sudden turn for the worse. He had told the nurse that afternoon that he was a little tired and was going to take a nap. He never woke up. He suffered a heart attack and died on January 16, 1959.

My father passed away just four months before I was to graduate from medical school. Perhaps hardest of all for me was the fact that he would now never see me become a doctor. When I walked into his room the first evening home, tears overflowed as my eyes fell on his starched shirt, navy-blue tie, handkerchief, suit, socks and hat carefully laid out across a chest of drawers. His dress shoes, polished to a gleam, rested neatly together on the floor. I knew without anyone telling me that these were the clothes Gus had planned to wear to see his youngest child awarded her medical degree. Friends and relatives told me that he'd spoken often of his impending trip to DC, and that his pride in me beamed out from his face. How often had I imagined my father sitting with my mother in the audience as I officially crossed the threshold of my life's most cherished dream? Instead, my father would be buried in those clothes.

In the days that followed, there was an outpouring of affection for my father from extended family, neighbors, members of his church and the larger Mount Vernon community. Townspeople who had ridden on his bobsled and hay wagon as children asked if they could bring their children to his funeral. Wreaths and floral arrangements filled our front room, and the phone rang constantly. In those days, it was highly unusual for a black person to be honored on the editorial page of the local newspaper, and yet following my father's death, an obituary appeared:

HE LEFT HIS MARK

There are few residents of Mount Vernon who have been so widely known as "Gus" Simmons whose death occurred the other day.

Simmons had been a familiar figure on the streets of Mount Vernon for a half-century or more in his capacity as a trash collector.

That he was a good collector and honest is evidenced by the length of the service he performed for several generations.

He was also a leader of the city's Negro population and the fact that we have such fine Negro people here must be attributed at least in part to his influence.

Simmons was superintendent of the AME Chapel Sunday School for 40 or 50 years and helped mold the character of thousands of young Negro children, which set the foundation for the high caliber of the Negro population of today.

Humble as he was, he left his mark on the city.

My mother did not attend my father's funeral, because she refused to enter any place of worship that was not of the Seventh-day Adventist faith. I have never been able to reconcile that she could not make an exception for my father, and eventually I gave up trying to understand. To this day, I feel such sorrow that my mother failed so completely to appreciate my father's goodness. All she could see was the life this humble, unschooled laborer had been unable to offer her, which blinded her to what he *had* given her—his lifelong and so cruelly unreciprocated love.

It seemed that everyone else in Mount Vernon, black and white, was at the service to honor my dad, with mourners spilling out the doors. I barely remember the service itself. I was in a daze throughout. I faintly recall the minister's voice intoning, "I am the resurrection and the life," and the congregation singing Gus' favorite hymn, "Nearer, My God, to Thee." And then it was over, my father laid to rest in a freshly dug plot in the churchyard.

The next day, January 20, 1959, I awoke to a steady drumbeat of rain. By afternoon it had turned into a torrential downpour that drenched the town all that day and into the night. The temperature plummeted from the mid-50s to the low 20s as the rain turned into a stinging hailstorm, then a blizzard whipped by a screaming wind, dumping snowdrifts several feet high in the neighborhood. And then it was raining again, the snow melting in rivers, water rushing through the streets, and radio newscasters were calling it the worst flash flood in Ohio's history, officially naming it the Great Flood of 1959.

In some areas, the water current was so strong that grown men were swept off their feet and parked cars floated away. Residents (thankfully not us) had to be evacuated from their homes, and Army Reservists, civil defense personnel and highway patrolmen poured into town to help with the rescue effort. The entire town was under twenty-four-hour surveillance by National Guardsmen with drawn bayonets, alert for looting. Watching the tumult from the sturdy front porch of the house on East Pleasant Street that my father had built, I could not help but think that even in this weather, my father would have been stepping into his galoshes, shrugging into his rain jacket, placing a worn fedora on his head, and heading out to see how his AME church was faring in the storm.

Gus Simmons was the hardest working man I would ever know, and on the day and night of the flood, my grief at losing him sat like a rock in the center of my chest. I tried to remember how optimistic he had always been, how outrageously hopeful. One memory in particular made me smile. "Get all the education you can and be the best you can be," Gus had told me repeatedly, and he always added, "because I promise you, baby, prejudice won't last. You're going to see colored folks running everything right alongside white folks, from the president on down."

This was my father's most profound, and to my mind most misguided, belief. Everyone knew America wasn't anywhere near ready to lay down the mantle of white privilege, much less elect a black president. But when I looked at Gus dubiously, he'd pat my shoulder and turn back to sorting his salvaged items on the side porch, or in his sitting room. "You mark my words, Ellamae," is all he'd say. "Sure as I'm standing here, it's going to happen. That day will come."

And now my sainted father was gone. Belatedly, I understood what he had tried to teach me, and it was simply this: No matter how steep the road or how far off the destination, there comes a day when the goal will be met, so long as we persevere. No force can forever stand in the way of a prized objective if you simply work hard and with purpose and refuse to quit. If you do this, whatever you dream can be achieved in your lifetime. This, Gus fully believed.

And so, when I marched with my medical school class on June 4, 1959, my father was in my thoughts the entire time. I imagined him looking down on me as I recited the Hippocratic Oath with my class. In my mind's eye, he was tall and dapper in the suit of clothes he had laid out for this very occasion, and whenever I conjured his gleaming brown face, he was smiling.

Lieutenant Colonel Price D. Rice belonged to an elite squadron of Tuskegee-trained fighter pilots who served as bomber escorts during World War II.

CHAPTER 19

My Tuskegee Airman

The first time Price D. Rice called me was a month into my internship at Wayne County General Hospital in Eloise, Michigan. It was the early fall of 1959, and I had just come back to my room after an exhausting three-day emergency room rotation. I was about to fall into bed when the phone rang.

"Hi, is this Dr. Ellamae Simmons?"

I didn't recognize the voice, deep and booming with a laugh tucked inside it, but it appealed to me instantly.

"Who is this?"

"Ellamae!" he said, and his tone had the quality of good friends heartily slapping each other on the back. "This is Lieutenant Colonel Price DeAlyon Rice of the U.S. Air Force. I met you years ago at Hampton when I was in flight school at Tuskegee. Virginia Sharpe gave me your number."

I remembered now. Virginia had been my good friend at Hampton. She had called me a few days before to tell me that one of her former boyfriends from our college days would be calling me. She said he'd been stationed near Detroit at Selfridge Air National Guard Base for many years. Virginia and the soldier had remained good friends, and she had mentioned to him that I'd recently moved to the Detroit area to do an internship. Virginia had apparently talked me up, mentioning my Army service, my various academic credentials, and Price had said he would like to meet me.

"Oh, she's not your type at all," Virginia told him. "Ellamae's a strong-minded woman who goes her own way."

Price had replied, "Well, let me be the judge of whether she's my type." For some reason, he told me later, he had been powerfully intrigued by my story. As I got to know him better, I knew it was because Price—who graduated from Tuskegee's flight

181

school and went on to earn a master's in public administration from American University while teaching air science and tactics at Howard University in the mid 1950s—prided himself on liking smart women.

At first, rather coyly, I tried to put him off. I told him I was much too busy with my internship to entertain his frankly flirtatious calls. And yet, I kept taking them. Our conversation was easy and wide-ranging. I enjoyed hearing his opinions on politics and music, and learning about his experience as one of the 450 Tuskegee-trained fighter pilots who flew combat missions over Europe and North Africa during World War II.[81] We had the war in common, both of us having confronted segregation to prove our worth in the military theater, me as an Army nurse integrating an officer-training base in Iowa, and Price as one of the first black aviators to serve as bomber escorts alongside white pilots during some of the war's most perilous missions.

Price told me how the planes the Tuskegee-trained pilots flew had distinctive red-painted tails to make them easily distinguishable from the enemy. As word of the Tuskegee Airmen's flying skill and courage in combat spread, they became an elite bomber escort squadron, the "Red Tail Angels," heavily requested by white pilots flying dangerous bombing raids over Germany. Sixty-six of the Tuskegee aviators would die in combat.[82] Price himself had flown 61 missions in North Africa, Sicily and Italy between 1943 and 1944 as a member of the 99th Fighter Squadron under the famed four-star general Benjamin O. Davis Jr.[83] Many of the Tuskegee pilots who survived combat would suffer persistent symptoms of post-traumatic stress syndrome, with a high percentage becoming heavy drinkers during and after the war.

I knew from the start that Price was from a culture of hard-drinking military men, but in the early days of knowing him, alcohol only made him more loquacious and amusing. He had a tender heart, and an abiding love for his daughters, four very pretty girls who at the time were fourteen, twelve, seven and five years old. Price and their mother had divorced four years before, shortly after the family moved to Denver when Price was transferred to the Air Reserve Records Center there. Price shared with me his deep hurt and sense of rejection when the girls' mother, Harriett, who was very light-skinned and looked more Native American than black, had begun dating an equally light-skinned man immediately after their divorce.

I realized that Price and I, both of a deep-brown complexion, had been subject to the toxic colorism that still infected so many African American families. In a world that bestowed favors on lighter-skinned blacks, teaching them that they were more attractive and therefore more worthy of notice, darker-skinned blacks had to fight harder for what was due to them—and sometimes to be seen at all. Perhaps the fact that both Price and I had been drawn to marriage partners who were much lighter-skinned than we were was evidence of our own vulnerability in this regard. In any case, we both took unspoken comfort in the fact that there would be none of the hurtful effects of unconscious colorism between us.

Price courted me for months with his phone calls, and in letters that began arriving two or three a week, with tales of his adventures overseas, stories of entertaining friends with full-course meals he had cooked himself, and moments with his cherished daughters. In return, I shared the details of my days and nights on the ward, and through my stories introduced him to the motley crew of other interns with whom I was sharing the experience. We exchanged photographs by mail, and Price sent me exquisite jewelry he had made himself. He told me a funny story about mastering the art of jewelry-making while on overseas assignment, as a compulsory activity designed to keep the soldiers occupied on base and out of local brothels. Apparently the arts and crafts worked, as rates of venereal disease among the soldiers went down during that period.

I began to look forward to the calls from my Tuskegee Airman after the long days and exhausting nights on rotation as an intern. I grew to love Price on those phone calls, and while reading his effusive letters, and holding his exquisitely made jewelry up to the light in my room. I could tell Priceless—as I had nicknamed him—was smitten with me, too. And so when at last we agreed to meet in person just before Thanksgiving 1959, with my Tuskegee Airman traveling to Detroit to escort me to a concert for which he had secured tickets, it was no surprise that we fell into each other's arms.

During my internship year at Wayne County General, I rotated through all the medical disciplines, including pediatrics, surgery, obstetrics and gynecology, infectious diseases and internal medicine. Perhaps because of my nursing training, I was a natural at internal medicine and the bedside care it required. Treating a diabetic through a critical coma, a sickle cell anemia sufferer through a crisis, or a cardiac patient through congestive heart failure—all of these stimulated my interest in the body's defense mechanisms. I also enjoyed the pediatric service as I found interacting with children rewarding. But many of the youngsters who ended up as patients were ill because their parents had failed to provide adequate oversight and care. I wanted to yell at these parents in frustration, but of course I had to maintain a rigorous professionalism. I quickly decided I was not well suited to this service.

Ironically, at the time I did not particularly like treating asthmatics. My medical ward might be filled with critically ill patients with gastrointestinal diseases, ulcers, renal infections, cardiac arrests, and then inevitably at two or three o'clock in the morning, people would show up complaining, "I can't breathe." While I thought they were taking valuable attention away from those who were truly ill, I would diligently administer the recognized treatments of epinephrine, sedation, oxygen tents and the inhaled bronchodilator. Secretly, I believed their affliction was emotional. I had allowed myself to be unduly influenced by medical staff muttering among themselves that asthmatics were just hungry for attention, that what they needed was a head doctor, not an internist. This was the prevailing view of asthma at the time. Imagine such ignorance!

I never dreamed I'd go on to specialize in asthma, allergy and immunological disorders. In fact, at the time I knew of no such specialty—it was still being created by a handful of mostly male, mostly Jewish doctors who had discerned the physiological mechanisms of asthma earlier than the rest of the medical profession. I would later learn that asthma, a chronic disease, tends to worsen nocturnally, which is why asthmatics tended to appear at the emergency room in the hours after midnight. I was to spend the next twenty-five years of my life completely absorbed with treating these patients, about whose illness I had once been so biased and ill informed.

My own path to illumination spanned six years, during which I completed the one-year rotating internship and two years as a resident at Wayne County General, followed by three years of specialized training in Denver. I ultimately selected a subspecialty in chest medicine, working at the world-renowned National Jewish Hospital in Denver and training with a leader in the field of asthma, allergy and immunology, Dr. Irving Itkin.

Moving to Denver in 1962 completely changed the trajectory of my medical career. For this, I have Price D. Rice to thank, as my initial reason for moving to Colorado was so that he and I could be together. Throughout my years at Wayne County General, our courtship of letters and phone calls and intermittent visits had continued, our relationship deepening despite Price's fourteen-month tour of duty in Korea, a hardship assignment that would allow him to choose the location of his next transfer. He chose to return to Denver, wanting to be close to his four daughters, and he urged me to consider moving there as well. When he proposed marriage over the Christmas holidays in 1961, surprising me with a diamond engagement ring, which he presented on one knee, I agreed to seek a position at a hospital in Colorado.

I hadn't expected to marry again; the memory of my first failed marriage was still fresh, and I'd convinced myself that my passion for medicine was as much fulfillment as I would ever need. I also hadn't wanted to deprive a man of the opportunity to have children, should he be unwilling to adopt. But this wasn't an issue for

Price, who already had four daughters. If I'm being honest, I did not truly understand what the handsome Tuskegee Airman saw in me. But he insisted he'd been looking for me his entire life, and despite my years, I swooned like a schoolgirl. I was enticed by his dark, smooth skin and laughing eyes, his muscular soldier's build, and his singing voice, which could wake the angels. And so, the following summer, I packed all my possessions into my metallic blue Karmann Ghia and drove south to Denver, where I had been accepted as a resident in chest medicine at the University of Colorado Medical Center.

Price and I tied the knot just weeks later, on June 24, 1962, ten years almost to the day after my first wedding. We were visiting his three brothers and two sisters and their families in New Jersey. Most of his siblings still lived in and around Montclair, New Jersey, where they had moved with their mother from Shelby, North Carolina, when they were very young. Price's mother had taken the six kids with her to Montclair, where she found work as a teacher. She told her husband, a tailor, that he could follow them or not, as he wished, but she refused to live in the South any longer. Price's father often said that all a black man needed was a trade, but his mother believed differently—she intended for all her children to be college educated, and she felt their professional horizons would be severely limited in the South. Price's father joined the family within the year, and, as his wife had wished, all six of their children went on to college and professional careers. Price's brother Converse Deual became a minister, his second brother James DeLoin a teacher, and his third brother Robert DuBois a dentist. His sisters Dura and Delabian became a social worker and a nurse respectively.

On that visit to his siblings in the summer of 1962, Price asked his older brother Converse to marry us. His younger brothers Robert and James agreed to serve as our witnesses. It was an impulsive decision on our part, but we were both already in our early forties—why wait any longer? As both Price and I had been married previously, we thought a quiet affair held in Converse's home in West Paterson, New Jersey, would be just right. Everyone else, including my family back in Ohio, learned of our marriage after the fact. Price had not wanted to unduly upset his ex-wife, who had recently been diagnosed as clinically depressed, and who was not thrilled at the idea of him marrying again. By then I had met his four beautiful daughters—Delabian, now seventeen; Diana, fifteen; Daphne, ten; and Debra, eight. I had been relieved to find them open and warm with me. As I did not have children myself, these darling girls became my surrogates. While trying not to infringe on their relationship with their mother, I poured all the love I could into them.

My stepdaughters aside, life in Denver turned out to be a social minefield. Price was a great entertainer, and he loved having friends over to share in his elaborate home-cooked meals and drink his fine liquor. Unfortunately, I was often on call at the hospital and unable to play the good wife as he wished I would. Although this was often a source of tension, I thought my absence was probably for the best. Many of Price's cohorts were also friends with his ex-wife Harriett, and I suspected they viewed me as the woman who had erased all possibility of Price rekindling that marital relationship. Price's social circle—made up of military men and their wives, as well as doctors, lawyers, preachers, jazz men and teachers, the professional class of Denver's black society—were perfectly courteous to me, but one woman, the Southern-born wife of a fellow Tuskegee Airman, had all but called me an interloper during one of our gatherings. She had known Price and Harriett from the time they met, when Harriett was working as an accountant at the Tuskegee Flight School and Price was a hotshot pilot in training. One evening, regarding me in a bored manner, a cigarette holder in one hand and a glass of Scotch in the other, she had commented, "Well, I suppose our Harriett can stop hoping now."

"Hoping?" I asked, caught off guard. We were both in the kitchen of Price's apartment (I still thought of it as Price's apartment). I was refilling a small decorative silver bowl with peanuts.

"Oh, never mind, darling," the woman drawled in her thick Alabama accent. She waved her cigarette in a dismissive circle and raised the Scotch to her lips, adding, "It's hardly important anymore."

*My marriage to Price D. Rice made me a stepmother to his four beautiful
daughters, from left, Diana, Daphne, Delabian and Debra in 1972.*

Chapter 20

The Measure of A Woman

Finding myself politely relegated to the margins in Denver's black society, I escaped into my work. Not that the University of Colorado Medical Center was a hospitable place to be a black woman trying to specialize in internal medicine in 1962. I was the only black physician and the only woman on the chest medicine service at that time, and my first clue to what I was in for came during my initial meeting with the chief resident. "We've never trained a woman in medicine before," he told me as we sat facing each other in a small conference room, going over my duties. "Women don't go into medicine," he continued, his tone censuring. "They go into pediatrics or obstetrics or maybe psychiatry, but they don't go into medicine."

I did not ask him how he became such an authority on the specialties chosen by the universe of female physicians, given that he was only a chief resident in chest medicine, albeit nationally recognized in his field. I would later learn that he had chosen chest medicine after falling ill with tuberculosis during his residency. I wondered if this might be why he so often behaved as if I was not worthy of his field of specialization, as if I had not *earned* the right to practice chest medicine. In time, I realized it was simply that he was thoroughly infected with the attitudes of the day—he did not *approve* of having to train a woman, and a black woman at that, in chest medicine. I decided my best bet was to work around him as much as I possibly could.

I had never before encountered and would never again face a more challenging service. It was not the patients. I enjoyed bedside care as much as I ever had. It was not the area of specialty. Chest medicine held my interest clinically and theoretically. Nor was it anything to do with the nurses. I had taken pains to establish a pleasant working relationship with them, so much so that one of the other residents, in a moment of frustration, stopped me in the corridor one day. "Ellamae," he said, "you can get these damn nurses to do anything for you. They won't even help me by giving a message to a patient. I'd like to know your secret."

"I treat them the way I would like to be treated," I told him.

Another resident walking by overheard our conversation. "Man, don't you know she used to be a nurse?" he called over his shoulder.

I only smiled, because that was indeed my secret. I had seen that the lines of duty between doctors and nurses at the medical center were carefully drawn, the hierarchy of power strictly observed. The examination of a patient, for example, could not begin until the nurse (usually female) had placed the patient on the examining table, draped the patient and announced to the doctor (usually male) that the patient was ready, at which point the doctor would swoop in like a minor king. But having once been an RN myself, I made it a point to perform small duties that would make things easier on the nurses. I would clean up in the exam room in preparation for the next patient, for example, or I would perform the sterile draping of a female patient myself. A nurse's presence was mandatory whenever a male physician examined a female patient, so the fact that I was female often relieved the nurses of this particular responsibility.

But as friendly as my interaction with the nursing staff was, my working relationship with the residents and interns was anything but collegial. On the chest medicine service, interns were responsible for learning the medical history, treatment plan and prognosis of specific patients. On grand rounds, the interns would present the complete findings to the team, which was composed of the chief of the service, the chief resident, other residents, interns, nurses and any other therapeutic personnel assigned to the case. As a resident, I supervised a group of four interns, so it was incumbent upon me to also be well versed in the cases. To know the case did not always mean that one was prepared to present it, however, as every person on the team well knew. Yet almost daily, one or more of the white male interns on my team would approach me just minutes before rounds were to begin and say casually, "Oh, I haven't time to work up this patient. You present him because I'm not ready."

I found their disrespect staggering. I knew this ruse by the interns was meant to embarrass me and undermine my professional standing. They didn't appreciate being assigned to a black female resident, and they clearly believed that shirking their duties would go unchallenged, as indeed it did. The atmosphere on any service is set by its leader, and because the medical students were well aware of the chief resident's antipathy toward me, they saw no reason to defer to me as their supervisor.

There was nothing I could do on such occasions but present the cases myself and try to save face. I endeavored never to be caught unprepared after the first time this occurred, but I was so annoyed by these episodes that I would lock myself in the ladies bathroom afterward and cry. The hospital was an old concrete building, and the women's bathroom was cold and unpainted, a dingy gray box with cracked cement floors. I told myself that hiding and crying in there was cathartic, that it allowed me to release my pent-up frustration privately so I could maintain a professional demeanor publicly. This hiding and crying went on for the better part of a year.

One day, following the predictable lack of preparation on the part of my students, and a grand rounds during which the chief had peppered me (not my interns) with questions in a particularly antagonistic tone, I found myself once again in the women's bathroom, sobbing with anger and humiliation. Suddenly, I saw myself, crumpled against the wall, hugging my white physician's coat around my body, a soaked wad of tissues clutched in my hand. I was the image of defeat, and I didn't like the picture one bit. In that moment, I saw how counterproductive my crying had been, how useless this feeling sorry for myself actually was. Nothing had changed. In fact, things had only become worse. I stopped crying then, washed my face with cold water, patted my hair and straightened my coat.

I knew what I needed to do.

I just stood for a while, gathering my courage, studying myself in the mirror. I was thinking how, all across the South, black people were marching to demand their civil rights. They were risking their very lives at lunch counter sit-ins, calling for the end of the inhumane legacy of Jim Crow. In Birmingham, Alabama, policemen had turned high-pressure fire hoses and set attack dogs on a crowd of demonstrators that included children as young as six years old. These people had been marching for freedom—*my* freedom. A young minister from Atlanta by the name of Dr. Martin Luther King Jr. had been jailed in the protests, and on April 16, 1963, he wrote what would become his landmark "Letter from a Birmingham Jail." Addressing a fellow clergyman who'd criticized Negro activism as "unwise and untimely," Dr. King, then just 34 years old, argued that all persons had a moral right to stand against injustice, and to carry the cause of freedom. "We know through painful experience that freedom is never voluntarily given by the oppressor; it must be demanded by the oppressed," Dr. King had written.[84]

Now, standing in that dingy concrete box, staring at my swollen eyes in the bathroom mirror, it struck me forcefully that the least I could do in solidarity with those who were marching in Southern streets was to stand up for what was right in Denver. The ground on which I was to make my own bid for freedom was right here in this hospital, right now. I rehearsed the words I planned to say to the chief resident. I turned them over in my mind, and held them in my mouth like smooth stones. So what if he was acclaimed in his field and internationally known? He needed to address the woeful disrespect and racial intolerance on his team.

I left the ladies bathroom and walked straight to his office before I could lose my nerve. He was at his desk, immersed in a pile of charts. He looked up when I appeared in his doorway, surprised to see me.

"What is it, Dr. Simmons?"

I entered his office but did not sit down. "Dr. Marshall," I said (not his real name), "I think you need to be aware that the racial discrimination on this service is so harsh that it prevents me from doing my best work."

He shifted in his chair and removed his reading glasses.

"There isn't any racism here," he said. "I'm not aware of any."

"You're quite wrong," I replied. "There's a lot of it, though I am not surprised you don't see it."

This annoyed him. "You're just like that Dr. King fella," he shot back. "When something doesn't go your way, you cry racism."

I did not flinch. "This is not a matter of things not going my way," I said calmly. "This is about professional courtesy and your responsibility as the leader of this team to ensure that it is observed. There is racism here. I work very hard. My patients do not complain. The nurses do not complain. But every member of your service needs to be held accountable, just as I am held accountable."

"Oh, Dr. Simmons," he scoffed, "you don't work as hard as I did when I was a resident. I worked two and three days straight with little or no sleep."

"Yes, and you broke down with pulmonary tuberculosis," I pointed out. "Just because you worked that hard did not make it right. That's why the rules were changed."

"Look, I went to Harvard and there was no prejudice at Harvard," he said finally. "If I had been prejudiced, Harvard would have taken it out of me."

"Apparently not," I said dryly.

The longer I stood there, the more courage and conviction I seemed to gain. I forged ahead, speaking to the chief resident as he had surely never been spoken to by a black woman. "Dr. Marshall, I am convinced you know exactly what I'm talking about here. It is incumbent on you to make sure all members of this team pull their weight. Now, I know I'm pulling mine. Can you say the same for everyone else?"

He regarded me through narrowed eyes. Clearly startled by my refusal to back down, he seemed at a loss for words.

"Very well, Dr. Simmons," he said at last, "I'll look into your concerns."

I walked out of his office feeling redeemed. This was the woman I knew myself to be, not that wilted, crying girl in a dank ladies room.

The incidents of my interns being unprepared decreased dramatically after my meeting with the chief resident, although I now had to deal with a certain sullenness from some of them. No doubt, the chief had spoken with them, and they believed I had turned them in. I did not let their demeanor concern me unduly. I was there to practice medicine, to heal patients, not to make friends. I should note that whenever the chief resident saw me after that, he took great pains to recognize me publicly—once even acknowledging me from the dais of the lecture hall as he addressed the residents—and to inquire as to my well-being. Perhaps, like many others in America, he was waking up to the fact that the world was changing. But even as the civil rights demonstrators gained ground in the fight for equality, black America would sustain unimaginable losses.

It was now the summer of 1963. Protest marches, lunch counter sit-ins and voter registration drives were being staged all through the South, despite the violent response from police and local whites. Then, on June 12, African Americans suffered a fresh heartbreak when a white assassin shot NAACP's field secretary Medgar Evers in his driveway in Jackson, Mississippi. Two months later, on August 28, Price and I watched on television with the rest of country as Dr. King delivered his galvanizing "I Have a Dream" speech from Washington. This speech remains one of the greatest moments of oratory and bedrock human faith. None of us will soon forget these lines, or the haunting cadence of Dr. King's voice, rising as if to the heavens as he addressed the quarter of a million souls gathered that day on the Washington Mall[85]:

> *I have a dream that one day on the red hills of Georgia the sons of former slaves and the sons of former slave owners will be able to sit down together at the table of brotherhood.*
>
> *I have a dream that one day even the state of Mississippi, a state sweltering with the heat of injustice, sweltering with the heat of oppression, will be transformed into an oasis of freedom and justice.*
>
> *I have a dream that my four little children will one day live in a nation where they will not be judged by the color of their skin but by the content of their character.*
>
> *I have a dream today.*

Leaning against my husband on our living room couch, I could feel the hairs prickling along the back of my neck.

"Priceless," I whispered. "Do you *see* this?"

He moved his arm around my shoulders and pulled me closer. On the TV, the cheering crowd stretched as far as the eye could see, and then beyond that, and for the first time in my life, I dared to believe that America might finally address its festering racial wounds.

But hate and violence weren't done with us yet. Just weeks later, on September 15 in Birmingham, Alabama, four little black girls attending Sunday school were incinerated when a bomb exploded at the Sixteenth Street Baptist Church, the staging ground for many of the city's civil rights protests. The faces of those four girls—Addie Mae Collins, Cynthia Wesley and Carole Robertson, all 14 years old, and 11-year-old Denise McNair[86]—are seared into my mind. I could have been any one of them, had my father's people ended up in the South instead of in Ohio. Any one of those beautiful brown girls could have been my child. Indeed, they were now the children of us all, martyrs in the struggle for freedom. My heart and mind cried out that so many brave souls were living and dying for my rights, and what was I doing to help them?

When I mentioned to Price my desire to be a more active participant in the struggle, he looked at me seriously and said, "You're doing your part, Ellamae. Every day you're pushing open doors for other little black girls who dream of becoming doctors just like you. You're active in the struggle right here."

My own father would have said the very same thing, had he still been alive. Price's words did allay my self-reproach at not being among the demonstrators carrying placards in the streets. He reminded me that there are many ways to advance the cause of equality, all of them worthwhile. And so my rotation on the chest medicine service continued and was ultimately served in full. At the end of the year, out of courtesy, I stopped by the office of the chief resident to let him know I was leaving.

"Well, Dr. Simmons," he said, "you're getting away with your hide."

"Barely," I said, only half-joking.

Dr. Marshall thanked me for the way in which I had handled my time on the chest medicine service. He confessed that his past contact with black people had been minimal, and that he'd learned a lot from me. He then commented that he had noticed that blacks tended to "ghettoize" themselves. "Why do blacks always want to hang around together?" he asked me. I was tempted to point out that whites also tended to hang around together, and weren't they also "ghettoizing" themselves? But I refrained, because I could see that despite his discomfort about matters of race, he was being sincere, so I simply responded, "Perhaps they are seeking out people who are friendly toward them."

"Fair enough," the chief said as he shook my hand and wished me luck. As I left his office, I thought that even though we had managed to negotiate a truce, he was probably as happy to see me go as I was to leave. I knew that I was not alone in what I had experienced at the University of Colorado Medical Center. Across the country, and especially in the South, other black doctors could recite similar tales. But at least we were now at the table, serving residencies, supervising interns and specializing as physicians in numbers never before seen. As black people, we weren't free yet. But it seemed to me we were getting there.

Working at the National Jewish Hospital in Denver in the early 1960s, I became the first African American woman in the United States to specialize in asthma, allergy and immunology.

CHAPTER 21

Breath

After my yearlong residency in chest medicine, I decided to seek subspecialty training in the field, because it was an area in which I still felt weak. And I wasn't yet ready to hang out my shingle as a private practitioner, especially given that Price didn't know where he'd be stationed next. It made no sense to begin building a practice, only to then uproot myself and move to another city. I had played with the idea of moving back to Emporia and starting a practice there, as I still had my little house on the edge of town, which was rented. I had once been warmly welcomed in Emporia, but when I thought about it now, the vision of coming home that winter to an emptied house swamped all other memories of the place. Realizing I could never again be happy there, I resolved to sell the house and use it to finance my next move.

Price and I had been talking about relocating to California in another year or two. Price thought that when his current tour of duty was complete, he might be able to negotiate a transfer to one of the Air Force bases near San Francisco. My older sister Georgeanna and her husband Braxton had moved to Los Angeles in 1960, and we had recently visited them there. Georgeanna, who was studying for her real estate license, had told me that our grown niece Cheri Jackson would soon be joining her in LA, along with her son, Jeff. I liked the idea that in California I would have family members nearby.

That summer I attended a national medical meeting being held in Denver, and by chance I started a conversation with another attendee. She turned out to be the wife of a local physician who could not take time away from his busy practice to attend the meeting. She had come to audit the conference for him. Our conversation moved to my desire for further residency training. "You want a residency in chest medicine?" she asked me. "I think I know where you can get one. I have a friend who is the director of the chest service at National Jewish Hospital. I'll call him for you." And so she did.

This is how I came to be interviewed by an administrator and the department chief of National Jewish Hospital (NJH) and to be accepted into the residency program in chest medicine there. What followed were two extraordinary years of subspecialty training within an institution that was blissfully free of the taint of racism. NJH was, and still is, a world-class research and treatment facility dedicated to pulmonary, cardiac and immunological diseases. Patients suffering from conditions like emphysema, cystic fibrosis, pulmonary tuberculosis, cancer and serious allergic disorders were accepted from all over the country and the world, without regard to race, creed or ability to pay. The only criteria were that the patient's illness must fall within the hospital's specialties, and the patient must be unable to pay for comparative private hospital care. Everyone was welcome there, and a patient's family traditions, ethnic culture and geographic circumstance were all taken into account when devising plans for care. NJH's guiding principle was that good medical care is a birthright. That was nothing short of revolutionary, and I was thrilled to be annexed to an institution guided by such lofty ideals. Indeed, walking up to the building on my very first day, I had been impressed by the inscription over the door: "None who can pay may enter—none can pay who enter."

Since opening its doors in 1899, NJH had relied entirely on fundraising and philanthropic sponsorship to provide services of last resort to patients who had been treatment failures at other facilities. NJH took only the most serious cases, and only by referral from a local doctor, and patients might stay for months at a time undergoing treatment. The staff at NJH was trained to treat not just the patient but also his or her family, training all concerned to manage the patient's illness. The most exhaustive clinical summaries I have ever seen were written about each patient, comprehensive personal histories were compiled, and treatment protocols were meticulously evaluated. If it was determined a patient could not get well, then that patient would be taught to live to the maximum physiological limits of his disease.

It was at NJH that I witnessed up close the horrifying results of tobacco smoking. I saw the miserable quality of life of smokers in their forties and early fifties, men who should have been at the prime of their lives but who were chronically ill and dying, whether from primary or secondary tobacco smoke. The U.S. Surgeon General at the time, Dr. Luther Terry, had already begun sounding the alarm about cigarette smoking, but for more than three decades, such warnings would be largely ignored. Smoking would remain widespread, even in hospitals.

My own husband was a pack-a-day smoker when I joined the chest medicine team at NJH. Within weeks, I told him quite clearly that unless he quit smoking altogether, I would divorce him. I was deadly serious, and he knew it. He did manage to stop smoking within the year. His motivation, he told me, was that he now had a better understanding of the fate that awaited smokers, as I brought home graphic stories daily. I also had no desire to have my own health compromised by living with a smoker. I had noted that second-hand smoke triggered dry coughing spasms and copious mucous production, more so it seemed in the bystander than in the smoker himself.

Each morning, I would be the attending doctor on a ward composed almost entirely of men who were at NJH because they had smoked. At the time, not many women smokers were being admitted. Whether this was because there were relatively fewer of them, or because their doctors failed to refer them to us, I cannot say. Of the men who were referred, their diagnoses ran the gamut from chronic bronchitis and emphysema to chronic obstructive lung disease and lung cancer. Occasionally, we might see a patient with bronchiectasis (bronchial tubes that become distended, flabby, scarred and infected due to mucous blockage), chronic occupational lung disease such as asbestosis (due to the inhalation of asbestos particles, causing mesothelioma), or pneumoconiosis (such as black lung disease, the kind of pulmonary impairment seen in coal miners or silica and iron workers). But even these patients were at NJH because they also smoked, heaping further insult upon their occupational, genetic or metabolic injury. Most of these patients would never return to normal life. They lacked the lung capacity to walk even a short block on level ground. They had no sex life and no family life. Some prayed to die and cursed each day they lived to draw breath. Some were tied to their oxygen tank, and treatment was only palliative.

Perhaps most perplexing to me, who had never so much as sampled a cigarette, was the degree to which these patients craved the nicotine to which they had become addicted. A number of them continued to dance with the very agent of their destruction, sneaking cigarettes when they thought they could get away with it. Of course, the doctors and nurses could generally tell, although we often did no more than scold the patient, as this infraction could result in the patient being discharged from the hospital. Although I understood the need for such discipline, discharge felt like a defeat to all concerned.

My patients with far-advanced pulmonary tuberculosis, many of whom had previously been diagnosed as drug-resistant, were a more hopeful story. In these patients, an experimental cocktail of potent anti-tuberculosis drugs were used to attack the disease. This was the value of being treated at a research institution; healing protocols were at the leading edge. My role as a resident was to observe and track the level of these drugs in the patient's bloodstream so as to maintain an effective therapeutic dosage. Most of these patients were ultimately restored to complete health.

The chest medicine residency program also included rotations on the cardiac and asthma-allergy services. I found the cardiac service rotation to be a pleasant learning experience, and I even briefly contemplated becoming a cardiologist. Then came my asthma-allergy rotation.

I had secretly dreaded this service. I had observed that the chief of the service was difficult, or to be more accurate, he appeared in interactions I had witnessed to be an arrogant perfectionist, exacting to a fault. I thought he might also be sexist, as most male doctors of the time were, and I wondered if he might be prejudiced against black people, too, although to be honest I had not detected any whiff of racism at the institution. It didn't help that I still thought asthma was psychosomatic and that asthmatics needed a psychiatrist more than they needed a medical doctor. It pains me to confess that at this point in my medical training, I still held such an archaic and idiotic view. I dared to voice my false impression to the chief of the chest medicine program. He smiled, humoring me, but reminded me that the asthma-allergy rotation was an important part of my training and could not be avoided. The full rotation was for two months. He suggested that I try it for two weeks and check in with him at the end of that time.

The chief obviously calculated that the way asthma-allergy was practiced at NJH would completely reorient my thinking. And he was right. After just one week on the service, I had grown fascinated by the varied causes of asthma and the allergenic agents that could aggravate attacks. By the end of the second week, I had determined to stay and complete the full two-month rotation. I had begun to grasp the environmental subtleties of the allergic response. To my surprise, I even enjoyed working with the demanding chief of the asthma-allergy service, Dr. Irving Itkin, who was Jewish and had come to NJH from the famed Massachusetts General Hospital. A gruff but brilliant clinician, he took pains to share knowledge of his emerging field, but he was also known to bark at residents who did not execute treatment protocols precisely. Ironically, given his chosen specialty, Dr. Itkin had a pipe perpetually clamped between his teeth. He never lit it, of course—one did not smoke around asthmatics—but he was always chewing on that pipe, and he spoke around it through clenched teeth in a kind of Humphrey Bogart growl.

It was perhaps this growl—which suggested irritation or even contempt—that had made Dr. Itkin unpopular with many members of the hospital staff. They were afraid of him, and I, too, kept my distance at first. But in time, I realized that his fierce demeanor masked the heart of a true educator, one who welcomed any question his students might pose. In fact, he thrived on our inquisitiveness, which he took as a sign of commitment and a working brain, prompting him to step more fully into his role as teacher. And so, when Dr. Itkin took me aside at the end of my two-month rotation and asked me to consider doing a fellowship in asthma-allergy with him, I didn't hesitate.

"All right," I told him.

He was pleased. I know, because he flashed that smile of his that was more like a grimace. He growled, "Ellamae, you are a gifted clinician, and you're going to be the foremost black female allergist in the country."

Dr. Itkin managed to convey the sense that at NJH, we were all in the trenches together, patient and medical team, all of us arrayed against life-threatening illnesses as the line of extreme defense. Consider being uprooted from your family, your school, your working environment, your friends, and being sent to a distant state to yet another hospital for treatment. You know that you haven't gotten well in your home environment, surrounded by friends and loved ones, and treated by doctors who have known you for years, and now you are facing a new roster of doctors. Imagine the responsibility that placed on NJH's medical staff.

The asthmatics at National Jewish ended up knowing more about their illnesses than the doctors who had referred them, because once a week, patients and the medical staff would assemble around a conference room table to discuss the many facets of their disease. The goal was to give patients insight and knowledge about their illness, so that they could take the reins of control for their overall health. A patient might learn something from questions asked by fellow patients, in a kind of group therapy. As they began to realize they were not alone, feelings of fear and hopelessness started to dissipate.

Of necessity, these patients had built their lives around their illness. They never knew when an asthma attack would strike. Some of the more chronically ill patients might have to remain at NJH for months, even years. Some young people went to college in the Denver area while undergoing treatment at the hospital; some adults got jobs in Denver and went back and forth to the hospital for treatment. The asthmatic patients even formed their own softball, tennis and swimming teams, competing against local leagues and winning. Before landing at NJH, these same patients could only sit and watch while others played sports, too breathless themselves to walk a short distance, much less run.

Nowhere else in my medical career would I experience such a holistic approach to patient care. Even though we treated only the most severe cases at NJH, I saw very few deaths from asthma there, which speaks to the level of care. But there was one girl who still haunts me, a 16-year-old who had spent several months at the hospital learning to take care of her asthma. She was doing well and was ready to be discharged. She would be staying for the time being with family friends in Denver, because her parents lived in another state.

What none of her doctors knew is that the friends lived in an apartment where a cat had previously been present. The family, knowing that cat dander is highly allergenic, had boarded the cat with relatives and then cleaned the apartment thoroughly. They felt confident that all the dander had been cleared away, and therefore, when we asked if they had any pets, they said no, without thinking to mention the recent presence of a cat in their apartment. But apparently traces of dander remained, because on her first day in the apartment, this young girl started wheezing. That night, she couldn't breathe and was rushed back to the hospital. We went to work on her immediately, trying to break up the thick, viscous mucus in her lungs triggered by her allergic response. The mucus had completely clogged her main and secondary airways, and although we tried everything, we couldn't seem to break it up. The girl suffocated right there on our table.

When I looked up at the clock in the room to call the time, I saw that Dr. Itkin, this gruff, scowling man, had tears in his eyes. "Ellamae," he said, "I never thought we could lose a patient if we got there in time." He meant if we got there while the patient was still alive. But this young girl was so severely allergic that our usual treatments failed her. We spent many hours studying her case afterward to see what we could have done differently. And the only thing we came up with was that we had failed to discern a single environmental detail.

There is always a patient that crystallizes for a doctor the professional path he or she will follow. For me, that patient was the asthmatic 16-year-old girl in Denver, whose lungs filled up with mucus after a single day of exposure to cat dander. I'll never forget the night we lost her, and the painful lesson she taught us about the need to thoroughly assess a patient's non-therapeutic environment. I vowed to not waste the lesson of her too-brief life, or to ever forget her needless death. That was the night I truly became an allergy doctor.

In the mid-1960s, many patients at Kaiser Permanente's allergy clinic had never before encountered a black doctor.

CHAPTER 22

The Interview

My fellowship with National Jewish Hospital would come to an end on June 30, 1965. Price and I had made plans to relocate to California after that. My husband knew I felt socially out of my element in Denver. Perhaps that played a role in his decision to retire from the military altogether and to enter civilian life out West, finding a position as a teacher or professor of aviation science. He had the gift of gab and would excel in such work. I did not doubt for a moment that he would find his place on the West Coast. Now, I just needed to find mine.

When I told Dr. Itkin of my plan to move west at the end of my residency, he was full of advice. "If you're going to California," he told me, "there are only two places you should consider. One is the Scripps clinic in La Jolla in Southern California, and the other is Kaiser Permanente in Northern California. Now," he continued, warming to the subject of my future training as an allergist, "Scripps is just another National Jewish. They write the same papers and conduct the same research. You'd basically be doing the same thing you did here. At Kaiser, on the other hand, you'd round out your experience in a well-established outpatient allergy center, where asthmatics are well maintained on an established anti-allergenic regimen. And I recommend Ben Feingold, the chief of asthma-allergy at Kaiser. He's a good allergist, does fine research. Of course, he's difficult. He's a little Caesar—nobody else knows anything as far as he's concerned—but I recommend you go there and learn everything he has to teach you about asthmatics whose condition is well controlled, who are ambulatory, who go to school or to work. After that you'll be well set up to take care of anybody in this field." Chewing on his unlit pipe, he added, "I always told you I'd make you the foremost black woman allergy specialist in the country."

207

I was, in fact, the first black woman to specialize in asthma, allergy and immunology in the country. In that sense, you could say that for a period of time at least, I was also the foremost, which meant Dr. Itkin was true to his word.

On the strength of Dr. Itkin's recommendation, I established contact with Dr. Feingold at Kaiser Permanente's allergy clinic based in San Francisco. I forwarded my resume and subsequently received an appointment for an interview. In May 1964, I had traded in my 1958 Karmann Ghia for the only car I had ever really coveted, a white 1964 Porsche 356C. Two months later, departing just after midnight, I drove that car across the country, through the wide, dusty plains of Wyoming, the red hills of Utah and the flat desert of Nevada to San Francisco.

The trip took almost two days, but I refused to stop except for gas and to use the restroom and buy coffee and a sandwich in the gas station convenience store. I had no idea of the racial climate in the white towns I was passing through, especially given the footage on the nightly news of battles erupting during voting registration drives down South. While the struggle for civil rights advanced, visible and invisible bigots railed against the protests, with many of them committing brutal acts of violence.

Only one week before, three young men—James Chaney, Michael Schwerner and Andrew Goodman, a black Mississippian and two white New Yorkers respectively—had gone missing. It was thought that they'd been kidnapped and murdered by the Ku Klux Klan. The search for the killers dominated the news blaring from my car radio, along with ugly rants from white citizens threatening the college students and other volunteers pouring into town by the busload.[87] But while this social conflagration had opened the eyes of some whites to the injustices suffered by blacks, it had further enraged others, calcifying their prejudice and hatred of black people. I did not want to chance which side of the fence the whites I might encounter in the vast and dusty heartland might fall.

It was almost eleven o'clock on a Wednesday night when I checked into an airport motel in San Francisco, exhausted from the long drive. I unpacked and hung my good blue suit with its patriotic red buttons and white trim, and spread my white silk blouse and hosiery over the chair. Then I showered and fell into bed. I would meet with the famous chief of Kaiser Permanente's allergy department bright and early the following morning.

Dr. Ben Feingold sat back in his large bronze-studded black-leather chair, scrutinizing me. He questioned me about my previous residencies, always calling me "Miss," never "Doctor." He asked me about my asthma-allergy fellowship, and more superficially about my chest medicine residency. After about 30 minutes, he tented his fingers on his desk and said, "Well, I have my doubts about hiring anyone whom I have not trained, but please go out and see my secretary. We'll have to continue this another day, as I have another meeting." He told me to make an appointment with his secretary for the following Tuesday, which was five days away. I could ill afford the expense of additional nights at my hotel, plus meals, but I did not say this. Instead I made the appointment and spent the next few days exploring downtown San Francisco and biding my time.

I returned the following Tuesday for the continuation of our interview and entered Dr. Feingold's office as scheduled. Again the department chief sat back in his chair and viewed me intently. He asked a few questions about specific allergic reactions and how they might be treated at the institution of my residency. I answered easily and in meticulous clinical detail. At last he said, "Well, I see you know your stuff, but I'm afraid I cannot hire you, as I've never hired anyone whom I have not trained."

I wasn't sure I'd heard him correctly. "Doctor, are you telling me that you've trained every physician who works under the Kaiser allergy plan?"

"Every one of them," he replied, his voice more than a little bit self-satisfied.

A little Caesar, Dr. Itkin had said.

I forged ahead. "Well, Doctor, have you ever hired anyone whose residency training compares with mine?"

"No, no I guess I haven't," he answered.

"And are there any black doctors here in any of the departments?" I continued.

Dr. Feingold thought for a minute, his long fingers stroking his chin.

"No, no, I guess there are none," he said finally.

"Have you ever hired a black woman?" I asked him then.

"No, I haven't," he replied. I had caught him off guard, but now he gathered himself. "Do you always ask questions like this when you apply for a job?" he demanded, adding, "And I've never hired a black woman because I've never interviewed one who I found to be sufficiently qualified."

I paused, regarding the elegant little Caesar carefully. I rather liked the man. He was known to be brilliant, and I appreciated the fact that he had entertained my rather intrusive questions. But I wasn't done yet.

"Dr. Feingold," I said, my voice steady, my gaze direct, "I've never applied for a job for which I was not fully qualified. In fact, I've usually been overqualified. So tell me, is the real reason you've decided not to hire me the fact that I'm black?"

My interviewer seemed to be lost in thought. I wondered for a moment if he had heard me. Suddenly he blurted out, "We've got one! We've got one!" He held up his right hand with his index finger jabbing the air. "We've got one black doctor on staff. He's in radiology. I'll call him and you can talk with him."

The single black doctor turned out to be Dr. Granville Coggs, a Harvard-educated Phi Beta Kappa physician and former Tuskegee Airman who had joined the staff of Kaiser some months before. Dr. Coggs walked with me to an adjoining office, where we talked briefly about his work for Kaiser and about our paths to becoming physicians. A native of Pine Bluff, Arkansas, Granville Coggs' early life had been defined by Jim Crow laws, but his parents, like mine, had encouraged his ambitions, and like me, he had financed medical school on the GI Bill. "Harvard was the first place that treated me as a person, rather than as a black person," he told me. "I lived in a mixed dormitory there and experienced a level of integration that would have been impossible in the South. Harvard has been training black doctors since the mid-1800s, yet I would never have been able to afford the tuition there but for the GI Bill."[88]

Afterward, I returned to the office of the chief, thinking that at least my visit to Kaiser had not been a waste; I had met and talked with Dr. Coggs. I felt resigned, knowing I had done all I could to acquit myself, and now it was time to go home. I thanked Dr. Feingold for his time and told him I would be heading back to Denver early in the morning to complete the final months of my residency. I added that I hoped to hear from him in the future.

Dr. Feingold didn't respond at first. He just stared at me in that fixed way I was already becoming used to. I realized he was wrestling with a decision.

Finally, he spoke. "Stop by my secretary on your way out and sign your contract," he said. "I'll take you after all."

And so I was hired, with instructions to return to San Francisco by June 30, 1965, so that I could begin work in the outpatient allergy clinic on July 1. I didn't know it then, but I would spend the next twenty-five years working for Kaiser.

I returned to Denver to complete my final months of training at National Jewish Hospital, an institution that had given me so much more than an academic education. It was here that, for the first time in my medical career—indeed, in my life—race had been transcended. I had been accepted on the basis of my clinical performance, and my skin color had been entirely incidental. I had felt at home. I would forever feel grateful to the institution where I had known this privilege, and where I had gained a level of experience that would serve me for life.

All too soon, I was saying misty-eyed farewells to my patients, colleagues and staff, and heading across the country once more in my sporty white Porsche, our black-and-brown Doberman, Dede, perched like a queen in the passenger seat. The plan was for Price to join me in July after his tour of duty at the Air Reserve Records Center was completed and his military discharge came through. In the interim, he would also arrange for our furniture to be shipped to our new home. Scanning newspaper ads, I had found a vacancy for a large apartment in a neighborhood not far from the clinic where I would be working. The landlady had taken our rental information by phone. She seemed pleased to learn that I was a Kaiser physician and my husband an Air Force lieutenant colonel. She did not have any idea that we were black, as I had not seen fit to mention it. I mailed our first and last months' rent to her in the form of a personal check, and trusted there would be no problems once I arrived.

This time, as I drove across the country, I encountered a series of good omens disguised as car trouble. I once again took the route through Wyoming, and in its most barren, unpopulated terrain, I had a flat tire. There was not a soul in sight, not a house or gas station or truck stop on the horizon. I didn't panic. I knew how to change a tire. I got out my tools and had the car jacked up and the spare tire on the ground beside me as I struggled to unscrew the lugs of the flat rear wheel on the left. Suddenly, out of nowhere, two young Wyoming state highway patrolmen appeared in their cruiser. They were jovial and friendly. "You're doing it wrong," they told me cheerfully as they exited their vehicle. In less than ten minutes they had the spare tire in place and the flat carefully stored.

"Now you be careful and get that flat repaired right away," they advised.

I thanked them and got back on the road, thinking how different this encounter with law enforcement was from that long-ago road trip when I was an Army nurse leaving Louisiana and heading for Iowa. I thought of writing a letter of appreciation to the Wyoming Highway Patrol department, but not knowing the officers' names or their badge numbers, I never did. But I have never forgotten their kindness.

I reached Central Nevada as night was falling. With the benevolence of the Wyoming patrolmen fresh in my mind, and Dede at my side, I decided to chance overnighting at a Holiday Inn in Salt

Lake City. My stay was without incident. The next day, I drove through Reno to Highway 80 West, crossing into the state of California by early afternoon. I was sailing along on the road toward Sacramento when my engine sputtered, then died and refused to restart. I raised the hood and waited at the roadside, hoping for the appearance once again of the highway patrol. A middle-aged African American man saw my disabled car and pulled over to offer his help. He pushed the car and tried to jumpstart it, to no avail. Fortunately, he was a member of AAA, so he drove Dede and me to the nearest gas station and called their roadside assistance service. Then he drove us back to my car and waited with me until the mechanic arrived.

The technician could not start the car either, so he towed me to the nearest auto repair shop, which was little more than a gas station next to the highway in the middle of the dusty desert. The mechanic there raised the rear hood and observed the engine.

"I don't see anything wrong," he said, squinting against the sun. He reached in and tightened a screw that secured a wire, then tried the motor again. The car sputtered to life. "That's it, then," the mechanic said. "I guess you're good to go."

"What's the charge?" I asked him gratefully.

"Nothing, I didn't do nothing," he said.

"At least let me pay you for servicing my car," I insisted. I thought of my father, who had taught us never to take a person's effort for granted.

"Lady," the mechanic said again. "You don't owe me anything, but if it makes you feel better, you can give me a couple of dollars."

At that point the good Samaritan who had stopped to help and who had called the tow-truck service for me, mentioned that he lived in the Bay Area and, in case I had further engine trouble, he would follow me as far as the Bay Bridge. He did so, but there was no further problem. In fact, my prized Porsche never again behaved as temperamentally as it did on that road trip, when a flat tire and a loose wire under the hood showed me a more hopeful America than the one I had experienced all those years ago as an Army nurse traveling through Shreveport.

*With the help of my friend and Kaiser colleague, Dr. Louis Chardon
(with me in his living room), I found my dream home, a semi-Victorian
in Presidio Heights, a neighborhood that in 1965 was all white.*

CHAPTER 23

The House on Clay Street

You've probably heard the saying: "The coldest winter I ever spent was a summer in San Francisco." The quote is generally attributed to Mark Twain, although some literary scholars claim he never actually said it. Whoever coined the witticism, I quickly understood why it was so often repeated by newcomers to the city. As soon as I crossed the Bay Bridge, the drop in temperature shocked me. I was wearing a sheer sundress suitable for warm summer days. It was the height of June, after all. And yet the sky was overcast and the fog lay thick and damp on my shoulders, chilling me to the bone in a way never matched by Denver's dry sub-zero temperatures. It was clear I had a lot to learn about Bay Area weather.

The first thing I did was drive to my landlady's home to retrieve the keys to my rented apartment. She was surprised to discover I was black and said as much. "I've never rented to colored before," she told me, "but you're a doctor and you work for Kaiser, so I imagine it will be okay."

"I imagine it will be," I replied pleasantly, taking possession of the keys.

The second thing I did, after setting down my bags and exploring the spacious six-room apartment at 1545 Lake Street where Price and I would live, was to go out and purchase flannel jumpsuit pajamas with feet attached. I wore them every night, turning the thermostat up to eighty degrees Fahrenheit and zipping my sleeping bag up to my neck when I settled down at night on the bare wood floor (our furniture hadn't yet arrived). I was still cold. I didn't lose my perpetual chill until about six months in.

At Kaiser Foundation Hospitals' Allergy Clinic, I quickly

settled into the routine. As Dr. Feingold had confirmed, there were no other African American women doctors in the entire Kaiser system, and only three black male physicians had ever been on staff. I was prepared for this, and I refused to allow some of my patients' initial discomfort with my color to rattle me unduly. One mother hissed at me not to touch her child and requested another physician. Other patients, usually white and male, would ask me, "Where did you get your degree?" Typically, I would reply, "I have several degrees. Which one would you like to know about?" This was usually enough to put that line of questioning to rest.

I came to understand that it wasn't so much that these patients were biased against me personally as that they had never before seen a black woman doctor. But it is difficult to hold malice toward a person who is expending every effort to relieve one's illness, and so with few exceptions, the skeptics became my permanent patients and did not wish to see any other physician when I was available. Patients tend to respond to how you make them feel about themselves. I had long ago learned that if you make them feel valued and worthy of attention and care, then they will cooperate with you to get themselves well.

As life-changing as my time at National Jewish Hospital had been, and as much as I had grown from treating critically ill patients, I grew to love the way medicine was practiced at Kaiser. Although I was the only black woman doctor on staff for some time, it was a truly multicultural experience, with people of all races and economic circumstances having access to the highest professional care. Because Kaiser had such a diverse patient population, its doctors became very attuned to cultural nuances that could impact a patient's ability to get well. A lot of African American children, for example, lived in poorer neighborhoods where landlords tended to be less vigilant and asthma allergens proliferated; this had to be taken into account when prescribing treatment.

Kaiser ultimately became a leader in what came to be known as "cultural competencies," which simply meant that doctors developed targeted treatment plans with the socioeconomic and cultural realities of patients top of mind. It also meant that patients could request the doctor they felt would most understand them, whether a woman doctor, a white doctor, an African American or Latino doctor, or an openly gay or lesbian doctor. Appreciating this, I didn't take offense when a patient who had been assigned to me asked for a white male, just as my white colleagues did not take offense when a black patient requested me, or a white or Latina or Muslim woman would ask to be transferred to my care.

At Kaiser, I saw more clearly than I ever had that you don't learn medicine from books; you learn medicine from patients. While books will give you a necessary background and provide a critical context, it is your patients who will ultimately teach you everything you know.

By the time my husband Price joined me on July 18, I was already well on the way to becoming established in my new life. We shared a big, empty, unfurnished apartment until July 31, when our furniture finally arrived. We slept in sleeping bags on the hardwood floor, walked our dog together in the evenings and dined out for most of our meals. It was all a grand romantic adventure, as if we were newlyweds again. During the days when I worked, Price painted the apartment and investigated getting his California teaching certification, as his plan was to teach aviation science at a local college.

As soon as our apartment was properly set up, family members began visiting—my sister Georgeanna and niece Cheri from Los Angeles, my sister Rowena from Columbus, my brother Lawrence's daughter Varian, from Mount Vernon, and Price's four beautiful girls. San Francisco was clearly a more appealing destination than Detroit or Denver had been, and I was thrilled at the prospect of seeing my relatives more regularly than in years past. Along with a few friends who had gone to medical school with me at Howard, and a couple of fellow Hamptonians, I had also made some good friends among my colleagues at Kaiser, most notably my fellow allergist Dr. Louis Chardon.

Louis' office was next to mine, and we fell into an instant camaraderie. Our irreverent humor matched seamlessly, and our conversations about our medical cases could occupy us for hours. Louis had never married. He never told me explicitly, but I understood fairly quickly that he was gay, although in that day and age, a prominent professional such as Louis still tended to be circumspect, simply never speaking about his life away from work. With me, however, he soon felt free to share whatever was on his mind, which only bonded us more closely. Louis was not very tall and slight of build, silver haired and handsome in the Old World way of Renaissance paintings. He was a true aristocrat, perhaps the first I had ever known, descended from both French and Spanish royalty. His parents had settled in Puerto Rico, where his mother was born, and where he was raised, so he also had the flair of the tropics about him. It was present in the riotously colored Hawaiian shirts he liked to wear when not working, in the spicy fare he served and the rum punch that flowed like water at his lavish dinner parties.

He and his live-in partner Darrel loved to entertain. Many weekends they would invite Price and me, and any family member who happened to be visiting us, to join them for a meal at their Spanish-style home perched on a hill overlooking the sweep of San Francisco. He encouraged us to bring our dogs and seemed unperturbed when they invariably wanted to frolic in the cascading waterfall of the massive stone fountain that adorned his rather grand circular driveway. When the dogs then ventured into the house, still wet from the fountain, Louis merely shrugged and pointed out that his floors were tiled; they would dry naturally, and were easily cleaned.

Price in particular loved Louis' parties. He, too, was a natural born host, a master cook who could taste the most intricate dish once and go home and recreate its flavors. Before long, we were throwing dinner parties of our own in our apartment, and when too much time passed in between them, our friends would start calling to inquire when Price would be cooking one of his famous spreads again and to please make sure they were invited.

It was true my husband sometimes drank more than I was comfortable with during these festivities, but this had always been the case. I had long ago chalked up his excessive drinking to a form of PTSD, as I'd observed that most of the Tuskegee war veterans I had met were also heavy drinkers. They had gotten into the habit of using alcohol to numb the terrors of combat, and now, in peacetime, the habit remained. Despite the bickering Price and I sometimes fell into about his alcohol consumption, we still enjoyed each other's company tremendously and had wonderful conversations, especially about politics and family. In general, I thought our married life was going well.

Upon his honorable discharge after twenty-three years of distinguished service, Price had been made a full colonel at a ceremony I had traveled back to Denver to attend. On arriving in the Bay Area, he'd found a job almost immediately as an executive with the U.S. Customs Service. He also taught at a local community college, and he got together frequently to drink or go fishing with military buddies who lived in the area. He would later help to found a San Francisco Bay Area Chapter of the Tuskegee Airmen, and he and the other famed black fliers were in constant demand for lectures to community groups and schools.

By October of the following year, with our lives humming along comfortably, we began to think in terms of putting down more permanent roots. In San Francisco, I felt more at home in my skin than I had ever felt anywhere else, the only exception being my three years as a nursing student at Hampton. As both my job and Price's seemed stable, and we were occupied with an active social life with our combined groups of friends, it was clear to both of us that we were in the Bay Area to stay. But our apartment, although fairly large by Bay Area apartments standards, had only one bathroom, and that was a challenge during the periods when my stepdaughters came to visit. I wanted us to have enough space to welcome them as often and for as long as they wanted to stay. I even dreamed of them each having their own permanently assigned rooms. Obviously, we would have to move to larger quarters. The next logical step was to buy a home.

Price and I looked at houses for sale all over the Bay Area before deciding to concentrate on San Francisco proper. We would drive through different neighborhoods after work to get a sense of where in the city we might like to live. We wanted to be located reasonably close to our places of employment; neither of us relished a long commute. I had no previous experience in home-buying, despite my father having always expounded on the desirability of home ownership. "When you've decided on the city where you want to live, buy a house!" he had frequently admonished. It pleased me to think I was following his advice, finally selling the house John and I had built in Emporia to help finance the down payment. I would assume the mortgage payments, because much of Price's income was needed to support and educate his four growing daughters. I was completely comfortable with this plan, and I innocently believed that when we found the house we wanted and could afford, I would simply write a check.

Price shook his head ruefully at my naïveté. Having moved often with the Air Force, and being called on to set up fresh living arrangements in any number of new locales, he was better informed than I was. Not only was I totally ignorant of real estate terms, I was also blissfully unaware of the restrictive covenants, redlining practices and predatory subprime loans that too often bedeviled African Americans seeking to purchase a home. Just as I had spent years learning the complexities of medicine while picking my way through a minefield of racial hostilities and ambiguities, my true education in the field of real estate was about to begin.

In September of 1967, I found the house I wanted. It was at 3711 Clay Street in Presidio Heights, which my colleague Louis

Chardon had assured me was a top-flight neighborhood, among the most exclusive in fact. It was he who had first noticed the listing, a semi-Victorian selling for $50,000 on a street where most houses went for $75,000 or more. "Why don't you go look at it?" Louis had said, showing me the notice in the newspaper one morning at work. I called the realtor and made an appointment to see the house during my lunch hour the very same day.

An older couple and their dog occupied the house, which was badly in need of repairs. There was dry rot around the window frames, old wiring, outdated plumbing with no copper piping anywhere, and crumbling plaster and peeling paint indoors and out. The realtor told me the house had been built in 1907, right after the Great San Francisco Earthquake. The current owners had purchased the property in 1933, and they had raised their children there, living there continuously without ever making repairs. Now, thirty-four years later, it was the classic "worst house in the best neighborhood," an ideal home-buying scenario.

Despite the costly restorations needed, I knew at once I had found my home. Open, gracious and flooded with light, its location and proximity to our workplaces, as well as its size—3,600 square feet—was perfect. And I loved its Victorian details. The house was three stories plus a basement, and it was built into a hill at the back, so the basement opened to a sloping terraced back yard. There were four bedrooms, three and a half bathrooms, and two kitchens, the second one on the top floor, which I suspected had been used as the servants' quarters. The ground floor had two sitting rooms, a library with plenty of room for my grand piano, a dining room and a TV room in addition to the kitchen, but there was no garage. This didn't concern me because I could see how the dining room or one of the sitting rooms could easily be converted to house my precious white Porsche.

I informed the realtor of my strong interest in the property and made an appointment for six that evening to have my husband look at it after work. At about 5 P.M., when I called the realtor at his office to tell him we were on our way, he said, "Oh,

Dr. Simmons, I was going to call you. There's no need for you to come by; the house has been sold."

This made absolutely no sense to me. I had seen the property just four hours earlier. It had been available then, with no mention of a pending sale. I expressed my surprise to the realtor and asked if we might look at the house again anyway, so that my husband could see the location and the type of house that had caught my interest. The realtor adamantly refused. "You knew the house was priced $25,000 below market value and that it would not be on the market very long," he said. "The owners are not interested in showing it again."

Although disappointed, I took him at his word. Price, however, was skeptical about this strange turn of events, and so was my colleague and friend, Louis. He was absolutely convinced that there had been "some skullduggery" with the owners, and he was determined to find out what was behind it. The next day, a Saturday, Louis called me at home. "Ellamae, are you really interested in buying that house?" he asked me. When I confirmed that yes, I absolutely was, he asked me to meet him at Kaiser's allergy clinic in an hour.

"That house has not been sold," Louis told me as soon as I appeared at his office door. He was pacing up and down next to his desk, visibly steaming. "These damned white folks make me so mad. The owners refuse to sell to a Negro. The realtor told me that a Negro lady had come looking at the house, but someone from the block association must have seen you, and they made the owners take it off the market till you went away. That neighborhood is all white, Ellamae, and the bigots who live there seem to believe they own this country and can tell you where to live. But if you really want that house, well, goddammit, I'm going to buy it and deed it to you."

I was dumbfounded. After the warm collegiality at National Jewish Hospital, followed by the general friendliness of San Franciscans, I had let down my guard; I had stopped looking behind the screen for the racial driver of all events, and to be frank, it

had been a relief to stop dancing for a while with that particular bogeyman. Price had tried to warn me that I was being too
trusting, and now I saw that he had been right.

I asked Louis to give me time to discuss his proposal with my
husband, and I promised to give him our answer by the following
Monday.

When I told Price what had transpired, he gave a short, bitter
laugh. "Well, Ellamae, did you think you could go out and buy a
house wherever you wanted it?" he asked me.

"Why not?" I said. "Why the hell not! My money is as good
as anyone's!"

Price just kept shaking his head. "No, no, no, Ellamae. You're
dreaming. Look, we don't need that house. There are many other
houses for sale. You don't need to get sneaky to buy that house.
The whole scheme Louis is proposing is just too messy."

But now I was angry. I felt duped and humiliated, and I had
something to prove. I wanted to accept Louis' offer to buy the
house and then deed it to us. Not only would this be an answer to
our immediate housing needs; not only were there significant tax
advantages in home ownership; but I also didn't think I should be
denied the right to purchase the home I wanted simply because
the white people of Presidio Heights didn't want black people
living next to them.

I had one precedent for this. My brother in Ohio in 1938
had negotiated to buy the land upon which he had decided to
build his home. He had met my future sister-in-law Isabelle, the
woman he planned to marry, and he wanted to complete the
house before their wedding day. They would move into it for
their honeymoon. When the white neighbors across the street
learned of Lawrence's plan, they offered the lot owner twice the
amount of money my brother had agreed to pay. The lot owner,
who respected my brother, told his neighbors, "You own every
old piece of run-down property in this town. You have more
money than I'll ever see, but you don't have enough money to
buy that lot, because I'm selling it to that colored boy." And thus

Lawrence acquired the land and built his family's home.

The reason his white neighbors had given for attempting to buy the land out from under him was, "We don't want any little pickaninnies running up and down our street." I imagined the neighbors in Presidio Heights had expressed similar sentiments when they tried to bar me from purchasing the house on Clay Street. And so, despite Price's protestations, I decided to go ahead with Louis' plan.

The acquisition of that San Francisco house—the entire shaky arrangement of it—became a threat to my marriage, as Price wanted nothing to do with what he saw as our legally ambiguous trickery. I appreciated that my husband was a military man who wanted always to stand on the right side of the law, but I did not see the situation in the same way he did. To my mind, Louis and I were balancing the scales of economic justice. I gave Louis the money for the down payment; we both signed a contract outlining our agreement; then he followed through with the purchase of the house in his name. A couple of months after the sale had been concluded and all paperwork properly filed, Louis then began the process of transferring the title to my name. This took longer than we had anticipated, as the bank sat on the application for months, refusing to act on it. My husband's skepticism deepened. He continued to insist that he wanted no part in any of our planning and scheming to get into that house.

The first order of business, while we waited for the title transfer to be approved, was to clean the premises from top to bottom. The house was filthy, and I knew I would have to clean it by myself. One Saturday, with buckets, scouring powder, Mr. Clean solution, Lysol, cleaning rags and steel wool in hand, I approached the overwhelming task. Fresh in my mind as I walked around to the side door were the recent Watts riots in Los Angeles, the burning of Newark and Detroit in violent demonstrations during the summer just past, the police beatings, the anger boiling over into violence across the country. The ugly racial climate of the decade made me nervous about reprisals from neighbors who might see me coming and going from the house.

In the weeks that followed, occasionally someone would approach me on the street and ask, "Who bought that house?"

"I don't know," I'd tell them. "I'm just the cleaning lady."

One day an Asian woman dressed in a maid's uniform stopped me. "Everyone is wondering who bought that house," she said.

I told her I thought some physician had bought it, and that I had been hired to clean. She seemed satisfied with my explanation, but I continued to feel apprehensive at my neighbors' inquisitiveness. I did not own a dog at that time, as our Doberman, Dede, had recently died, but I planned to get one as soon as we acquired the title to the house. This was as much for our protection as anything else. I truly feared some act of violence toward Price and me, or vandalism of our property. Fortunately, so far there had been nothing of the sort. I reasoned that no one really knew yet that a black couple had bought into lily-white Presidio Heights. As far as everyone who saw me was concerned, I was just the hired help.

I slowly grew more comfortable moving about the neighborhood as I scrubbed and scraped and plastered and painted my new home, getting it ready for habitation. Louis helped me find professional contractors to refurbish the exterior of the house, as well as carpenters, plasterers, plumbers and electricians to repair the inside woodwork and walls and upgrade the house's internal systems. It would be many years before I was able to convert one of the downstairs sitting rooms into a garage for my Porsche, but I was already calculating which rooms I would demolish and how I would move the staircase from the front to the back of the house to make that happen.

From October through December of 1967, I spent evenings and weekends cleaning and overseeing repairs to 3711 Clay Street. It had turned out to be a mammoth undertaking, during which Price refused to even visit the house. He had never seen the inside. The most he would do was drive by and look at the exterior progress from his car. I had to admit that until the title of the house was securely in my name, this was probably for the best. For a black couple to be seen at the house would have raised suspicion, and who knows what action the neighborhood association might then take against us.

We finally moved in on January 2, 1968, mercifully without incident. Some of our white neighbors did stop and squint hard at us as we moved in our furniture, and one of them even walked over to volunteer that a few weeks before, Willie Mays, the legend of baseball, had been rejected from purchasing a residence just around the corner. My husband harrumphed curtly and carried the crate of kitchen utensils he was holding into the house. "What was she trying to say?" he complained to me, once inside. "Did she even realize I'm not the moving man and you're not the maid?"

It made us somewhat uncomfortable that the title transfer had still not been finalized, but at least we had now heard from the bank and the process was moving forward. However, in my estimation, the transfer fee was unusually large. By this time, the minister at the Methodist church that Price and I regularly attended had told me of an organization in San Francisco called M-REIT, which stood for Mutual Real Estate Investment Trust. Founded by the successful real estate developer and devoted integrationist Morris Milgram, the organization secured investors to go into all-white neighborhoods where minority home ownership was systematically blocked. These investors would purchase homes and apartment complexes and subsequently rent or sell the homes without regard to race, religion or creed, thereby quietly integrating neighborhoods where de facto segregation had previously existed. In essence, they were doing exactly what Louis and I had done, but they had formalized the arrangement, and they had money and influence behind them. I was thrilled to learn of the existence of such a group, and I immediately bought shares in the organization and became a member.

One of the leaders of the group, Fortney Stark, agreed with me that the title transfer fee the bank had levied on the Clay Street house was excessive. "Don't pay it!" he advised. "You go down to that bank and you threaten them with every civil rights organization you can think of—the NAACP, the Urban League—"

"SCLC," I added, referring to the Southern Christian Leadership Conference founded by Dr. King.

"Absolutely," he said. "But whatever you do, don't pay it!"

Price grumbled that this was an easy position for a white man to take, but it might not work quite as well for black people. Nevertheless, we made an appointment for Friday, March 29, 1968, and went down to the savings institution that held the title. The loan officer was a young white man who looked as if he was barely out of college. He had previously lived in Columbus, Ohio, and had done courses at Ohio State, so we began by making light conversation about our mutual experiences there. Then, with no warning, he remarked, "You used subterfuge to buy that house. Don't you know that is no way to buy a house? Why didn't you come to me?"

Price was quiet, bristling with attentiveness.

"How would I know that you would be any different from all the others who did not want us to have that house?" I said.

The loan officer shuffled through the title papers in front of him and didn't respond to my question. "This is the savings branch of our bank," he said after a while. "We don't handle loans and mortgages. That branch is in San Jose. You'll have to take these papers and go down there to take care of this title change on your loan."

"We thought you were the loan office," I said. "The appointment letter originated from this address."

Price had been totally silent during our meeting. Now, for the first time, he spoke. "Look, this isn't reasonable," he said. "She's a physician and her time is just as valuable as yours. If she has to waste time going down to San Jose, why can't you pick up the phone and make an appointment for her and make sure that all the paperwork will be in order when we get there?" The loan officer shifted uncomfortably. My husband kept going. "You know, I'm a retired World War II colonel. I flew missions over Italy and Sicily during the war. But a black soldier still can't come back to this country and buy a house for his family, can he?"

The bank officer's face and ears turned beefy red. His voice was tight as he excused himself to make a phone call from another office. After several minutes, he returned to us, saying he had contacted the loan office in San Jose. We would hear from them shortly and need take no further action regarding the title transfer until we received written communication from San Jose. He added that he had also talked to them about reducing the title transfer fee, and he believed we would find all was to our liking when we went there to sign the final papers.

We thanked him and got up to leave. But then I had an idea and sat back down. I wanted to tell him about M-REIT, and to help him understand that our experience in buying a house was not an isolated incident, that too often black people faced similar obstacles when they sought to purchase a home. I explained to him that M-REIT had been organized around this problem, and I invited him to come to one of our seminars, which Price and I happened to be hosting at our home on Clay Street in one week. I explained that Morris Milgram, president of M-REIT, who was known for building and managing multiracial housing complexes all over the country, would conduct the seminar.

I handed him a flyer that further explained the program, and I shared with him that in 1963, President John F. Kennedy had commissioned Morris Milgram's investment group to buy up 633 housing units in the Washington, DC, area so that non-white diplomats would be able to find housing.[89] I was trying to make the point that what had happened to Price and me was happening all across the country, and that even highly distinguished diplomats faced the same difficulty in finding housing if they happened not to be white.

I didn't add that the damage caused by these discriminatory housing practices rippled down through generations, resulting in an ever-widening wealth gap between white and black families. That year, for example, affluent black homeowners' potential property values averaged only $50,000, compared to $105,000 for well-heeled white homeowners and $56,000 for poor whites.[90] In other words, when black people who could afford to buy in high-value neighborhoods were instead steered to homes in lower-value neighborhoods, their children reaped a lesser return on their investment, resulting in less generational wealth than their white counterparts.

"Why don't you come and hear what Mr. Milgram has to say?" I suggested to the loan officer enthusiastically. "Be a part of the solution."

But the bank officer said he had an out-of-town meeting on the date of our seminar and would be unable to attend.

One week later, on Thursday, April 4, 1968, the world suffered a shattering loss. Dr. Martin Luther King Jr. was assassinated. In Memphis, Tennessee, a shooter's bullet had pierced the preacher's neck, ending his life at the age of 39.

I was at work at Kaiser when the news came over the airwaves. Doctors, nurses, patients, administrators, everyone stopped what they were doing, in shock. I felt utterly destroyed; tears rolled down my face. Throughout the clinic, people were hugging each other and crying, all too aware that the violence that had stilled the heart and silenced the voice of the prince of non-violence had deprived America of an irreplaceable anchor. Dr. King had represented the greatest hope of our nation, not just for blacks but also for many whites. His stirring speeches and leadership of boycotts, protest marches, lunch counter sit-ins and voter registration drives had led to groundbreaking advances like the Civil Rights Act of 1964, which ended segregation in public spaces and banned job discrimination based on race, gender, religion or national origin, and the Voting Rights Act of 1965, which dismantled poll taxes and other unfair practices that had effectively barred blacks from the vote.[91]

That night, Price and I watched newsreel footage of mostly black rioters looting and burning down neighborhoods in cities across the nation. It seemed the entire country had gone up in flames, as people vented their anger, sorrow and despair at the murder of Dr. King. I knew this violence was the opposite of what the great man would have wanted. I remembered when Price and I had gone to hear him speak at GLIDE Memorial Church in San Francisco's Tenderloin district the year before. Dr. King had talked of forming a coalition of the disenfranchised, with poor blacks and poor whites, women and gay people and conscientious objectors all joining forces to fight against poverty, joblessness, sexism and homophobia, and to oppose the Vietnam War. I could only imagine the bridges that Dr. King might have constructed to a more just future, if only he had lived.

The next day, a Friday, I remained at home. At six that evening, we were scheduled to host the M-REIT seminar with Morris Milgram in our living room. I was in anguish, feeling sorry for myself and for our country. There were moments when it all seemed like a terrible dream, as if the assassination had not actually happened, and Dr. King was still with us, but in the next moment, I knew that the deadly aim of the sniper's bullet had robbed us of a portion of our humanity. In the midst of these ruminations, the phone rang: It was the loan officer with whom we had met the previous week. He began by expressing his condolences over Dr. King's assassination, then he told me that he really did have a previously scheduled out-of-town meeting and so would be unable to attend our M-REIT seminar that evening. However, he had asked one of his bank's associates to represent him.

That evening, when the seminar led by Morris Milgram convened, the bank officer's associate did indeed attend.

Less than a week later, on April 11, 1968, President Lyndon B. Johnson signed into law the Civil Rights Act of 1968, which prohibited discrimination based on race, religion, gender or national origin in the sale, rental and financing of any real estate.[92] This law, also known as the Fair Housing Act, was widely considered to be Dr. King's last, great legislative victory.

Inspired by the passage of the law, I was more determined than ever to help carry forward the work of M-REIT. I had not marched at Selma. I had not been on the National Mall in Washington when Dr. King had told us about his dream. I had not sat in at any lunch counters down South, nor registered a single person other than myself to vote. But I could do this. I could give my whole heart to breaking down the barriers faced by people of color when it came to finding and purchasing fair housing. Real estate, I decided, would be the frontier on which I would continue the good fight that Dr. King had started.

As I wrote in my annual Christmas letter to family and friends that year, "Surely the urgency to free all people from the ills of communicable disease, cancer, heart disease, is no greater than the urgency to free all people from the ills of segregated housing. Bad housing deteriorates society just as disease deteriorates the human body. We do not reserve the use of new antibiotics, vaccines and other medical discoveries for a special group of citizens; in the same way, we cannot preserve good housing for a special group without demoralizing all groups in a democracy. M-REIT's investors believe the privilege of open housing is profitable and right and imperative for our country. We're going to work, and work vigorously, toward that end."

Not long after, I began serving on M-REIT's board, and ultimately became co-chair of the Northern California branch of the organization. It seemed fitting that protecting the ability of the disenfranchised to acquire property, and therefore generational wealth, was the battle I had chosen, especially considering where my story had begun—with two brothers from West Africa, James and York Simmons, staking their claim as American landowners at the end of the Underground Railroad.

In 1976, I joined my brother, Lawrence, sister Rowena, niece Varian and her husband, Larry, for a family reunion in Mount Vernon.

CHAPTER 24

The Wide World

The Bay Area, as it turned out, would become my last home. Since leaving Mount Vernon in 1937 to attend nursing school at Hampton, I had lived in eleven different cities, relocating every few years in pursuit of a moving target—life as a fully trained and practicing physician. I had been among the first eight nurses chosen to integrate the U.S. armed forces; I had become the first black woman to live on campus at Ohio State; I was the first black woman physician to specialize in asthma, allergy and immunology in the nation; and I had become the first African American female doctor to join the Kaiser Foundation Hospital staff, where I would later help found the Kaiser African-American Professionals Association (KAAPA). I would also serve on the admissions committee of the University of California, Davis School of Medicine as the program retooled its admittance protocol in the years after Allan Bakke—a white applicant who had twice been denied admission—challenged the school's affirmative action minority quotas all the way to the Supreme Court.

Bakke, an engineer and former Marine, argued that he was better qualified than some of the applicants who had been admitted under a 16-seat quota for minorities. In 1978, Bakke, who was in his late thirties by then, won his case, and admission to Davis. But his victory was ambiguous, because the Supreme Court simultaneously upheld the right of colleges and universities to consider race as one of several factors in determining admission. Specific quotas, however, were ruled impermissible.

My initial fear that the Bakke decision would have an adverse effect on minorities being admitted to medical school would turn out to be unfounded: Ten years after the landmark Supreme Court case, the number of blacks enrolled in medical schools across the country was holding steady at 6 percent, the same as it had been when Bakke first filed his lawsuit.[93] But while there had been no reversal in numbers of blacks entering the medical profession, we were still woefully underrepresented. When I accepted a position on the admissions committee of UC Davis Medical School, I confess that my main agenda was to help facilitate the admission of students like me, for whom medicine was a passion and a calling, a desire that could not be extinguished by all the social and economic obstacles that America might throw in their path.

Less visibly, I had become the first black person to purchase a home in the exclusively white area of Presidio Heights, with former Black Panther associate and San Francisco State University professor Angela Davis and her husband Hilton Braithwaite buying a few years later at the other end of the neighborhood. I ran into Hilton on the street one weekend, and we greeted each other as comrades in the struggle: "You integrate the neighborhood from your end and we'll integrate it from our end," he said to me, laughing.

It's worth noting that twenty years after I moved into that house on Clay Street, when I fell ill briefly, my neighbors who had once so resisted my presence rang my doorbell constantly with pots of soup and just-baked casseroles. Through years of exposure, we had come to know one another as individuals beyond the color of our skin, and we had forged more than a truce. Some of us had developed true understanding, which one might argue has always been the goal and the promise of integration.

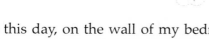

To this day, on the wall of my bedroom, hung over my bed, is a signed, framed lithograph of the Norman Rockwell painting, *The Problem We All Live With*. Escorted by four federal marshals, the brave little brown schoolgirl with her crisp white dress and sweetly braided, silk-ribboned hair, spoke to me from the very first moment I laid eyes on her in the window of a downtown art gallery. I had just moved to the Bay Area, having won the position at Kaiser, and that little girl in the painting embodied all it had taken for me to get there. Just looking at her proud bearing and determined stride would forever after give me the courage to face whatever challenges or sorrows might come my way. And there would be many.

First, my mother died on February 9, 1969, two weeks before her eightieth birthday. I had dreamed of her and my brother Lawrence and his wife Isabelle visiting me in California, but it was not to be. Ella died of a heart attack in her sleep at 6:15 A.M. on a bitter-cold Friday morning. As I viewed her exquisitely peaceful countenance at the funeral home later that week, the full tragedy of her eight decades of life came home to me. I saw so clearly how beautiful and brilliant she had been, and how racism had thwarted her ambitions, so that her vast potential had finally withered inside her, and she had devoted herself instead to the achievements of her children while growing bitter and disillusioned with her husband. I realized that I had spent my entire life trying to make her proud, and yet, other than my graduation from Hampton Institute back in 1949, when she had danced in the aisle, I was never quite sure that I had succeeded. Standing at her gravesite with the rest of the family, I silently thanked Ella Sophia Cooper Simmons for the fire of ambition she had ignited in my young heart, a fire that was burning still.

The year 1973 was also particularly painful. In the winter of that year, Price's ex-wife Harriett, the mother of my four cherished stepdaughters, took her own life in Denver. Six years earlier, Harriett had been diagnosed with breast cancer and had undergone a radical mastectomy. The surgery had left her horrifically scarred; always a beautiful woman, she now felt maimed and broken beyond recognizing herself. Soon after, she was diagnosed with clinical depression. Later, as her mood swings grew more extreme and manic, the diagnosis became bipolar disease.

There were years when Harriett rallied. When her two youngest, Daphne and Debra, were 17 and 15 and both still living at home, she took them on an extended tour of several African countries. The travelers had returned home in good spirits, and for a while, the crisis of Harriett's spiraling depression seemed to ease. Her medication seemed to be working, and everyone exhaled. But in 1972, while teaching African American studies at East High School in Denver, she suffered a complete breakdown and was briefly hospitalized. She was beyond exhausted, she'd told her principal one afternoon on the school stairs. She felt wretched and unable to manage anymore.

The following year Debra, who had recently turned 18, started her freshman year at Brown University, leaving her older sister Daphne, 21, at home with their mother. Daphne had completed community college and was working for a department store in town. Their sister Diana, 26, was also living and working in Denver, but she had moved into her own apartment. Delabian, 29, was already married and pursuing her master's in urban planning at George Washington University in DC.

On the evening of February 21, 1973, Daphne went out to a movie with friends. She came home to find her mother's light still on, but the house was eerily quiet. She looked in on Harriett, who appeared to be propped up in bed sleeping, a book held loosely in her hands. Daphne took the book from her mother, placed it on the bedside table, turned out the light and went to get herself ready for bed. But something didn't feel right. Something about Harriett's stillness frightened her, so she went back to look in on her mother. She tried to wake Harriett but couldn't. She watched for the rise and fall of her chest, noticing that her breaths were shallow and infrequent. Realizing that something was terribly wrong, she called her sister Diana, who told her to call the family physician. Dr. Gibson sent an ambulance immediately, but it went to the wrong house. By the time the ambulance got to the right location, Diana had arrived, and the two girls traveled with their unconscious mother to the hospital. There, doctors revived Harriett briefly, but she slipped back into a coma almost immediately and died the next morning.

The autopsy showed that Harriett had apparently taken an overdose of prescription medications, Darvon and Demerol, then climbed into bed and waited to die. Price wept for his daughters, and also for Harriett, who had never stopped hoping they would one day be reunited. How cruel that the girls should lose their mother, especially in this way. Price wanted to close ranks. He suggested that I stay behind in San Francisco while he went to Denver alone; he thought my absence would be easier on Harriett's family. But his four girls called me the evening he arrived and asked me to come and be with them, and to sit with them in the church at Harriett's funeral. I caught the next flight to Denver, but I have always wondered whether that was a mistake. At the funeral, when I walked into the church with Price, I felt the eyes of Harriett's family members and friends boring into me, and I couldn't help wondering if perhaps I should not have come at all. But I had wanted to be there for Price, and for his and Harriett's four heartbroken girls, who would carry this sorrow forever.

This difficult time was further complicated by the fact that Price and I were not doing very well as a couple. We hadn't really told anyone, but it had been clear to both of us for some time that our marriage was no longer working. Price's drinking had grown worse; by the early '70s, he was downing highballs at lunchtime and was usually in a surly mood come dinnertime, with the two of us squabbling endlessly. I maintained he was an alcoholic and needed to stop drinking altogether; he maintained that I was just being overdramatic and would I please get off his case.

To make matters worse, he had been diagnosed with diabetes and cardiac trouble, but he routinely flaunted his doctor's treatment recommendations, with the result that I needled him endlessly to take his medication and to stop consuming alcohol and sugary foods. I hated the nagging, complaining woman I was turning into, and I hated when my husband's moods turned mean. I also strongly suspected that Price had been unfaithful, because when he drank, his inhibitions came tumbling down, and he would flirt outrageously with any woman in the room. Oh, he was a terrible flirt. It had charmed me once, but now it only annoyed and humiliated me.

I clearly remember the last straw. It was Thanksgiving of 1975, and we had invited company to join us; we still sometimes tried to pull off these social occasions with friends. At the start of the meal, as I was dishing out plates, Price became angry at me for some reason—what exactly I had said or done, I cannot recall, but he obviously felt I was acting high and mighty, and he meant to cut me down a notch. I was wearing a hairpiece that day, and without warning my husband reached over and snatched it off my head, right there in the midst of our guests. Delabian was visiting us at the time, and she gasped with dismay at her father's drunken behavior. Wanting to spare her further embarrassment, I merely took the hairpiece from my husband's hands, repositioned it on my head, and did as I had heard my father do countless times with my mother—"Oh, Price," I said mildly, "just stop." And I went on serving the meal.

But I had had enough, and when he was sober the next morning, Price understood as well as I did just how badly things had broken down.

I filed for divorce the following February, asking one of my patients, an attorney, to handle the proceedings. Like so many of my regular patients, he had become a dear friend, and I trusted his discretion. The final judgment was issued in January 1977. Soon after that, Price moved out of our house on Clay Street and in with another woman. Despite the woman's claim to be a lesbian, I am quite sure she and Price had a physical relationship, and perhaps it had begun while we were still married. I didn't know, and at that point, I no longer cared. It wasn't that I wished Price ill; I still believed that at his core he was a decent man, a good father and a heroic soldier. In truth, I was glad someone else was there to make sure he didn't destroy his health entirely.

I cared more about maintaining a close relationship with my stepdaughters. They knew their father's drinking had gotten out of hand, and they knew of his flirtatiousness with other women, so I hoped they would understand my decision to leave the marriage. Thankfully, shortly after the divorce was final, Delabian sat me down to say that while I had divorced their father, I would never be allowed to divorce his daughters. She cannot know how those words lightened my heart.

Around the time I began to realize that Price and I weren't going to make it to happily ever after, I started thinking seriously about providing for myself in retirement. I had four stepdaughters and several nieces and nephews, many of whom I was close to, but I had no natural-born children, which made me very conscious of the need to secure myself financially. By this time I had been involved with M-REIT for some years and had a good sense of the factors affecting real estate in the Bay Area, but I needed to master the nuts and bolts of personal investment. I enrolled in a semester-long evening course at San Francisco State called Profitable Real Estate Investing, which emphasized that buying real estate is all about timing and location. Fortunately, one of my patients, a state employee by the name of Arthur Goldberg, was a real estate investor on the side, and he was able to help me identify some promising properties.

During this time, I worked with the same loan officer who'd helped us get our Clay Street title change. Through him, I got approved for a series of mortgages, but I held off on buying until after my divorce was final, because I didn't want Price to automatically become half-owner of everything. The day after the divorce decree came through, I put my plan into motion, making offers and following through on purchasing two investment properties in San Francisco, one in Sonoma Valley, one in Palm Desert and one in Lake Tahoe. My life's second act as a real estate investor had officially begun.

The '70s and '80s were a busy time for me, filled with medical conferences, the buying, selling and management of multiple properties, and a regular rotation of houseguests, some of whom moved in for weeks at a time. Most of my guests were family members, like my grandnephew Jeff Jackson, who lived on my top floor during his final year of high school after his mother Cheri asked me to help get him away from LA. They didn't live in a great neighborhood, and Cheri was concerned about some of Jeff's friends. I put the boy in private school in San Francisco and tried to talk to him about where he was going with his life. At the time, I didn't think I was making a dent, and at the end of the year,

I sent him back to his mother. But something clicked, because Jeff straightened himself out and married a lovely young woman, and they now live in South Carolina and have four bright girls.

My niece Varian Wilson and her family also visited frequently, and I grew particularly fond of my grandniece Shawna, an inquisitive child with a spark of ambition that reminded me of myself. I used to take Shawna to medical conferences with me, hoping she would feel the call of medicine, but Shawna went into business instead. She did follow in my footsteps in one way, however: She did her undergraduate years at Ohio State University, and even lived in Baker Hall, the same dorm I had integrated more than four decades before.

I loved it when my family and friends were in town, and I think Louis Chardon and his partner Darrel Ozenbaugh got as much of a thrill from showing my relatives a good time as I did. Darrel, unlike Louis, was tall and stocky, his dark hair thinning, while Louis, for all the years I knew him, had a gleaming silver-white mane. Louis and Darrel's dinner parties continued to be fabulous and sought-after events. Darrel loved to cook, and he had a state of the art kitchen in which to create his magnificent meals. My grandniece Shawna thoroughly enjoyed these occasions. After earning an M.B.A. from Northwestern University's J.L. Kellogg Graduate School of Management, she had moved out West, and she visited me often in the Bay Area. Shawna had grown up to be a beautiful young lady, poised and soft-spoken, with a laser-like intelligence and an organizational gift that in later years would lead me to make her my trustee and power of attorney. Shawna was loyal yet clear-sighted, and I did not hesitate to put my business in her hands.

Louis and Darrel were also very fond of my grandniece. Shawna was an animal lover, and Louis had a lot of animals— several goats and a Russian wolfhound named Princessa; Darrel told me that every dog Louis ever had, he named Princessa. I remember Shawna's dog, Abercrombie, an Airedale-Irish wolfhound mix, used to jump into Louis and Darrel's fountain and try to smash the foam bubbles. Shawna couldn't quite believe how easygoing her hosts were about that. Shawna also enjoyed the pomp and circumstance that was second nature in Louis' world— the massive French antique furniture, the sixty-foot-long ballroom-sized living room, the stone fireplace in the den where everyone sank into plush leather couches and sipped after-dinner liqueurs. She never tired of the classical music playing through speakers in every room of the house, nor the wall of windows that looked out over the pool and hundreds of rose bushes to a breathtaking view of the hills of San Francisco below us. Coming from Ohio, Shawna had never had a steak that wasn't well done, nor tasted an avocado, nor dined with such a varied and eclectic mix of people as she was exposed to in Louis and Darrel's home. Louis, of course, was the chief eccentric, holding court during dinner, then standing up unceremoniously at some point in the evening and bidding everyone a good night. He would then disappear to bed and leave Darrel to fulfill the rest of the evening's social obligations.

During one period, Louis and I had a falling out. Louis was a functional alcoholic and would make outrageous and sometimes offensive statements when inebriated. After my divorce from Price, I had little tolerance for it. We soon reconciled, even though Louis never did quit the bottle. But even when Louis and I weren't on speaking terms, Shawna still went to visit him and Darrel whenever she was in town.

In our enduring camaraderie, Louis was a soulmate, and our friendship would last a lifetime. We did bicker sometimes, but our bond would prove resilient. Louis would later ask me to legally witness his last will and testament, just as I would ask him to legally witness mine, the two of us depositing copies with each other for safekeeping. Louis, Darrel and I even traveled the world together, taking trips, sometimes with other friends, to China, Russia, Brazil, Jamaica, Argentina and Italy. I can still see us, bags in hand, artwork and other artifacts we had acquired tucked under our arms as we rushed to catch the bus, the train, a taxi, the plane. I enjoyed these travels with my friends, but it was the excursions to Africa—to Addis Ababa in Ethiopia, Johannesburg in South Africa, Monrovia in Liberia, Tanzania, Zimbabwe, Kenya, Ghana—organized by the Howard University medical school alumni association during the '70s and '80s, that would affect me most profoundly.

I remember in Addis Ababa we visited Emperor Haile Selassie in his mansion. There were about eighty of us, black physicians from the United States and South America, and Haile Selassie shook hands with every one before sitting down to a meal with us. He had two little dogs that traveled with him always, and his aides would offer them a taste of every dish before offering it to the emperor. If the dogs wouldn't eat it, Haile Selassie wouldn't eat it. As I recall, he ate heartily with us that day.

It was on these trips that I began my collection of African art. I quietly pledged never to visit any country in Africa without bringing home a piece of artwork or some meaningful artifact of the place. For me, these works expressed my pride in being black, and I wanted evidence of the pleasure I took in my racial heritage adorning my home. I also wanted to support African artists financially, but sometimes they wouldn't take my money. I have an ivory piece that I acquired from an 82-year-old carver in Zimbabwe, for example. I was walking down a street early one morning, and I saw him carving this piece, an abstract circular shape, with exquisite geometric details. I asked him what it was, and he told me that it was whatever I saw. I fell in love with the piece and asked the ivory carver how much to purchase it. He told me it would be an honor to have a piece of his art go to America, and there would be no charge. I argued with him at length, but he refused to take anything. I hand-carried that heavy piece of sculpture back to San Francisco and put it on a pedestal in a place of honor in my library.

The wooden carvings and ivory and stone pieces I found in Africa immersed me in the history of my ancestors, the chieftain and his family who went aboard a slaving vessel to trade their carvings of ivory and wood. Somehow, when I touched those pieces of art, I felt connected to the Gold Coast princes who became the root of the Simmons family in America. It was a deeply emotional experience, as if, standing on the African continent, I was discovering some lost portion of myself for the first time. I was not alone in this feeling; my fellow travelers, the physicians who like me had graduated from Howard medical school, experienced it too. It was a homecoming, a reintegration of the black self, born of a sense of pride and wonderment at the richness of our culture, which white America had so ruthlessly tried to misappropriate or erase.

Until I visited Africa, I did not begin to fathom the depth and breadth of what was taken from us. For survival, we became accommodated to our lives in the New World, and adopted the cultural norms of a white world. And so when I traveled to the People's Republic of China with white friends, I chose not to be offended when children followed me through the streets, touching my skin to see if the brown color rubbed off, and wanting to hear me speak to see if I spoke in a human tongue like my white companions. When my friends asked me how I managed to remain unruffled, I pointed out that black people experienced such things in America all the time. Another time, when I was walking through a hotel lobby in Saint Petersburg, Russia, with Louis, he remarked that every eye was upon me, and yet I seemed unconcerned, as if unaware that I was being so intently watched. I laughed and reminded him that for much of my life I had been the only black person in the room. I was used to the white gaze. Saint Petersburg felt not much different from my life back in America.

Africa, on the other hand, had been a revelation. In every African country I visited, I felt completely at home. Everywhere I looked, I saw my people, and they embraced me as a daughter who had at long last returned. It filled a place in my soul that I had not known had been so starved. And when at the end of my first trip to Monrovia, Liberia, I told a young clerk at the hotel front desk that I was checking out and going home, he corrected me gently: "You are already home, Dr. Simmons. You belong to us. We only loaned you to America."

With my grandniece Shawna Wilson, I traveled to Washington, DC, to attend the 2008 inauguration of the nation's first black president.

Chapter 25

"That Day Will Come"

In 1989, after two-and-a-half decades as a specialist in asthma, allergy and immunology with Kaiser Permanente Medical Group, I retired from active service. I was 71 years old, a three-mile-a-day walker, and I was not about to go quietly into the good night: I had arranged a post-retirement position as an allergist at Martin Luther King Family Health Center in Riverside, California, where I treated uninsured and under-insured patients, most of them African American. But I knew I needed more.

One afternoon, while I was out walking with my cockapoo, King Tut, I ran into an old colleague from Kaiser, a physician like myself, also retired. He told me he was on his way home from classes at the University of San Francisco, where he had enrolled in the Fromm Institute for Lifelong Learning. He was studying the history of Russian opera in one class, and learning about the aesthetics of Bay Area architecture in another. As he spoke about the eight-week college-level program, I saw how lit up he was, how the years fell away from his features.

I questioned him closely about the program, which he explained had been founded in 1976 by California vintners Alfred and Hanna Fromm to provide intellectual stimulation to retirees age 50 and over. The Fromms, both of whom had come to America fleeing the rise of Nazism in Europe, wanted to express appreciation for their adopted country, where they had been able to regain status and wealth as California winemakers. The Fromm Institute was their way of giving back to the country that had embraced them. "The body might wear out," Hanna Fromm liked to say about the elderly, "but their minds will never rust away."

The peer-learning model had been the brainchild of her husband, Alfred Fromm. It had been inspired by a question

Hanna had put to him one day in the early 1970s. "What would you do if you had to retire?" she had asked, to which her husband had replied, "I hope never to retire, but if I have to, I would like to go back to the university and study all the things I never had time for; but I don't want to study with my grandchildren, nor do I want to be taught by professors who could be grandchildren of mine, but by people my own age group who have had much the same life experiences."

I was intrigued. I understood at once that lifelong learning was exactly what I had been seeking, although I hadn't known it consciously before. My own passionate engagement with the Fromm Institute began the very next day. I went down to the University of San Francisco and enrolled myself for the next semester in a creative writing seminar and a class titled "Freedom, Democracy and Responsibility." From that day forward, my so-called golden years never again felt anything less than intellectually rich and purposeful. There was such a bounty of courses offered at the institute, classes with titles like "The Shakespearean Festival," "Visions of Heaven and Hell," "Why Good People Hate Each Other" and "Maintaining Independence as You Age." There were no tests, grades, course credits or homework, just lively exchanges and shared learning between the retired university professors who taught the classes and the thousand or so retirees enrolled at USF. The ninety-minute classes began at ten in the morning and ended by three in the afternoon and were held Monday through Thursday. Daily, I interacted with men and women who had led the most fascinating lives and who were now at the Fromm Institute simply for a revitalized life of the mind, and the invigorating access to the larger world provided by lifelong scholarship.

Adult learning programs were the key to a fulfilling retirement, I realized, and I immediately wanted to start such a program at my beloved alma mater, Hampton University. I called the school's president, Dr. William R. Harvey, and discovered not only was there no adult learning program at Hampton, but none existed on any HBCU campus at the time. It seemed to me a significant oversight, because there was a large retired population in the Tidewater area where the Hampton campus was located, not to mention a generation of baby boomers who would soon comprise the largest group of retirees in history. And so I resolved to work with the Fromm Institute to bring the first lifelong learning program to Hampton and by extension to the HBCU community.

With this goal in mind, I approached Hanna Fromm after class one day. As the executive director of the institute, she often sat quietly at the back of the classroom in her classic Chanel suits, a gracious and dignified woman, soaking up the instruction along with the rest of us. Her husband had passed away by this time, and she was running the institute, the first of its kind, with the help of program director Robert Fordham. When I explained my plan to establish an adult learning center at Hampton, they were enthusiastic. Hanna at once offered to put me in touch with Mary Bitterman, then president of the Bernard Osher Foundation, which was looking to expand its Osher Lifelong Learning Institute (OLLI) model to campuses across the country.

The Osher Foundation was fully on board with the idea of bringing its program to Hampton University. In 2005 it awarded a $100,000 first-year operating grant to establish an OLLI center on the campus, with a full academic curriculum serving retired citizens of Hampton Roads who were 50 and older. Just two years later, the center had become so successful that it was named the winner of the Association for Continuing Higher Education's Older Adult Model Program, making Hampton's OLLI eligible for a permanent million-dollar endowment from the Bernard Osher Foundation. I was both ecstatic and humbled by this achievement, which I felt was as monumental a triumph as that of a Negro girl born in 1918 in a rural Ohio town growing up to become the nation's first black female allergist.

But even as I continued to push the intellectual and artistic boundaries of my own life outward through my involvement with lifelong learning, I had reached the point where my circle of family and friends began to shrink before my eyes. In those pre- and post-retirement years, I experienced one devastating loss after the other. My sister Rowena, at age 70, had succumbed to multiple myeloma in August 1979. I had flown from the Bay Area to be with her at Grant Hospital in Columbus, and I was at her side, her hand clasped in mine as she took her last breath. My ex-husband Price, with whom I had remained on friendly terms, would die of complications from diabetes in 1999. My sister Georgeanna followed, suffering congestive heart failure in 2005. She was 95. My dear friend and colleague Louis also passed away that year from a brain aneurysm.

It seemed that every year, and then every month, and then every week, I received news of another death, classmates at Hampton and Howard, friends from Detroit, Denver and Washington, and my first ex-husband, John, whose passing I learned of from a notation in the obits section of Ohio State University's alumni magazine. I had not seen him since the night, some years before, when he had shown up at my door out of the blue, just as I was headed out to dinner with my niece, Varian, and her family. John—who was living in Folsom with the German man who had been his housemate on and off for decades—joined us for dinner that evening. Varian believed he was trying to rekindle our friendship, but I had no interest in rehashing the past with him. Still, he had been such an important part of my young life, and I mourned his loss.

I was grateful that my brother achieved some longevity, although Lawrence often complained that he'd lived too long, because his wife Isabelle and all of his friends were gone. He died on May 12, 2011, on the first day he entered hospice. He'd been "traveling" in the weeks before, and had told his daughter Varian that his help was needed "on the other side." Varian knew then that his time was close, and she called her daughters to come and see their grandfather one last time.

I am now, at age 97, the last surviving child of Gus and Ella

Simmons. I have been afforded the rare privilege of bearing witness to almost a century of American history crystallized through the experience of one whose life's deepest yearning had always been to practice medicine, and who despite the almost overwhelming barriers of race, gender and economics, saw every door she endeavored to walk through, finally opened wide.

In the span of my lifetime, I would also see my father's most outrageous prediction come to pass, with Barack Obama being elected the nation's first African American president on November 4, 2008. What a momentous night that was! I was 90 years old by then, and a less-than-successful right knee replacement two years earlier had slowed me down a bit, forcing me to rely on a rolling walker. Nevertheless, I was determined to be on the National Mall to witness President-elect Obama take the oath of office the following January. I will be forever grateful to my grandniece Shawna, then living in Dallas and working as a regional vice president at PepsiCo, for making it possible for me to stand in the presence of history being made.

Months before Barack Hussein Obama was elected as the nation's 44th president, Shawna had booked flights to Washington for inauguration week, and reserved hotel rooms at the Marriott Hotel in Dupont Circle. She was convinced that whoever won the Democratic nomination—Barack Obama or Hillary Clinton—would win the general election, which meant the inauguration would be epic, with the nation swearing in either the first black president or the first woman president. Shawna made sure we would have a room in the city for the event.

The whole year before, I had followed the presidential campaign with my jaw hanging open, unable to believe that an African American might actually be installed as commander-in-chief in my lifetime. Every time I heard the Democratic senator from Illinois chant, "Yes, we can!" I felt a shiver of certainty, an insistent whisper that this seemingly impossible achievement was to be his destiny. The night Obama won his decisive victory—winning twenty-eight states with 53 percent of the popular vote and a 7.2 percent margin of victory over the Republican contender, John McCain[94]—I was in the bedroom of my apartment at Lake Park Retirement Residence in Oakland. I had recently moved there after family members became concerned about how I was managing alone in my house on Clay Street.

I had been reluctant to leave my beloved home on Clay Street, but after my knee surgery, I'd suffered a couple of falls. Then my dog, King Tut, died in 2007, and the house was suddenly silent and cavernous. I finally allowed myself to be convinced that the upkeep of a four-story semi-Victorian might be too much for me. And so, I had agreed to sell my home and move to assisted living at Lake Park, where I would take my meals in a communal dining room, attend piano recitals and church services right on the premises, walk down the hallway to the hair salon, do daily yoga and ride a stationary bike in an exercise studio right upstairs, and enjoy the company of neighbors who were at the same stage of life as I was.

That night, as Barack Obama gave his soul-stirring acceptance speech from Grant Park in Chicago, I was watching from my bed, the light from the television flickering against the walls of my otherwise dark room. It was after midnight, long past my bedtime, but I could not turn away from the jubilant celebration unfolding on my TV screen. Since I couldn't shout my own joy from the very rooftops, I just kept repeating in an awed whisper, "My father told me this day would come. My father told me. My father told me."

The next day, Shawna swung into action on a mission to get tickets for the actual inauguration, which was to be held on January 20, 2009. It wasn't easy. Everyone in the whole world wanted to be there on the National Mall to witness the swearing in of the nation's first black president. But my grandniece was resourceful: She secured two purple tickets from an associate who was the head of security at her company, a man who had previously worked for the Secret Service, and then another colleague got her two yellow tickets from the law firm in Washington where she had worked before joining PepsiCo. Apparently the yellow tickets would put us even closer to the action than the purple tickets. We were set.

Shawna rented me a wheelchair for the day itself, even though I tried to insist I could get there on my own two feet with the help of my rolling walker. She refused to indulge me. "Aunt Ellamae, you have no idea how far we're going to have to walk," she said. "And the crowd is going to be insane." I let her boss me around a bit, because after all, she was the one making all the arrangements. She also went out and bought me a black one-piece zip-up snow suit, the kind you might see little children wearing to grade school. To complete the ensemble she added a white puffy jacket, a black wool hat, matching mittens, a scarf and furry snow boots. It was no use trying to object. The weather report called for below-freezing temperatures, and Shawna did not intend for me to meet the East Coast winter in my thin Bay Area overcoat. And so there I was, bundled up like a compliant preschooler in my rented wheelchair. I grumbled aloud that my niece was going overboard. I did not yet have a clue how grateful I would be for every layer of clothing that day.

The trek to the mall proved to be a major undertaking. We started out at four in the morning, because we knew the lines would be long. Shawna pushed my wheelchair through the pre-dawn cold and, with the help friends to whom she had given the purple tickets, she literally carried me down onto the Metro-rail Station platform. There, a reporter from NPR interviewed us: a young African American corporate vice president bringing her 90-year-old great-aunt to see the inauguration of the nation's first black commander-in-chief. I imagine there were thousands of such stories that day. Some two million people flocked to the mall for the swearing-in, the largest crowd ever assembled for any public event in the history of Washington, D.C., and the largest attendance of any inauguration of an American president ever.[95]

Shawna and I had to find our way through that throng to get to our seats in the yellow section, an endeavor that would prove ferociously challenging despite our pre-dawn departure.

Shawna had some trouble maneuvering the wheelchair onto the train, and then back out of the station, and over rough patches of ground, but at every pass, people would step up and help: A woman showed her how to tip the chair back a little to get me onto the train; a group of young men picked up my chair and carried me out of the station. Another man helped Shawna get me across a crowded, rubbly intersection and then finally, we were on the grassy mall. The yellow-ticket line seemed to stretch for miles, despite the early hour. Daylight was only just beginning to streak the far edge of the sky as we found our place in line and began inching forward. But because I was low to the ground in my wheelchair, from a distance it looked as if there was a gap in the crowd right in front of Shawna, and so people kept making for that spot to cross to the other side of the mall. Again and again I was jostled as people kept running into my wheelchair.

And then, a lovely thing happened. A nearby group of young women saw that I was getting bumped and shoved and they spontaneously surrounded me. They formed a tight circle, creating a human barrier against the pressing crowd. In their midst, Shawna and I moved forward slowly, protected by these radiant young women, who identified themselves to us as Georgetown University law students. They were a mix of African Americans, Caucasians, Latinas and South Asians, all of them coming together to assure the progress of a senior citizen huddled in her snowsuit in a rented wheelchair. These eight or nine young women could not have known what their kind gesture meant to me, or the profound metaphor I drew from their protection.

I imagined them relatively unencumbered by the racism and sexism that had made it so difficult for me to pursue professional training in decades past. In my own life, the sheer climb to the top of that mountain had often felt unbearable, but I had persevered. And now here I was, encircled by these optimistic young women who were not only living their dream, but who had also come out on a bitter-cold morning in January to watch the nation live *its* dream—the impossible dream that Dr. King and my own dear father had prophesied.

As I watched the winter sun rise around the beautiful young women, the light bouncing off them and the throngs of humanity beyond, it occurred to me that on this historic day, through the grace of these students, the law was making a way for me, as indeed it would make a way for every committed dreamer who came after me.

We had been shuffling forward in the yellow-ticket line for about an hour when a police officer broke through the cordon of students and said to me, "You, ma'am, please come with me." He escorted Shawna and me all the way to the front of the line and handed us off to an usher. The usher, after checking our tickets, took us to an area designated as wheelchair seating, but there was no room left, not even for my single chair. The usher thought for a moment, and then she said, "Okay, follow me." She took us through the crowd on a roundabout path to a roped-off area right at the foot of the steps of the Capitol building, just under the balcony where our president-elect would take his oath of office and deliver his inaugural address. It turned out to be a section reserved for Tuskegee Airmen and their families, which could not have been more perfect, as I had been married to a Tuskegee Airman. Better yet, as most Tuskegee Airmen were as advanced in age as I was, members of the Marine Corps had been assigned to take care of us, supplying us with blankets and hand warmers and refreshments.

It still was not yet 7 A.M., but I was exhausted. I had flown in from San Francisco the evening before and had been up since four that morning, so when a young Marine wrapped me snugly in a blanket, I nodded off, Shawna's arm around my shoulders. I woke to Aretha Franklin belting out "My Country, 'Tis of Thee" in that extraordinary voice of hers, and I rose to my feet. My mittened hands were clasped over my thudding heart when the president-elect took his oath of office, and immediately afterward, everyone was cheering and crying and taking pictures and waving little American flags, in awe that as a nation we had arrived at this moment. As our new president gave his twenty-one-minute inaugural address, his dazzling wife, First Lady Michelle Obama, and their two gracious daughters, Malia and Sasha, sat beaming behind him. I hung on his every word. And when he finished up in his soaring incantation, my tears were icy on my face.

"Let it be said by our children's children that when we were tested we refused to let this journey end, that we did not turn back nor did we falter; and with eyes fixed on the horizon and God's grace upon us, we carried forth that great gift of freedom and delivered it safely to future generations,"[96] the new president said. Those words, spoken on that bright morning, summed up the entire meaning of my life. I had the strange sensation that Barack Obama was addressing me personally, but how could he have known so exactly the nature of my life's struggle—and *this*, my great reward.

The feeling stayed with me late into the evening, my many decades unspooling like a film reel in my mind's eye. I was a child again, only this time, I was full of hopeful anticipation, because now I knew how the story ended. Now I knew I would be alive to experience the power and the glory of this day. I had watched a brilliant and courageous black man sworn in as our nation's president. A black family, complete with a wise and resilient grandmother, would be moving into the White House that very evening. Two precious brown girls would grow up playing in the rose garden, and no white child would ever turn away from them because of the color of their skin.

That night, Shawna and some of her friends went out to the inaugural balls, but I stayed back at the hotel. I was tired. I felt the full portion of my 90 years settling deep in my bones, but it was gentled by a sense of wonder, almost like the hushed reverence one feels in church. I had witnessed the thing I never imagined could happen in my lifetime. My heart was bursting. My soul was lifted up in song.

Oakland, California, 2012.

Epilogue

Forgiveness and the Holy Ghost

Five days later, on January 25, 2009, I had the pleasure of being once again in Ogden Hall on the campus of Hampton University, to receive an Honorary Doctorate of Humane Letters. It was the 116th Annual Founder's Day ceremony, and sitting with my grandniece Shawna and my nieces Varian and Cheri in that grand auditorium, I remembered keenly the exhilaration I had felt in 1940 when my mother jumped to her feet, cheering and clapping and calling, "She's mine!" as the dean conferred my bachelor's degree in nursing. Now here I was, 68 years later, my hair almost snow white and cropped in a neat natural close to my head, my body shrunk to the size and shape of a skinny adolescent. I looked down at my hands resting in my lap; they looked square and utilitarian, the nails neatly clipped but unadorned. They reminded me of my father's hands, working hands that had toiled with an unquenchable faith in the future. As much as I had wanted to please my mother, it was my father who had taught me never to quit, to just keep taking the next step, and the next, until the prize was within my grasp.

Listening to Dr. William R. Harvey, the school's president, cite the litany of my achievements now, I thought, *Hampton saved my life.* I was filled anew with gratitude for this place that had shown me so clearly who I was and what was possible for me in this world. My eyes brimmed as Dr. Harvey ended with the capstone of my career as a Hampton alumna: the establishment of the Osher Lifelong Learning Center at my beloved school. *I did all that,* I marveled, as Dr. Harvey called me to the stage. *And it was Hampton that opened the door.*

As I made my way up the aisle to the stage at the front of the auditorium, pushing my rolling walker ahead of me, I allowed myself to contemplate what my life might have been like had my mother never encountered the professor who told her about Hampton. In truth, I could not imagine it. And then I wondered, would the civil rights movement even have been possible had there been no historically black colleges and universities, no Hampton, Howard, Meharry, Morehouse, Spelman, Fisk and all the rest? Who would have educated the Negro intelligentsia? Who would have shown them their true worth and untapped potential? What institutions would have been there to instill not just learning, but also pride of self and courage in the future in those who would one day lead marches and sit-ins, who would put their bodies on the line, being fire hosed and attacked by police dogs, their most innocent bombed while attending Sunday school, all so that we might gain the rights and privileges of full citizenship in the nation of our birth?

After almost one hundred years, I knew the fight was far from won. Even though I have achieved the deepest yearning of my soul—to practice medicine—I knew that in urban ghettos across America, the talents of black and brown children were still being suffocated by the institutionalized bias of substandard schools, neighborhoods torn apart by poverty, crime and drugs, clashes with police, and people robbed of all sense of possibility, so that they could see no further than the struggle to survive one more day. Despite the best efforts of so many, there were still two Americas, one white and wealthy, one colored and poor, and the fact that a class of African Americans had managed to gain an education and straddle the divide despite the obstacles did not negate that truth.

I returned home to the Bay Area the next day, chastened,

a new fire burning inside me. I saw that I needed to do what I could for motivated black students with outsized dreams who were as disenfranchised as I had once felt. And so I sat down with Shawna, whom I had appointed as my trustee, and I arranged to endow scholarships at all my alma maters, for students of color who aspired to enter the medical profession but who did not have the means that the GI Bill had afforded me so many years before. Setting up endowments to cover the cost of tuition, room and board was easy for me to reconcile when it came to Hampton University and Howard Medical School. I wrote these institutions into my will and felt my heart swell with joy as I signed the first check.

Ohio State was a different story. In the beginning, I had no intention of leaving anything at all to the school that had almost crushed my life's ambition in thirteen impersonal words: "We have no facilities for training colored girls in our school of nursing." All these decades later, the memory of those words still stung, as did the recollection of how hard I had fought to be allowed to live on campus when I reapplied under the GI Bill and was admitted to the pre-med program after the war. *Look at what they did to me,* I thought. I had taken their rebuffs so personally, and now it seemed the only vehicle I had to fight back was to leave them nothing in my will.

I was just beginning to understand that the many times Ohio State had turned me away—from their nursing school, from their dorms, from their medical school—had filled me with secret shame, because the intimation had been that I was simply not good enough for their halls of learning. I had earned a pre-med undergraduate degree and a master's degree in social work from Ohio State almost out of vengeance; I'd had something to prove to the school—or perhaps it was to myself. In any case, I resolved not to give Ohio State a red cent of the means I had amassed over the course of my life as a doctor and investor in real estate, and initially at least, I felt as if I was at last balancing the scales.

But the decision rankled. While everyone who loved me applauded my position, something in my soul shriveled because of it. After a couple of years, I finally decided to sit with my discomfort long enough to understand its source. And it was this: Ohio State did not care one iota whether or not I contributed to its coffers through my estate planning. The pittance I could offer would make no difference to them at all. But it would make a difference to *me*. And it would make a difference to a student who looked like me. You don't meet evil with evil, I decided. That was not what God would have me do. Besides, what had happened to me at Ohio State was not personal; it was the tenor of the times, and I had become a stronger and more determined soul because of all I had faced there. I had earned two degrees there on which I had been able to build. Perhaps it was time to heal.

The truth was, Ohio State didn't need my money, but I needed to give it. And so I called Shawna, and I asked her to include Ohio State University in my will. What better way to honor my experience as a Buckeye than to endow a scholarship that would allow other students of color to attend the school, and excel there, and gain the credentials to climb the ladder of achievement in a powerful way. This was my quiet act of forgiveness. It felt like freedom.

As it happened, just a few years after I decided to include Ohio State in my will, the school took an unprecedented step forward in the matter of race. In February 2014, former University of California, Irvine chancellor Dr. Michael Drake was appointed the first African American president in Ohio State's 144-year history. "Transforming lives is a tall order, but this university is sharpening its focus in ways that will improve lives close to home and around the world,"[97] Dr. Drake said after his appointment was announced. It was impossible for me not to hope that he would increase minority representation at the school, whose faculty was still only 4 percent black, with a mere 6 percent of students who were African American.[98]

Many alumni suspected that the appointment of this highly qualified black administrator was intended to ameliorate continuing racial tensions at the school. The most notorious recent incident had occurred when graffiti had appeared on a campus building proclaiming "Long Live Zimmerman!" The graffiti was a reference to the Sanford, Florida, neighborhood watch captain who in 2012 had taken the life of 17-year-old Trayvon Martin, an unarmed African American youth who had been walking back to his father's house from the store. To George Zimmerman, the black teen with his hoodie pulled up against the rain had looked threatening. Their encounter ended with the youth dead on the sidewalk from a gunshot wound and Zimmerman holding the discharged weapon. The case had inflamed the nation, with African Americans convinced that Trayvon Martin had been profiled to death, and Zimmerman claiming self-defense.

As I watched the news of national protests in months that followed, I knew quite clearly that young Trayvon had looked suspicious to Zimmerman simply because he was black. We had come a long way in terms of race relations, but we had not yet rooted out the treacherous stereotypes that so often led to such tragedies. I thought again about my encounter with a white law enforcement officer when I was an Army nurse passing through Shreveport in the 1940s, and how I had feared for my life. Since that time we had elected a black man as president, but America was not even close to being post-racial. And so, when Zimmerman was acquitted of second-degree murder and manslaughter charges on July 13, 2013, I believe the verdict must have splintered the heart of every black person in America, reminding us all of the great distance we had still to travel.

And yet the university that had once told me no because of the amount of melanin in my skin had just appointed an African American president. And I had mustered enough faith and forgiveness to endow my pittance of a scholarship to allow a bright and hopeful student of color to graduate from Ohio State. In this small way, I could help change the tide that once upon a time had threatened to swallow me whole. Except it hadn't. Hampton, Howard, Meharry and, yes, even Ohio State had helped me stand firm in the swirling water. With God's help and for God's purpose, I had overcome.

I was alone in my apartment at Lake Park, a month before my ninety-seventh birthday. It was mid-morning, the breakfast dishes cleared, lunch not yet served. My home attendant, a no-nonsense Filipino woman named Irene, was across the hall doing laundry. Outside my window, watery sunlight fell through the trees and dappled the stone and ivory Shona art sculptures on my terrace. I was sitting at my dining table, writing in my notebooks, a habit from childhood that had never left me. Suddenly, the air went still. The birds stopped chirping, the leaves stopped rustling, the light grew bright and clear. Time itself seemed to pause. I felt suspended in space, carried on a soft, elusive wind, and I knew it was God. I had never felt anything like this before, and I knew I might never experience it again. I felt lifted from the earth, enveloped in a moment of living faith, of pure love, and everything was infinite peace.

All my life, I had been a churchgoing woman, and yet I had never felt the immensity of the Holy Spirit as I did that morning.

It was indescribable, an awakening, and in that opening of faith I was able to look back over my life and see that at every turn, God had been there. I finally understood that none of it had been an accident. All of it had served to strengthen me, so that I could pursue the life of medicine that my own questing heart had identified for me when I was still a child. And now, the Holy Spirit had one more task for me. I was to tell my story.

And so I have.

On August 8, 2009, the descendants of Abraham Simmons and Amelia May Briggs Simmons marked our 100th reunion with this family portrait in Mount Vernon, Ohio.

ENDNOTES

1   Clayborne Carson: *In Struggle: SNCC and the Black Awakening of the 1960s* (Harvard University Press, 1995)

2   "History of the Kaiser Permanente Medical Care Program" www.kaiserthrive.org/kaiser-permanente-history (accessed 7/11/15)

3   "All About Allergies" http://kidshealth.org/parent/medical/allergies/allergy.html

4   "Dr. Ben F. Feingold Dies at 81; Studied Diet in Hyperactivity" *The New York Times* www.nytimes.com/1982/03/24/obituaries/dr-ben-f-feingold-dies-at-81-studied-diet-in-hyperactivity.html (accessed 2/23/15)

5   *"The Problem We All Live With*—The Truth About Rockwell's Painting" http://kenlairdstudios.hubpages.com/hub/The-Problem-We-All-Live-With---Norman-Rockwell-the-truth-about-his-famous-painting (accessed 3/27/15)

6   www.history.com/topics/us-states/ohio

7   Frederick N. Lorey: *History of Knox County, Ohio 1876–1976*

8   David Chalmers: *Hooded Americanism: The History of the Ku Klux Klan* (Duke University Press Books, 1987)

9   *Ibid.*

10   *Ibid.*

11   "The History of Historically Black Colleges and Universities" www.collegeview.com/articles/article/the-history-of-historically-black-colleges-and-universities (accessed 4/18/15)

12   *Ibid.*

13   "Jesse Owens Biography: Olympic Triumphs, Olympic Sized Struggles" www.biography.com/news/jesse-owens-biography-olympic-triumphs-olympic-sized-struggles-20892201

14   *Ibid.*

15   "Jesse Owens Biography" www.biography.com/people/jesse-owens-9431142#rising-star

16   Tamara Jeffries: "Remembering Hampton," personal writings, August 2015

17   www.hamptonu.edu/about/history.cfm

18   *Ibid.*

19   www.blackpast.org/aah/hampton-university

20   http://nursing.hamptonu.edu/page/History

21   Robert Francis Engs: *Educating the Disfranchised and Disinherited: Samuel Chapman Armstrong and Hampton Institute, 1839–1893* (University of Tennessee Press, 1999)

22   "Mary Peake" www.womenhistoryblog.com/2014/11/mary-peake.html

23   mas.hamptonu.edu/about/ogden.cfm

24   "Civilian Pilot Training Program Fact Sheet" National Museum of the US Air Force www.nationalmuseum.af.mil/Visit/MuseumExhibits/FactSheets/Display/tabid/509/Article/196137/civilian-pilot-training-program.aspx

25   "James Weldon Johnson Biography" www.biography.com/people/james-weldon-johnson-9356013

26   William P. Winter: "A Brief History of Sickle Cell Disease"
      www.sicklecell.howard.edu / ABriefHistoryofSickleCell-
      Disease.htm

27   "Mystery Solved: How Sickle Hemoglobin
      Protects Against Malaria" www.sciencedaily.com/
      releases/2011/04/110428123931.htm

28   www.blackpast.org/aah/moton-robert-r-1867-1940

29   "Booker T. and W. E. B.: The Debate Between W. E. B. Du
      Bois and Booker T. Washington" www.pbs.org/wgbh/
      pages/frontline/shows/race/etc/road.html

30   Cary D. Wintz: *African American Political Thought, 1890–
      1930: Washington, Du Bois, Garvey and Randolph* (New York:
      Routledge, 1995) pp.114-115

31   Letter from W. E. B. (William Edward Burghardt) Du
      Bois to Robert Russa Moton, April 17, 1916, W. E. B. Du
      Bois Papers (MS 312), Special Collections and University
      Archives, University of Massachusetts Amherst Libraries

32   *Ibid.*

33   www.tuskegee.edu/about_us/legacy_of_leadership/
      robert_r_moton.aspx

34   "Tuskegee VA Medical Center Celebrates 85 Years of
      Service," Central Alabama Veterans Health Care System
      press release, www.centralalabama.va.gov/Press_Release.
      asp (accessed 7/13/15)

35   Lerone Bennett: "Chronicles of Black Courage: Robert R.
      Moton Risked Life in Fight for Black Doctors at Tuskegee
      Veterans Hospital," *Ebony*, July 2002

36   *Ibid.*

37   American Chemical Society: "Discovery and Development of Penicillin" www.acs.org/content/acs/en/education/whatischemistry/landmarks/flemingpenicillin.html (accessed 7/13/15)

38   "The Making of a Miracle Drug" http://smellslikescience.com/the-making-of-a-miracle-drug (accessed 7/13/15)

39   Phil Hickey: "Homosexuality: The Mental Illness That Went Away" www.behaviorismandmentalhealth.com/2011/10/08/homosexuality-the-mental-illness-that-went-away (accessed 7/13/15)

40   "12 States Still Ban Sodomy a Decade After Court Ruling" www.usatoday.com/story/news/nation/2014/04/21/12-states-ban-sodomy-a-decade-after-court-ruling/7981025

41   Centers for Disease Control and Prevention: Syphilis Fact Sheet www.cdc.gov/std/syphilis/stdfact-syphilis.htm

42   *Ibid.*

43   Rebecca Kreston: "Pyromania! On Neurosyphilis and Fighting Fire With Fire," *Discover* May 31, 2014 http://blogs.discovermagazine.com/bodyhorrors/2014/05/31/pyromania-syphilis-malaria (accessed 5/24/15)

44   "Studies Show 'Dark Chapter' of Medical Research" www.cnn.com/2010/HEALTH/10/01/guatemala.syphilis.tuskegee/index.html

45   *Ibid.*

46   "Tuskegee Syphilis Study" https://explorable.com/tuskegee-syphilis-study

47   *Ibid.*

48   History Channel: "Pearl Harbor" www.history.com/topics/world-war-ii/pearl-harbor (accessed 7/13/15)

49 *Ibid.*

50 YWCA of the City of New York: Emma Ransom House Y.W.C.A. price list, ca. 1938 W. E. B. Du Bois Papers (MS 312). Special Collections and University Archives, University of Massachusetts Amherst Libraries

51 Alain Locke: "Harlem," *The Survey Graphic*, Harlem Number (March 1925) http://xroads.virginia.edu/~drbr/locke_2.html (accessed 7/8/15)

52 Kevin Baker: "Jitterbug Days" *The New York Times*, January 22, 2006 www.nytimes.com/2006/01/22/nyregion/thecity/22feat.html?pagewanted=all&_r=0 (accessed 7/13/15)

53 *Ibid.*

54 http://abyssinian.org/about-us/history

55 *Ibid.*

56 Judith A. Bellafaire: U.S. Army Center of Military History brochure www.history.army.mil/books/wwii/72-14/72-14.htm (accessed 7/11/15)

57 Patrick Feng: "Executive Order 9981: Integration of the Armed Forces," https://armyhistory.org/executive-order-9981-integration-of-the-armed-forces (accessed 8/31/15)

58 From essay "Women's Army Corps: WAAC and WAC" by Colonel Betty Morden, USA (Ret.) in *In Defense of a Nation: Servicewomen in World War II*, edited by Major General Jeanne M. Holm, USAF (Ret.) and Judith Bellafaire, Ph.D., Chief Historian of the Women's Memorial Foundation (Arlington, Virginia: Vandamere Press, 1998)

59 War Department: W.A.C. Field Manual *Physical Training* (FM 35-20) (United States Government Printing Office, Washington, D.C., July 15, 1943)

60   Mattie E. Treadwell: *The Women's Army Corps: United States Army in World War II* (United States Army Center of Military History, ed. 1991)

61   From essay "Women's Army Corps: WAAC and WAC" by Colonel Betty Morden, USA (Ret.) in *In Defense of a Nation: Servicewomen in World War II*, edited by Major General Jeanne M. Holm, USAF (Ret.) and Judith Bellafaire, Ph.D., Chief Historian of the Women's Memorial Foundation (Arlington, Virginia: Vandamere Press, 1998)

62   *Ibid.*

63   Judith A. Bellafaire: U.S. Army Center of Military History brochure www.history.army.mil/books/wwii/72-14/72-14.htm (accessed 7/11/15)

64   Ellamae Simmons: "Understanding Homosexuality," pre-med undergraduate thesis, Ohio State University, 1948

65   Mary T. Sarnecky: *A History of the U.S. Army Nurse Corps* (University of Pennsylvania Press, 1999)

66   "The Death of President Franklin Roosevelt, 1945" www.eyewitnesstohistory.com/fdrdeath.htm (accessed 7/11/15)

67   Kansas Historical Society: "Karl Menninger" www.kshs.org/kansapedia/karl-menninger/17218

68   U.S. Department of Veterans Affairs www.benefits.va.gov/gibill/history.asp (accessed 7/18/15)

69   David Callahan: "How the GI Bill Left Out African Americans," *Demos*, November 11, 2013 www.demos.org/blog/11/11/13/how-gi-bill-left-out-african-americans (accessed 12/18/15)

70   *Ibid.*

71   "The GI Bill," Wessels Living History Farm www.livinghisto-ryfarm.org/farminginthe40s/life_20.html (accessed 7/20/15)

72   *Ibid.*

73   "Leslie N. Shaw Dies; First Black Postmaster of a Major U.S. City" *Los Angeles Times,* March 10, 1985 http://arti-cles.latimes.com/1985-03-10/local/me-25790_1_los-an-geles (accessed 8/18/15)

74   "Honor for Postmaster" *Los Angeles Times,* April 28, 1988 http://articles.latimes.com/1988-04-28/local/me-2863_1_downtown-los-angeles (accessed 8/18/15)

75   "Black Milestones in Higher Education: Buckeye Edition" July 21, 2007 https://twilightandreason.wordpress.com/category/ohio-state-university (accessed 7/29/15)

76   National Library of Medicine, National Institutes of Health: "The Rise and Fall of a Kaiser Permanente Expan-sion Region," *The Milbank Quarterly* ncbi.nlm.nih.gov/pmc/articles/PMC2690244 (accessed 8/1/15)

77   "Kaiser Permanente Plan," *Online Archive of California* oac.cdlib.org/view?docId=kt7s2005p0;NAAN=13030&doc.view=frames&chunk.id=d0e1423&toc.depth=1&toc.id=d0e1180&brand=oac4 (accessed 8/1/15)

78   Meharry Medical College: "The Salt Wagon Story" mmc.edu/about/salt-wagon-story.html (accessed 8/17/15)

79   "Little Known Black History Fact: Howard University" http://blackamericaweb.com/2013/12/18/little-known-black-history-fact-howard-university/2

80   Howard University College of Medicine: "A Short History" http://healthsciences.howard.edu/education/colleges/medicine/about/mission/short-history (accessed 8/31/15)

81   CAF Red Tail Squadron: "Airmen in Combat" www.
      redtail.org/the-airmen-a-brief-history/airmen-in-combat
      (accessed 8/29/15)

82   *Ibid*.

83   Larry D. Hatfield: "Col. Price Rice of the Famed Tuskegee
      Airmen" *San Francisco Chronicle*

84   Dr. Martin Luther King Jr.: "Letter from a Birmingham
      Jail," www.africa.upenn.edu/Articles_Gen/Letter_
      Birmingham.html (accessed 9/7/15)

85   "Civil Rights Timeline: Milestones in the Modern Civil
      Rights Movement" www.infoplease.com/spot/civilrights-
      timeline1.html (accessed 9/6/15)

86   *Ibid*.

87   Wisconsin Historical Society: "What Was the 1964 Freedom
      Summer Project?" www.wisconsinhistory.org/Content.
      aspx?dsNav=N:4294963828-4294963805&dsRecordDe-
      tails=R:CS3707 (accessed 9/12/15)

88   Janice O'Leary: "Dr. Granville Coggs: Gold Rush" www.
      coggs-granville.com

89   Lawrence Van Gelder: "Morris Milgram, 81; Built Inter-
      racial Housing" *The New York Times*, June 26, 1997 www.
      nytimes.com/1997/06/26/us/morris-milgram-81-built-in-
      terracial-housing.html (accessed 9/15/15)

90   The Editorial Board: "How Segregation Destroys
      Black Wealth," *The New York Times* www.nytimes.
      com/2015/09/15/opinion/how-segregation-de-
      stroys-black-wealth.html?_r=0 (accessed 9/15/15)

91   "Civil Rights Act" www.history.com/topics/black-his-
      tory/civil-rights-act

92   "Fair Housing Act of 1968" www.history.com/topics/
      black-history/fair-housing-act

93   Joseph Berger: "The Bakke Case Ten years Later" *The New
      York Times*, July 13, 1988 www.nytimes.com/1988/07/13/
      us/education-the-bakke-case-10-years-later-mixed-results.
      html (accessed 10/11/15)

94   Richard Baehr: "The Obama Victory Reconsidered" www.
      americanthinker.com/articles/2010/07/the_obama_
      victory_reconsidered.html

95   Joint Congressional Committee on Inaugural Ceremonies:
      "Swearing-In Ceremony for President Barack H. Obama"
      www.inaugural.senate.gov/swearing-in/event/barack-
      obama-2009 (accessed 9/20/15)

96   www.whitehouse.gov/blog/2009/01/21/presi-
      dent-barack-obamas-inaugural-address (accessed 9/20/15)

97   Kristin Mitchell: "Ohio State 'Making History' with 1st
      Black President" *The Lantern,* February 3, 2014 thelantern.
      com/2014/02/ohio-state-making-history-with-1st-black-
      president (accessed 10/21/15)

98   *Ibid.*

ABOUT THE AUTHORS

ELLAMAE SIMMONS, M.D., was the first African American woman to specialize in asthma, allergy and immunology in the United States. A graduate of Hampton University and Howard University's College of Medicine, she was also the first black woman to join the staff of Kaiser Permanente's medical group, based in San Francisco. She later founded the first Osher Lifelong Learning Institute in the HBCU system at her beloved alma mater, Hampton.

ROSEMARIE ROBOTHAM, a former senior editor at Simon & Schuster and deputy editor of *Essence* magazine, is the author of five books. A graduate of Barnard College and Columbia University's Graduate School of Journalism, she has collaborated on numerous other literary works. She lives in New York City with her husband and two children.

CPSIA information can be obtained at www.ICGtesting.com
Printed in the USA
BVOW02*1443130316

440044BV00001B/2/P